Experiments in Metropolitan Government

James F. Horan
G. Thomas Taylor, Jr.

The Praeger Special Studies program, through a selective worldwide distribution network, makes available to the academic, government, and business communities significant and timely research in U.S. and international economic, social, and political issues.

Experiments in Metropolitan Government

Praeger Publishers   New York   London

PRAEGER SPECIAL STUDIES IN U.S. ECONOMIC, SOCIAL, AND POLITICAL ISSUES

Library of Congress Cataloging in Publication Data

Horan, James F
    Experiments in metropolitan government.

    (Praeger special studies in U.S. economic, social,
and political issues)
    Bibliography: p.
    1. Metropolitan government—United States.
2. Toronto metropolitan area—Politics and government.
I. Taylor, G. Thomas, joint author. II. Title.
JS422.H67   1977   352'.0094'0973   77-7816
ISBN 0-03-022336-9

This research was funded by a contract with the Office of
University Research of the U.S. Department of Transportation and
the U.S. Government assumes no liability for the contents or use
thereof.

PRAEGER SPECIAL STUDIES
200 Park Avenue, New York, N.Y., 10017, U.S.A.

Published in the United States of America in 1977
by Praeger Publishers,
A Division of Holt, Rinehart and Winston, CBS, Inc.

789   038   987654321

Printed in the United States of America

ACKNOWLEDGMENTS

Any study as broad in scope as this study attempts to be is dependent on the efforts, cooperation, and encouragement of many persons other than the authors. In the preparation of the study, the authors would like to acknowledge the assistance received from the students of the Urban Regional Governments seminar at the University of Maine. Without their probing questions and observations, research projects, and continued interest, this study would not have been possible.

We are greatly indebted to a number of scholars whose landmark work provided an incentive for this study. We would especially like to mention the work of Brett Hawkins and Daniel Elazar in Nashville, York Willbern in Indianapolis, John DeGrove in Jacksonville, Edward Sofen in Miami, Harold Kaplan and Albert Rose in Toronto, Robert Warren in Los Angeles, and Stanley Baldinger and Ted Kolderie in Minneapolis-St. Paul.

We would also like to thank Sally Horan and Fran Walsh for their perseverance and their excellent job of typing this manuscript. Ann Hambrock's clerical assistance proved invaluable to the completed text.

Finally, we would like to acknowledge the support of the University of Maine for granting us a faculty research award, which facilitated this research.

CONTENTS

PART II: THE TWO-LEVEL ALTERNATIVE

LIST OF TABLES AND FIGURES

INTRODUCTION:
COMPARATIVE METROPOLITAN
SYSTEMS

Experiments in Metropolitan Government will attempt to
describe and analyze the basic techniques that have been utilized
in different metropolitan areas to meet the challenge of urban
problems. The study examines in detail eight specific cases of
metropolitan governmental reform. The cases include seven cities
in the United States and one Canadian city, the latter chosen because
of its unique development and potential. [1] Each city was selected as
an example of a certain type of political response to metropolitan
problems that involves a significant change in the structure of
government. In short, this is a comparative study of some rather
unique approaches to governmental reform.

The study utilizes an analytical framework developed by Bollens
and Schmandt who suggested three approaches for the analysis of
metropolitan government—the one-government approach, the two-
level approach, and the cooperative approach. [2] We have added a
fourth category entitled metropolitan councils and have included in
this category an example of a council of government (COG) and the
Twin Cities experience. While these examples are definitely cooperative in nature, we have concluded that they merit a separate classification because of their differences from the other forms of the cooperative approach such as the Lakewood plan and interlocal agreements.
Accordingly, the study will examine four metropolitan alternatives:
the one-level alternative, the two-level alternative, the cooperative
alternative, and the metropolitan council alternative. The comparative
metropolitan systems framework presented here should illustrate the
advantages as well as the problems of conceptualization. Each city
was selected because it fits within a specific component of the framework or represents a more subtle variation within a component. In
each of the eight cases, the study employs a variation of the systems
approach (input-output analysis) as developed by David Easton. [3]

First, in each case, the metropolitan environment will be
explained in a brief sketch that will include the history, socioeconomic
data, political culture, and governmental structure of the area before
the change in government was effected. Second, the "politics of
acceptance" will be analyzed. Here the emphasis will be on how
and why the basic changes occurred. The inputs, which include both
demands and supports, will be stressed. Inputs may be viewed as
demands (requests) or supports (commitments) or resources by
individuals or groups that are intended to influence the choices of

decision makers and thereby possibly affect public policies. The inputs are transmitted from the environment through such channels as political parties, elections, interest groups, and even mass demonstrations.[4]

Third, the new governmental structure will be described in an attempt to determine the exact nature of the structural changes that took place and to assess their impact on the metropolitan environment during the period of transition. Fourth, the record of the new government since its inception will be reviewed with emphasis placed on the following questions:

1. Did the change in governmental structure result in a change in policy for the metropolis?

2. What were the "outputs" or goods and services that the new governmental units produced?

3. What were the consequences or "outcomes" of the policies for the general public?[5]

Thus, the analysis will attempt to evaluate the policy outputs and their effects by focusing on the accomplishments, problems, and styles of leadership in each metropolitan area.

Finally, the study will seek to determine whether each experiment in metropolitan government can be replicated. In other words, is there any potential for borrowing all or parts of each technique and what would appear to be the limitations of replication for other communities confronted with similar types of problems?

ONE-LEVEL ALTERNATIVE:
CITY-COUNTY CONSOLIDATION

Since the turn of the century, many urban reformers, including civic leaders and political scientists alike, have argued that the centrifugal social and economic aspects of the modern city should be brought within the actual legal boundaries of the city. These "centrist" reformers have long favored the creation of a single government for an entire metropolitan area because, in their view, such a unified structure would be more efficient, effective, and economical. This proposal has been opposed by a number of local officials who maintain that its implementation would bring about the loss of local control, decreased citizen access to public officials, and reduced attention to local services.[6]

Within the past decade, two major proponent groups for a unitary form of city government have sought to convert national audiences to their cause. In 1966 the Committee for Economic Development, which is a private research group of prominent businessmen and educators, recommended a reduction of at least 80 percent in the number of the nation's local governments. [7] Two years later, the National Commission on Urban Problems recommended the use of financial incentives to encourage smaller units to consolidate due to its conviction that the multiplicity of local units was contributing to the failure in solving housing and other metropolitan problems. Although both groups attracted a certain amount of attention at the time of their separate recommendations, their pleas to cause a change in metropolitan structure and politics have been largely unsuccessful.

The thrust of the reformers' single-government alternative is focused mainly on the older core city and can be accomplished by three basic techniques: (1) annexation (the absorption of nearby unincorporated territory), (2) municipal consolidation (the merger of two or more incorporated units such as two cities), and (3) city-county consolidation (the union of one or more municipalities with the county government).

This study will focus only on examples and variations of the third mechanism—city-county consolidation. Our purpose is to explore the boldest examples of structural change in the metropolis, and in the case of the single government alternative, this is represented by city-county consolidation. During the twentieth century, there have been few examples of municipal consolidation, as compared with the more frequent use of this mechanism during the nineteenth century. Historically, annexation also was frequently used as a technique of municipal expansion, but today it has only limited application, primarily to the southern and western cities that still have the potential for growth and are not completely surrounded by smaller urban municipalities. Moreover, annexation does not seem to alter the balance of power within a metropolitan area as much as some of the other techniques. This is true because annexation is usually accomplished in an incremental fashion, adding only a few square miles of annexed territory to the core city at any given time. [8]

From 1900 to 1945, there appeared to be considerable interest in city-county consolidation as a technique for establishing a single government at the local level. However, the supporters of this technique were unable to implement their reorganization plans in a single existing metropolis. The environment of metropolitan decision making had a definite effect on the outcome of these events. Suburbanites began to resist the absorption of their communities into unified governments. The traditional arguments of the proponents that consolidation would somehow result in greater efficiency, economy, and equity and, at the same time, create a government that was capable of solving area-wide problems were not accepted by the skeptical suburban leaders. Why, they reasoned, should they exchange their own desirable situations for a doubtful reform that made allusions to the "promised land?" Most of these suburban municipalities wished to retain their local autonomy in order to continue to control their land-use practices and financial resources. The smaller governments were usually rather professional and the services seemed more personal to the residents than those they would receive under the metro proposals. It seemed quite obvious that they would have more to say in the decision-making process with the status quo.

In order to achieve city-county consolidation, two legal battles normally had to be won. The first concerned the passage of a state constitutional amendment or legislative enabling act that would allow the metropolitan areas to pursue such an alternative, and the second involved approval of the proposal by the local voters, usually by separate majorities in the central city and the rest of the county. Most consolidation efforts from 1900 to 1945 did not get past these first political hurdles. As a matter of fact, only three city-county consolidation proposals ever got as far as being presented to the voters, and all three eventually were defeated: St. Louis-St. Louis County, Missouri; Macon-Biff County, Georgia; and Jacksonville-Duval County, Florida.

After World War II, interest in the technique of city-county consolidation continued to flourish as once again numerous merger proposals were submitted to the voters. In only a few cities, however, were the reorganization schemes approved. [9] Most of these attempts were directed at medium-sized metropolises in the South that required dual majorities—one in the core city and one in the rest of the county. In most instances, the propositions usually obtained sufficient support in the cities but failed to convince the suburbanites in the outlying areas of the county. The trend of city-county consolidation failures finally was reversed in 1962 with the consolidation of the city of Nashville and Davidson County, the nature of which is discussed in Chapter 2. Also considered in the study is the consolidation of Jacksonville and Duval County in 1967 and the merger of Indianapolis and Marion County in 1969. (See Table I.1.)

TWO-LEVEL ALTERNATIVE

Another variation of reorganization is favored by the so-called federationists. This school of reformers advocates a two-level alternative based on the theory of federalism. With this technique, area-wide functions—one or several—are delegated to area-wide governments while purely local functions remain with the local units, thereby creating a metropolitan-local or two-tier system. [10]

TABLE I. 1

City-County Consolidation:
Voter Support For Local Government Reorganization, 1945-74

		Reorganization Support (percent)	
Year	Reorganization Referendum	Success	Defeat
1949	Baton Rouge-East Baton Rouge Parish, La.	51.1	
1952	Hampton-Elizabeth County, Va.	88.7	
1953	Miami-Dade County, Fla.		49.2
1957	Miami-Dade County, Fla.	51.0	
	Newport News-Warwick, Va. [a]	66.9	
1958	Nashville-Davidson County, Tenn.		47.3
1959	Albuquerque-Bernalillo County, N. M.		30.0
	Knoxville-Knox County, Tenn.		16.7
	Cleveland-Cuyahoga County, Ohio		44.8
	St. Louis-St. Louis County, Mo.		27.5
1960	Macon-Bibb County, Ga.		35.8
1961	Durham-Durham County, N. C.		22.3
	Richmond-Henrico County, Va.		54.0[b]
1962	Columbus-Muscogee County, Ga.		42.1
	Memphis-Shelby County, Tenn.		36.8
	Nashville-Davidson County, Tenn.	56.8	
	South Norfolk-Norfolk County, Va.	66.0	
	Virginia Beach-Princess Anne County, Va.	81.9	
	St. Louis-St. Louis County, Mo.		40.1[c]
1964	Chattanooga-Hamilton County, Tenn.		19.2
1967	Jacksonville-Duval County, Fla.	64.7	
	Tampa-Hillsborough County, Fla.		28.4
1969	Athens-Clarke County, Ga.		48.0
	Brunswick-Glynn County, Ga.		29.6
	Carson City-Ormsby County, Nev.	65.1	
	Roanoke-Roanoke County, Va.		66.4[b]
	Winchester City-Frederick County, Va.		31.9
1970	Charlottesville-Albermarle County, Va.		28.1
	Columbus-Muscogee County, Ga.	80.7	
	Chattanooga-Hamilton County, Tenn.		48.0
	Tampa-Hillsborough County, Fla.		42.0
	Pensacola-Escambia County, Fla.		42.0
1971	Augusta-Richmond County, Ga.		41.5
	Charlotte-Mecklenburg County, N. C.		30.5
	Tallahasee-Leon County, Fla.		41.0
1972	Athens-Clarke County, Ga.		48.3
	Macon-Bibb County, Ga.		39.6
	Suffolk-Nansemond County, Va. [a]	75.7	
	Fort Pierce-St. Lucie, Fla.		36.5
	Lexington-Fayette County, Ky.	69.4	
	Tampa, Hillsborough County, Fla.		42.0
1973	Columbia-Richland County, S. C.		45.9
	Savannah-Chatham County, Ga.		58.3[b]
	Tallahasee-Leon County, Fla.		45.9
1974	Augusta-Richmond County, Ga.		51.5[b]
	Portland-Multnomah County, Ore.		27.5
	Durham-Durham County, N. C.		32.1
	Charleston-Charleston County, S. C.		40.4
	Sacramento-Sacramento County, Calif.		24.9
	Total outcome (Number)	12	37
	Local reorganizations attempted (Number)	49	

[a]Warwick, Virginia was a city at the time of the referendum. It had incorporated in 1952; it was Warwick County just six years prior to the referendum. A similar situation preceded the consolidation of Suffolk and Nansemond cities.

[b]The type of majority requirement is vital in consolidation referenda. In these four instances city-county consolidation was not possible despite the majority voting percentage in its support.

[c]St. Louis-St. Louis County portions of the 1962 statewide referendum.

Source: Vincent L. Marando, "The Politics of City-County Consolidation," National Civic Review 64 (February 1975): 77.

The two-tier system can take three basic forms:

1. Metropolitan district: A governmental unit that usually encompasses a substantial part or the entire geographic metropolitan area but is normally authorized to perform only one function or a few closely related activities of an area-wide nature;
2. Comprehensive urban county plan: The simultaneous transfer of selected functions from municipalities and other local units to the county government; and
3. Federation: The establishment of a new area-wide government that is assigned new responsibilities and customarily replaces the existing county government.

In this study we will consider examples of the comprehensive urban county plan and federation. The metropolitan district does not fall within the compass of the study because it has usually been restricted to a single special purpose and, thus, does not represent an effort at a systematic problem-solving capability. Metropolitan districts are the mildest form of the two-level alternative since most either do not have the power to tax at all or are strictly limited as to the amount that they can tax. [11]

Comprehensive Urban County Plan

Under this plan, through the redistribution of power and possible grants of additional authority, a county assumes those functions that are deemed to be of an area-wide nature, while the municipalities continue to administer those functions considered to be of purely local concern. Thus, the county is transformed into a metropolitan government with the simultaneous reallocation of a variety of functions from all municipalities to the county. The plan may also call for the distribution of responsibilities and functions not previously performed by any local government in the area.

Since a number of standard metropolitan statistical areas (SMSAs) include only a single country, the feasibility of this plan would appear to be quite broad. The plan also would seem quite appropriate in certain southern and western cities where the geographic boundaries of the metropolitan area have usually not spilled over into a second or third county. Some have argued that the comprehensive urban county plan could also be useful in those inter-county metropolises where the majority of the residents and the most serious urban problems are still concentrated in the central county.

Politically, the plan can have considerable appeal, if the county is viewed by the public as an acceptable unit of local government or can be reorganized to project this image. Unlike the metropolitan district and federation techniques of reform, the urban county plan does not require the creation of still another unit of government in what is already a very fragmented system. Instead, it merely strengthens one unit, the county, which will serve as the second tier. Although this model of reform has attracted many supporters, it has failed to produce the results that the reformers desired. In stressing the dismal track record of this reform technique, Joseph Zimmerman writes: "During the past twenty-seven years the concerned electorate have approved only . . . one charter establishing a two-tier system with a strong upper tier—Metropolitan Dade County, Florida."[12]

There are numerous factors that have inhibited the implementation of the comprehensive urban county plan. In many states, legal authorization to use the technique does not exist and may be gained only by amending the state constitution. Second, numerous county officials have often viewed the proposed changes as a threat to their continuation in office and, accordingly, have chosen to oppose the structural renovation. Another source of difficulty is the determination of the criteria used to establish the electoral district boundaries. The outcome of such decisions could well determine which parts of the metropolis could control the newly strengthened county government. The activities assigned to the county government can also be a controversial issue revolving around such questions as what are the problems that should be dealt with on an area-wide basis by the county and what degree of change will be acceptable to the voters? Finally, the inadequate financial powers of many county governments have proved to be a source of difficulty. Many counties are heavily dependent on the property tax and are often burdened with constitutional tax limitation terms that prohibit carrying out their added functional responsibilities.

The present study will examine the case of metropolitan Miami, or as it is officially designated—Metropolitan Dade County, as an exceptional example of the comprehensive urban county plan.

Federation

Another variation of the two-level alternative is that of a federation. This approach involves the creation of an entirely new area-wide government with either intercounty or one-county territorial limits. The newly created unit is usually designated as the metropolitan government and is charged with carrying out numerous area-wide functions. The original municipal units continue to operate and perform local functions that are not performed by the metropolitan tier. Most of the federation plans that have been proposed in the United States have called for the metropolitan legislative body to be made up of local representatives coming directly from the municipalities. Thus, federation, as a metropolitan concept, requires replacing the existing county government with a new metropolitan unit, while the previously mentioned urban county plan involves retaining the county unit as the area-wide tier.

The record of federation in the United States has been characterized by only a few fruitless attempts to implement this type of reorganization. Bollens and Schmandt summarize the record as follows:[13]

1. State legislative refusal to submit federation proposals to the Boston voters in 1896 and 1931.

2. Popular defeats of propositions in Alameda County (Oakland) and Allegheny County (Pittsburgh) in 1921 and 1929, respectively.

3. Lengthy discussions and a privately prepared plan in San Francisco-San Mateo County in the late 1920s and early 1930s.

4. Electoral disapproval in 1930 of a state constitutional amendment specifying detailed provisions to be inserted in a federation charter to be drafted for St. Louis and St. Louis County.

5. Revised interest in Alameda and Allegheny counties in the 1930s.

6. Preparation of a federation plan for metropolitan Miami in 1955 by a professional consulting firm for an official study group; the proposal, however, was converted into a comprehensive urban county system before adoption.

As with the urban county plan, there are numerous obstacles pertaining to federation as a metropolitan technique. Most federation efforts in the United States necessitated authorization in the appropriate state constitution before they could proceed further. Moreover, most federation plans were presented as charters, drafted by locally elected boards, and this proved to be much more difficult than seeking authorization through the process of state legislation.

Another characteristic of most federation experiences has been the requirement of the approval of the local electorate. Multiple majorities and majorities of a high percentage of the voters were required in most cases. For example, a majority of the voters was required in each of the ten cities in Alameda County, a country-wide majority and a two-thirds majority in each of a majority of municipalities in Allegheny County, and a majority in San Francisco and San Mateo County. Historically, federation plans have usually had to acquire more majorities than either the urban county plan or city-county consolidation proposals.

The method of selecting the metropolitan legislative board has usually been a controversial issue as well. Most federation attempts have called for a direct election to all seats of the governing body and for the nomination or election (and sometimes both) of at least some of the members from districts or smaller municipalities.

A final major issue that frequently provoked extended debate was whether the metropolitan government or the municipalities should have enumerated powers and whether the powers of each level should be individually specified. All of these alternatives have been attempted and all have failed.

Significant support for specific federation plans has declined in the United States, although many urban specialists still believe it is the most logical form of governmental organization for many of our cities. Ironically, in the 1950s, when this technique was losing support as a practical solution in the United States, it began to be tested in Canada in the metropolis of Toronto and later in other Canadian cities as well. Chapter 6 will consider the Toronto experience in some detail and try to answer the salient question of why federation was politically acceptable in Toronto while it was not in the United States.

COOPERATIVE EXPERIENCE

Those who support interlocal cooperation as a viable technique for dealing with metropolitan problems are often referred to as "polycentrists" because they favor retaining the large number of local governments in the metropolis. The supporters of the cooperative alternative view themselves as political realists because their proposals appear very moderate when compared with some of the other metropolitan experiments such as consolidation, the comprehensive urban county plan, or federation. Moreover, these reformers favor a dispersed local government and argue for the right of public choice between competing community locations, services, and tax bases. Interlocal cooperation is not a recent innovation, nor does it exist only in the metropolis. However, the major instances of its implementation have occurred since World War II in the larger urban areas.

For the proponents of the cooperative approach, the device represents a voluntary technique for confronting metropolitan problems while at the same time maintaining local control. They maintain that it represents a realistic alternative to those proposals that call for a strong metropolitan government at the expense of reducing the authority of many of the local units. In addition, polycentrists argue that the cooperative alternative contributes to greater governmental efficiency and lower cost since it eliminates the necessity of each local government's hiring its own personnel or constructing new facilities for each service that legally it is required to deliver.

Interlocal cooperation is a rather broad concept with numerous variations. There are, first of all, informal verbal agreements, often referred to as gentlemen's agreements, which may consist merely of the exchange of information by administrators who are employed by separate local governments. Other agreements are more formal, written documents among numerous local units that have decided, for example, to share the burden of constructing a new facility such as a cultural center or a sewage treatment plant. According to Zimmerman, of 2,248 municipalities over 2,500 in population responding to a 1972 questionnaire, 1,393, or 61 percent, reported that they were receiving services under provisions of formal and informal agreements. [14]

Where interlocal agreements are formal and relate to specific functions or services, they can take the following forms: [15]

1. a single government performs a service or provides a facility for one or more other local units;
2. two or more local governments administer a function or operate a facility on a joint basis; and
3. two or more local governments assist or supply mutual aid to one another in emergency situations.

The cooperative approach has been subjected to considerable criticism. First, critics argue that it really is a piecemeal approach since each service agreement normally involves only two governments and one service or facility. The usual result is a patchwork of agreements that relate to noncontroversial matters. For many critics, the most serious defect of interlocal agreements is their financial shortcomings. Although most agreements call for the provision of services for an exchange of money, often some local units in the metropolis do not have the financial resources to enter into a particular agreement. In short, cooperative arrangements are not devices that will equalize public resources among localities within the politically fragmented metropolitan environment. Accordingly, because communities are required to compensate each other for many of the services rendered, service contracts will probably continue to be of restricted value. They simply do not produce the equitable solution that the more systematic reorganization schemes call for.

The growth of interlocal service agreements probably will continue because of the demands of most suburban areas for better services, because of their capability for problem solving, and, of course, because of the persistent pressure to keep taxes as low as possible. However, these agreements do not appear to be as effective when dealing with such complex problems as low-income housing and environmental protection. Nevertheless, there is little evidence to suggest that most county governments are capable or willing to assume the same active role as Los Angeles County, where interlocal agreements are widely used. Few counties can perform like Los Angeles County as the supplier of services by contract, due to their own deficiencies in personnel, equipment, facilities, and programs.

Chapter 7 examines the development of interlocal agreements and their practical implementation in Lakewood, California in concert with Los Angeles County.

METROPOLITAN COUNCIL ALTERNATIVE

A final technique to be considered in this study is that of metropolitan councils. Here we have deviated from the framework of Bollens and Schmandt and will consider metropolitan councils as a separate category (Bollens and Schmandt, as mentioned earlier, consider them as a variation of the cooperative approach). While there is no doubt that these metropolitan councils involve cooperation, there are some key differences that merit a separate classification.

Metropolitan councils are permanent associations of governments that meet on a regular basis to discuss and reach agreement on remedies for mutual difficulties and needs. A metropolitan council can be defined as a voluntary association of governments designed to be an area-wide forum for key officials to conduct research, discuss, and debate issues and, eventually, determine how best to cope with their common problems. Due to its lack of authority, the council mechanism cannot be classified as a metropolitan government anymore than the United Nations can be considered a world government. Metropolitan councils lack mandatory financing and enforcement power. The legal basis for their organization is either a specific state law, a general state-interlocal agreement act, or nonprofit corporation legislation. [16]

Chapter 8 reviews the development of one type of metropolitan council—COGs—from their inception in 1954 to their present status. The specific case study that will be examined is the COG of Portland, Maine. As Vincent Marando suggests: "Political feasibility is the trademark of the COG, with its establishment in virtually all metropolitan areas. The politics of COGs occurs after their formation and is administrative in character."[17] In addition, a more advanced and politically developed type of metropolitan council as represented by Minneapolis-St. Paul will be examined in Chapter 9. The metropolitan council of the Twin Cities is an umbrella-type agency that acts as a coordinating and directing unit for metropolitan development. It has considerably more enforcement, recommendation, and review powers than do the COGs. Indeed, some reformers have viewed the Twin Cities experiment as the desirable prototype for the future evolution of COGs. Others have praised this approach because of its transfer of functions to state government. As Mogulof has commented:[18]

> The Twin Cities Metro-Council is the most impressive. Not because the Twin Cities Metro-Council itself has all the basic elements I see as necessary to metro-politan government—authority, adequate geographic scope, multifunctional capacity, and taxing powers— but because the Twin Cities Metro-Council is a creature of a stable government which does possess the scope and the power.

CONCLUSION

Communities in different regions are often confronted with similar problems but employ different approaches to resolve these problems. Metropolitan governmental reorganization has taken several major forms—the one-level alternative, the two-level alternative, the cooperative alternative, and the metropolitan council alternative. The present study explores the nature of these different alternatives of governmental reorganization to ascertain what factors contributed in each case to the adoption of one approach rather than another, how effective the structural change has been, and whether or not the reorganization scheme may be borrowed in whole or in part by other communities in different regions attempting to solve similar problems. In general, it seems that a pattern of political reform exists, but as Marando has cautioned, " . . . metropolitan reorganizations, where accepted, have been influenced more by political circumstances than the objective of establishing a metropolitan-wide approach to resolve metropolitan-wide problems."[19] This study seeks to examine the detail of these "circumstances" by investigating eight cases of experimentation in metropolitan government.

NOTES

1. Each of these seven American cities conforms to the federal definition of a metropolitan area, the Standard Metropolitan Statistical Area. See U. S. Office of Management and Budget (OMB) Statistical Policy Division, Criteria Followed in Establishing Standard Metropolitan Statistical Areas (Washington, D. C. : OMB, November 1971).

2. John C. Bollens and Henry J. Schmandt, The Metropolis: Its People, Politics, and Economic Life (New York: Harper & Row, 1975).

3. David Easton, A Framework for Political Analysis (Englewood Cliffs, N. J. : Prentice-Hall, 1965).

4. Robert L. Lineberry and Ira Sharkansky, Urban Politics and Public Policy (New York: Harper & Row, 1974), p. 6.

5. For a discussion of outputs, see Ira Sharkansky and Richard Hofferbert, "Dimensions of State Politics, Economics, and Public Policy," American Political Science Review 63 (September 1969): 872; and Robert L. Lineberry and Edmund P. Fowler, "Reformism and Public Policies in American Cities," American Political Science Review 61 (September 1967): 701, 702. For a discussion of the consequences of outputs or "outcomes," see Frank S. Levy, Arnold J. Meltsner, and Aaron Wildavsky, Urban Outcomes: Schools, Streets, and Libraries (Berkeley: University of California Press, 1974).

6. Bollens and Schmandt, op. cit. , p. 238.

7. Committee for Economic Development (CED), Modernizing Local Government to Secure Balanced Federalism (New York: CED, 1966), pp. 17, 44-47.

8. For a discussion of annexation, see Advisory Commission on Intergovernmental Relations, The Challenge of Local Government Reorganization (Washington, D. C. : Government Printing Office, 1974), chap. 5; and Richard L. Forstall, "Changes in Land Area for Larger Cities, 1960-1970," in Municipal Yearbook, 1972 (Washington, D. C. : International City Management Association, 1972).

9. For an account of such an exception, see "East Baton Rouge Parish" in National Association of Counties, Guide to County Organization and Management (Washington, D. C. , 1968), pp. 31-35.

10. Bollens and Schmandt, op. cit. , p. 264.

11. For a description of metropolitan districts, see ibid. , pp. 264-73; and John C. Bollens, Special District Governments in the United States (Berkeley and Los Angeles: University of California Press, 1957).

12. Joseph F. Zimmerman, "The Metropolitan Area Problem," Annals of the American Academy of Political and Social Science 416 (November 1974): 134.

13. Bollens and Schmandt, op. cit., pp. 280-81.

14. See Joseph F. Zimmerman, "Meeting Service Needs Through Intergovernmental Service Agreements," The Municipal Yearbook 1973 (Washington, D. C.: International City Management Association, 1973), pp. 79-88; Joseph F. Zimmerman, "Intergovernmental Service Agreements for Smaller Cities," Urban Data Service Reports, January 1973; and Joseph F. Zimmerman, "Intergovernmental Service Agreements and Transfer of Functions," in Substate Regionalism and the Federal System, ed. Advisory Commission on Intergovernmental Relations (Washington, D. C.: Government Printing Office, 1974), pp. 29-52.

15. Bollens and Schmandt, op. cit., p. 293.

16. Ibid., pp. 303-304.

17. Vincent L. Marando, "The Politics of Metropolitan Reform," Administration and Society 6 (August 1974): 256.

18. Melvin B. Mogulof, "A Modest Proposal for Governance of America's Metropolitan Areas," Journal of the American Institute of Planners 41 (July 1975): 252.

19. Marando, op. cit., p. 230.

PART

I

THE ONE-LEVEL
ALTERNATIVE:
CITY-COUNTY
CONSOLIDATION

1

THE NASHVILLE-DAVIDSON
COUNTY APPROACH

BACKGROUND

The metropolitan government of Nashville-Davidson County
is located in the north central area of the state of Tennessee.
Davidson County covers 533 square miles and consists of heavily
rolling terrain, structured like a bowl with Nashville in the middle,
bisected by the Cumberland River. Nashville was settled in 1780 as
a fort in then western North Carolina. It was incorporated in 1784
and had the first written city charter west of the Alleghenies. It
became the capital of Tennessee early in the nineteenth century
and subsequently developed into one of the most outstanding religious
and educational centers of the South. Today it has within its boundaries
783 churches and 13 colleges and universities including Vanderbilt
University, Meharry Medical College, and George Peabody Educational
College. The major historic sites include the Hermitage, Andrew
Jackson's home, and a full-scale replica of the Parthenon, which was
constructed to prove that the city is indeed the "Athens of the South."
Nashville is probably best known, however, as the "Country Music
Capital" of the world—the home of the Grand Ole Opry. In addition,
Nashville is a major recording center in the United States, producing
records and albums that generate approximately $100 million for the
Nashville economy. [1]
    Nashville is characterized by a diversified economy. It is
primarily a commercial city rather than an industrial one, although
it does have a moderate amount of manufacturing, such as DuPont,
Ford Glass, Gates Rubber, and Genesco. The city specializes in
insurance and banking establishments and also produces an above
average quantity of religious printing. Governmental services also

play an important part in the city's economy, since Nashville contains numerous municipal, county, state, and national agencies. Union Street in Nashville bristles with banks, investment houses, and loan associations and is often called the "Wall Street of the Central South."

In 1975, Nashville's population was estimated at 475,500, of which 19.6 percent was nonwhite. The white population is fairly homogeneous, with English, Scotch, and Irish surnames predominating. The area's citizens—black and white—are 99.5 percent native born. In the period 1940-60, Davidson County's population, including Nashville, grew from 257,268 to 399,743, while during the same period, the population of the city of Nashville remained almost constant. Table 1.1 shows this growth in terms of both the central city and the county outside.

From 1940 to 1960, Davidson County's pattern of growth was similar to that of other metropolitan areas in the United States— small or declining growth in the core city and rapidly expanding growth in the suburbs. Also consistent with the national pattern, the black population of Davidson County has become increasingly concentrated in the central city. In 1940, the percentage of nonwhites in Nashville was 28 percent; in 1950 it was 31.4 percent; and in

TABLE 1.1

Population of Nashville Standard
Metropolitan Statistical Area,
by Central City and County Outside, 1900-60

Year	Nashville	Davidson County Outside
1900	80,865	41,950
1910	110,364	39,114
1920	118,342	49,473
1930	153,866	68,988
1940	167,402	89,865
1950	174,307	147,451
1960	170,874*	228,869

*Including 4,587 persons annexed in 1959
Source: Brett W. Hawkins, Nashville Metro: The Politics of City-County Consolidation (Nashville: Vanderbilt University Press, 1964), p. 17.

1960 it had increased to 37.9 percent. In 1960, Davidson County, including Nashville, had the lowest percentage of population under the poverty level (10.4 percent) in Tennessee as well as the highest percentage of families with income over $15,000. [2]

Twelve roads lead out from Nashville, and for the most part the smaller communities in Davidson County have been located along these roads in a series of haphazard concentric circles fanning out from the central city. Each road serves as the main street for one or more of these communities and provides its major link with Nashville.

Prior to consolidation, Davidson County had 12 governments within its boundaries: the county, the city of Nashville, six incorporated suburbs (Belle Meade, Berry Hill, Lakewood, Oak Hill, Forest Hills, and Goodlettsville), and four special utility districts. The incorporated suburbs and special districts played only a tangential role in county politics.

The city of Nashville and Davidson County were, of course, the major governmental units before consolidation. Nashville had a strong mayor-council form of government. There were 21 councilmen, 20 elected from single-member districts, and the 21st, the vice-president, elected at large. The mayor appointed the heads of the 12 city executive departments with council approval. Also included within the governmental structure were some two dozen boards and commissions, and the major element of the judicial branch was the Nashville Metropolitan General Sessions Court. [3]

The county government was primarily designed to serve rural areas as an arm of the state. Legislative power was vested in a quarterly county court comprised of 55 members, called magistrates, who were popularly elected for six-year terms from 16 civil districts in the county and from the incorporated towns. The county court levied taxes for county purposes and provided such major services as public health, education, and roads and bridges. Since several of the communities outside of Nashville were unincorporated, the magistrates performed the political functions normally left to mayors and other city officials. [4]

The executive powers of the county government were vested in the county judge, who served as both the chief executive officer and as the judge of the monthly county court. His executive powers were fragmented among many boards and commissions, each of which governed in a separate field of authority. The county judge could not appoint persons to county boards or commissions, nor could he exercise authority over the county trustee, tax assessor, sheriff, or attorney general, all of whom were independently elected. Thus, the county judge was not as powerful a chief executive as the Nashville mayor. For all practical purposes, his real authority revolved around his responsibility for overall supervision of county fiscal affairs and his position as the central figure in county politics. In these respects, he could wield considerable influence. [5]

The county judiciary included a general sessions court, a criminal court, a circuit court, and a chancery court. These courts, with the exception of the general sessions court, were the general trial courts of the state's judicial system for Davidson County. [6]

The city and county each had planning commissions, which met jointly and shared a single staff. This joint agency played a major role in directing the growth of the community and took a significant lead in the development of the metropolitan government plan that was eventually adopted, the charter, and the campaign for voter approval.

Nashville-Davidson County politics are formally nonpartisan although Democratic party affilation seems to be necessary for election. [7] Before the 1962 consolidation, rivalry between city and county factions, rather than partisan politics, was the major political theme. Nashville's mayor, Ben West, led the city faction. West maintained a dominant position in city government and virtual control over the city council by using both patronage and his authority over city services. When he ran for office he could count on the support of "contingents of School Mothers' Patrols, assorted city inspectors, wives of city patrolmen, and so on. "[8] West was reputed to be more liberal than his chief political rival, Davidson County Judge Beverly Briley.

Briley, a fiscal conservative, was suburban-oriented rather than city-oriented. Although he never established an effective political machine, as did Mayor West, and, although the city appeared to be the stronger of the two factions, Briley himself felt that the county leadership had always been successful whenever it had challenged West and his supporters. [9] Daniel T. Grant has noted that the relative balance of power in the city-county factional rivalry "probably had the effect of militating against any major change in the status quo and, thus, in favor of the continued growth . . . of the metropolitan problems. "[10]

Nashville's two daily newspapers, the Tennessean and the Banner, played a major role in the area's politics. According to Bertil Hanson, both papers are "outspoken on public issues and almost invariably disagree; 'they can't even agree on the time of day' says a Nashvillian, recalling the papers' opposing stands on daylight savings time. "[11] The newspapers endorsed candidates in most elections, and it has been suggested that these endorsements are especially important in a one-party system in which personalities rather than party spokesmen compete for the voter's favor. In general, the Banner favored the West faction and the Tennessean opposed West.

STEPS LEADING TO CONSOLIDATION

The Nashville region's "metropolitan-type" problems—those problems uniquely related to the suburban spillover beyond the city boundaries—were quite similar to those of most other medium or small metropolitan areas in the United States. Those residents of Nashville who settled in the developing fringe area outside the legal city soon discovered that urban service needs continued but were no longer available. The most serious problem was the absence of sanitary sewers in the suburbs with an uncertain dependence upon septic tanks in the limestone base of Davidson County and the resulting inhibitions on the attraction of new industries. Since Nashville is underlain with hard limestone, housing developments had to be squeezed into relatively small areas where the soil cover was deep enough for septic tanks. At the same time, millions of dollars' worth of new industry was being lost because companies balked at building their own sewers. Thus, the necessity for a sewer to relieve the burden on septic tanks in the suburban areas became one of the major issues in the attempt to establish one government for the entire urbanized area.

There were also demands for police and fire protection, refuse service, and more and better schools. Nashville, the legally incorporated area to which the state legislature had granted broad powers to provide all needed municipal services, was actually only a 23-square-mile area in the center of the 100-square-mile urban region. County services were at a primitive stage. The county government even lacked the legal authority to own a fire engine. In the state of Tennessee, a county can repair roads, operate hospitals and schools, and provide sheriff's services, but it cannot perform such basic functions as setting speed limits without special state legislation. Because of this, Davidson County, parts of which were as thickly settled as Nashville itself, collected no garbage, erected no street lights, owned no parks or libraries, and provided no fire protection or water service. Nashville Fire Chief William McIntyre remarked, "It was as if there was a brick wall around the city's heart. Sometimes we had to let houses burn down a block across the city line."[12]

Thus, there existed a single metropolitan area with overlapping governments—one, the city, with plenty of power but little area, and the other, the county, with plenty of area but little power. This situation created constant buck passing to avoid responsibility, while each government tried to keep its own taxes low by taking advantage of the other's services.[13]

The Nashville region also provided an example of the tax dispute existent in many metropolitan areas between the city government and its "daytime citizens" from the suburbs. Most citizens in the region

paid taxes only to their "bedroom communities" beyond the city limits
in spite of the fact that their jobs depended upon the city of Nashville's
existence as a business center. They also, of course, used many city-
supported services. The city tried to combat these inequities by
overcharging county residents for city-supplied water and electricity.
In addition, in August 1959, the city passed an ordinance that levied
a $10 "wheel tax" on all motor vehicles using the streets of Nashville
for 30 days or more. County residents charged that this "green
sticker law," as it was called, was "taxation without representation,"
while the mayor pointed out that the city required additional revenue,
and he preferred this auto tax to raising property taxes as a means
of gaining the needed revenue. [14] Strict enforcement of the green
sticker law resulted in some arrests, and this, in turn, created
considerable resentment on the part of county residents. [15]

The situation described above contributed to poor city-county
relationships and a chain reaction of inefficiency and waste. City
and county police withheld crime information from each other, and
goods stolen from within Davidson County could be openly displayed
in city pawn shops without the city police even knowing that they were
stolen. The two school systems fought over how to split state education aid. On some roads where the city-county line went down the
middle, the speed limit was 35 m. p. h. in one direction and 45 m. p. h.
in the other. No libraries were built in the rapidly growing suburbs,
where they were badly needed. The city discontinued buying new
park land, while the population demanded more green space. Thousands
of acres of open space and woodland were cut up for residential subdivisions without reserving a single acre for public parks and playgrounds. County leaders declared they had no authority to operate
suburban parks, and city leaders said that the responsibility for such
parks was not theirs and even rejected offers of free park lands on
the ground that the county would refuse to contribute to their upkeep. [16]
Two hundred miles of suburban water lines of a size insufficient for
fire hydrants were installed over a period of decades. With only 282
hydrants in the whole county outside the city, fire departments had
to rely on pumper trucks or ponds for water and residents paid $50
to $100 more a year for fire insurance than did residents of the city.

The types of problems described above made it increasingly
evident that the needs of the residents in the Nashville-Davidson
County area were not being efficiently and effectively met by the
existing multigovernment arrangement. The events leading to the
successful 1962 governmental revision covered a span of roughly
ten years. In 1951, the Tennessee Taxpayers' Association, after
completing a study of Davidson County government, recommended
that the county's governmental needs "could be most efficiently and
economically served by one completely consolidated unit of local

government. "[17] In the same year, the Davidson County delegation
to the Tennessee legislature fought for and was successful in obtaining
the passage of an act establishing a Community Services Commission
for Davidson County and the city of Nashville. The city and county
both supplied funds for the commission, whose purpose was to
survey the governmental needs of metropolitan Nashville and
Davidson County and to suggest ways of filling these needs. In the
following year, the commission published a report entitled A Future
for Nashville. This study recommended that countywide functions
such as public health and public welfare be provided solely by the
county; that city and county home rule be authorized by the state
assembly; that Davidson County be reapportioned to correct for the
underrepresentation of city residents in county government; and,
most importantly, that extensive, surrounding, suburban areas be
annexed by the city of Nashville. Annexation would allow urban
services to be provided to suburban dwellers outside the city limits
who were not then receiving such services. In addition, the report
warned that Nashville probably would stagnate unless obsolete city
limits were extended to include 90,000 urbanites living on the city's
outskirts. The commission viewed city-county consolidation favorably, but it did not consider it to be a viable alternative to
annexation because of constitutional barriers in the way of implementation. [18]

There were few, immediate, tangible results of A Future for
Nashville. Some consolidation of city-county functions, such as
public health and public welfare, did take place, but the recommendation for annexation, the heart of the study, was not acted
upon. Nevertheless, the Community Service Commission's report
stimulated the establishment of a joint city-county planning agency
to examine area-wide problems, and it also gave impetus to state
legislative action that allowed Nashville and other similar metropolitan areas to begin to solve these problems. [19]

In 1953, Tennessee voters approved an amendment authorizing
the state legislature to provide for the consolidation of any or all
functions of cities and counties upon the affirmative vote of a
majority of those voting within the municipality and those voting in
the county outside. Although actual consolidation would still require
enabling legislation, the amendment at least made consolidation a
feasible alternative for planners and political leaders to consider.
Two years later, the Tennessee General Assembly enacted legislation
that permitted cities to annex contiguous, unincorporated territories
without the latter's consent. Before the adoption of this statute,
Tennessee municipalities had been unable to annex adjacent areas
except by means of a private act of the legislature or by petition of
the citizens of such areas. In 1956, the Advance Planning and

Research Division, an agency created three years earlier by the city
of Nashville and Davidson County planning commissions to undertake
long-range research and planning projects, produced a <u>Plan of
Metropolitan Government for Nashville and Davidson County</u>. This
study, which was conducted in response to the requests of businessmen, civic leaders, and public officials, proposed annexation as an
immediate solution for Nashville's problems, but it also recommended
the creation of a single metropolitan government to replace the
existing city and county governments. Consolidation was put forward
as the long-range solution for the wastefulness resulting from
duplicate governments, while annexation and functional consolidation
were viewed as only halfway measures and hence less desirable than
complete consolidation. [20] A major feature of the plan was the
creation of two service districts within a single governmental unit:
"a 'general services district' [GSD] would provide general services
required on an area wide basis and would include the entire county,
and an 'urban services district' [USD] . . . would provide additional
services normally required in an urban area. "[21] There would be
two separate tax rates, which would support the level of services
required in each district. In addition, the plan recommended that
the chief executive should have "strong mayor authority" and that there
should be a single legislative body for the entire county. [22] The
allocation of services to the two service districts would take the form
shown in Table 1.2.

     In the following year, 1957, the general assembly enacted
enabling legislation that implemented the 1953 amendment to the
state constitution providing for city-county consolidation. The
general assembly also authorized the establishment of a charter
commission to draft a charter consolidating city and county governmental functions under a metropolitan form of government. The
commission was comprised of ten members, five selected by Davidson
County Judge Briley and five selected by Nashville Mayor West.
The commission turned out to be a broadly balanced, representative
body consisting of business leaders, spokesman for labor and for
low-income interests, black leaders, and a distinguished woman
attorney. [23] The question of black support for consolidation entered
prominently into the deliberations of the charter commission.
Since consolidation could be interpreted as a means of diluting the
growing black vote in the central city, the commission drew up the
councilmanic districts so that at least two seats on the new council
would be held by blacks. In all, 15 councilmen were to be elected
from roughly equal districts and six were to be chosen at large.
This total was about one-third the existing number of representatives
on city and county legislative bodies. [24]

TABLE 1. 2

Allocation of Services in Two Service Districts

Urban Services District	General Services District
Police (class II)	General administration
Fire protection (class III)	Fire protection
Water	Assessment
Sewer, sanitary	Hospitals
Sewer, storm	Streets and roads
Street lighting	Parks and recreation
Refuse collection and disposal	Fair grounds
Wine and whisky supervision	Auditorium
Taxicab regulation	Public housing
	Urban redevelopment
	Electricity
	Building code
	Plumbing code
	Electrical code
	Housing code
	Transit
	Police
	Courts
	Jails
	Health
	Welfare
	Traffic
	Schools
	Library
	Airport
	Zoning
	Transit
	Planning

Source: Brett W. Hawkins, Nashville Metro: The Politics of City-County Consolidation (Nashville: Vanderbilt University Press, 1966), p. 45.

Under the terms of the charter, the new metropolitan government was to be divided into the two separate service-tax districts that were proposed in 1956 by the planning commission. Areas outside the USD would be annexed to the district by ordinance. In addition, the four incorporated communities in the county, excluding Nashville, were to retain their current independent status until they decided to merge with the consolidated government. [25]

The commission completed its proposed charter in 1958, and a vigorous campaign took place before it was presented to the voters. The campaign was largely a newspaper campaign. Both of Nashville's newspapers, the Banner and the Tennessean, set aside their usual differences and went all out in support of "Metro," the name by which the consolidation proposal came to be known. The fact that the two papers, which seldom agreed on controversial political questions, supported Metro was viewed by some voters with considerable suspicion: "When both of the papers supported it [Metro], there must be something fishy about it. "[26] The pro-Metro forces also included Mayor West, Judge Briley, various academics, the Nashville Chamber of Commerce and a majority of business leaders, the Nashville Trades and Labor Council, the Tennessee Taxpayers' Association, the League of Women Voters, and all ten members of the charter commission. In addition, a citizens' committee for metropolitan government supplied speakers for clubs and distributed pamphlets that summarized the provisions of the charter.

Opposition to the charter was slight until the final week before the referendum when it surfaced in the form of a flood of newspaper, radio, and television advertisements and thousands of handbills that were distributed throughout the region. Those opposed to Metro included the suburban private fire and police companies, sheriffs, constables, most of the operators of the small suburban business establishments, some Nashville businessmen, and about half of the members of both the city council and the county court. The opponents argued that Metro would mean bigger government, higher taxes, extended liquor sales, and the assumption of dictatorial powers by Ben West and his cohorts. [27]

On June 17, 1958, the voters went to the polls and rejected the proposed charter. The results of the election are reproduced in Table 1.3. The anti-Metro "scare campaign" appeared to be most effective in the lower-income suburbs and least effective in the higher-income suburbs. Perhaps the greatest weakness in the proponents' campaign was the lack of a grass-roots, door-to-door approach. [28] Hawkins describes the campaign and the reasons for the charter's defeat as follows:[29]

> The Nashville referendum appeared to be much like
> other referenda on government intergration. The
> actual proposal was put forward by such typically

TABLE 1.3

Vote on 1958 Metro Charter
by Nashville Wards and
Davidson County Civil Districts

Nashville Ward	Percent for	Percent Voting	Total Vote
1	40.9	15.2	987
2	44.8	14.1	746
3	65.7	22.3	1,775
4	78.2	34.1	3,793
5	50.7	18.6	2,144
6	52.6	19.8	1,186
7	61.5	23.7	1,969
Total	61.9	22.2	12,605

County "civil district"	Percent for	Percent Voting	Total Vote
2	21.3	45.5	1,131
3	31.9	44.0	3,013
4	17.5	47.2	1,891
5	21.7	42.3	539
6	35.3	40.4	3,836
7	72.3	50.4	4,585
8	53.6	40.8	2,600
9	12.0	47.5	332
10	9.3	50.8	1,210
11	26.1	40.4	2,155
12	24.9	34.8	1,748
13	20.9	37.6	728
14	6.9	45.9	596
15	44.4	44.7	4,742
16	67.1	45.9	3,923
Total	41.8	43.8	33,029
Grand total	47.3	34.5	45,634

Source: Daniel J. Elazar, A Case Study of Failure in Attempted Metropolitan Integration: Nashville and Davidson County, Tennessee (Chicago: National Opinion Research Center and Social Science Division, University of Chicago, 1961), p. 3.

reformist groups as a taxpayers' association, a
chamber of commerce study committee, a special
"community services commission" established by
private act of the state legislature, and by city and
county planners. It was then supported by numerous
civic associations, by businessmen and young lawyers,
and by the central city mayor in a largely amateurish,
upper-class, good government campaign . . . . The
opposition concentrated on the county area and
stressed such issues as higher taxes and city
dictatorship.

The outcome was a typical "yes" vote in the
city and a "no" vote outside. Similar results occurred
in the Louisville area in 1956, the Macon area in
1960, and the Richmond area in 1961.

There was, in short, nothing very different about
the Nashville referendum of 1958.

Another analyst suggested, "The whole consolidation proposal
lacked a crucial issue to arouse the interests of the citizenry."[30]

Following the defeat of the consolidation referendum, the
city of Nashville began to use for the first time the strong annexation
powers that had been authorized in 1955 by the Tennessee legislature.
Within two years' time, the city annexed nearly 50 square miles of
surrounding suburbs containing a population of approximately 87,000.
The first annexation occurred only two days after the unsuccessful
referendum, and the second was effected in April 1960. Neither of
these two annexations involved the consent of the persons living in
the areas being annexed, in spite of Mayor West's earlier promise to
give the affected persons the right to vote. Thus, the annexations
understandably generated a great deal of hostility toward West and
his administration, especially since the majority of those in the
annexed areas had voted against consolidation. The resentment
became even more intense when the newly annexed citizens discovered
that the city was unable to ensure that urban services would be
extended to their homes and that Davidson County was proposing a
property tax increase for unincorporated areas, including the
annexed territories.

In January 1960, after the first annexation was a fait accompli
and while the second one was under consideration by the Nashville
City Council, the Davidson County Quarterly Court enacted a
resolution calling for a new charter commission. The Nashville
City Council did not follow suit, however, since a majority of its
members felt that Nashville had gained enough already from its
extensive annexation program and would profit little from a new

consolidation campaign. [31] However, in March 1961, the Tennessee
General Assembly, primarily at the behest of the Davidson County
delegation, enacted into law a private act creating a second charter
commission for Nashville and Davidson County. Both city and county
voters approved the creation of the new charter commission on
August 17, 1961. Eight of the ten members serving on the new charter
commission had also served on the 1957 commission, and this
probably explains why the 1962 charter was so similar to the one that
was previously rejected. The main differences between the two
charters were an increase in the size of the metropolitan council
from 21 to 41 members; a three-term limit rather than a two-term
limit for the mayor and an increase in the mayor's salary from
$20,000 to $25,000; and provision for a referendum on the school
budget should two-thirds of the board of education deem the budget
adopted by the metropolitan council to be inadequate. [32]

On June 28, 1962, the voters of the Nashville-Davidson County
region approved the new charter. Since the 1958 and 1962 charters
were almost indentical, the 1962 success cannot be explained by
changes in the charter itself. The apparent consensus of observers
was that uniquely situational issues and a highly politicized, hard-
fought, grass-roots campaign were the key variables that resulted
in approval the second time around.

The roster of consolidation supporters remained the same as
in 1958 with the notable defections of Ben West and the Banner.
Mayor West argued that the city's annexation program should be
given a chance to succeed before anything new was attempted. However, his critics charged that he switched his position because his
chances of becoming metropolitan mayor were not nearly as good
as in 1962 as they had been in 1958. [33] Among the Metro proponents
were Beverly Briley, the Tennessean, the Nashville Chamber of
Commerce, the Jaycees, various black intellectuals, and such
so-called good-government groups as the League of Women Voters
and the Tennessee Taxpayers' Association. The anti-Metro forces
included, in addition to Ben West and his political supporters, the
Nashville Fire and Police Departments, officials and employees of the
six small cities, black "traditionalists," and the Banner.

The opponents charged that Metro was a utopian scheme that
would not, as promised, end overlapping and duplicating services
because it did not provide for the dissolution of the six city governments. Furthermore, they equated consolidation with "burning
down the house just to get rid of one rat."[34] The "rat" referred to
was Ben West and the "house" symbolized Nashville's city government.
The pro-Metro forces concentrated as they had in 1958, on such
rational, good-government issues as economy and efficiency in
government; elimination of city and county service disparities; and

the initiation of area-wide, long-range planning. The "gut" issues, however, were annexation and the obnoxious green sticker law. David A. Booth related these two issues to the various groups voting in the referendum as follows:[35]

> For the voter in the old core city, the question was whether or not to keep Ben West as mayor. A vote for the Charter was a vote against the mayor.
> For the voter in the newly annexed areas, the issues was whether to become a first-class citizen of a new metropolitan government, or to retain the second-class underrepresented status inherent in annexation. Another issue was whether to retain as a mayor a man who had broken his pledge (to give the people a vote on annexation) or whether to drive him from office . . . .
> For the voter in the rest of the county, there were also two issues: whether he wanted to be liable to annexation at any time, yet receive no guarantee of better services; or whether he wanted to adopt Metro which guaranteed services within one year after any property tax became part of the urban services district. The second issue was a choice between taxation without representation (such as the "green sticker" tax provided) and between a new plan wherein each voter would participate in the election of six members of the new council . . . .

The 1962 campaign was organized more broadly and in greater depth than the one in 1958. A good deal of effort went into such vote-getting activities as telephoning, doorbell ringing, and neighborhood coffees. On both sides, it appeared that the professionals and politicians had assumed the leadership positions that in 1958 had been occupied by amateurs. Competition between the Banner and the Tennessean made the 1962 campaign much more intense than the previous one. The Banner staunchly defended the status quo, while the Tennessean adopted a "beat-the-city-machine" approach and "in a barrage of editorials, news stories, cartoons, special feature articles, . . . pursued its goal zealously, obsessed by its intention to defeat the mayor and to achieve Metro victory."[36]

In the end, the charter was approved by a majority of both city and county voters. The newly annexed areas overwhelmingly endorsed Metro, and this provided enough of a margin to carry the entire city. The fringe areas adjacent to the city also voted heavily in favor of consolidation, thereby delivering the country in spite of

TABLE 1.4

Vote on 1962 Metro Charter by Nashville Wards and Davidson County Civil Districts

County District	Percent for	Percent Voting	Total Vote
2	37.5	40.3	674
3	69.2	45.1	4,065
4	35.6	49.7	2,245
5	57.2	45.7	1,141
6	68.2	44.4	2,527
7	59.1	54.6	2,383
8	71.2	52.7	2,205
9	32.8	47.6	393
10	24.7	45.8	1,399
11	47.9	37.4	2,521
12	57.7	35.7	1,859
13	38.7	41.9	1,231
14	31.0	44.5	693
15	66.7	44.3	3,543
16	56.6	54.4	1,529
County totals	55.9	43.9	28,408

Nashville Wards	Percent for	Percent Voting	Total Vote
1	32.9	31.9	2,246
2	24.9	31.4	1,784
3	50.7	37.7	2,825
4	62.4	39.0	4,490
5	42.2	31.9	4,079
6	38.3	26.9	1,649
7	42.3	33.7	2,887
Totals 1-7	45.1	33.7	19,960
8	64.4	40.6	4,533
9	79.2	50.2	8,953
10	63.6	41.5	3,240
Totals 8-10	72.2	45.3	16,726
Total city	57.4	38.1	36,686
Grand totals	56.8	40.4	65,094

Source: Brett W. Hawkins, Nashville Metro: The Politics of City-County Consolidation (Nashville: Vanderbilt University Press, 1966), p. 151.

substantial rural opposition. (See Table 1.4 for the results of the referendum.)

The new metropolitan government successfully withstood several challenges to its legality. In November 1962, Beverly Briley was elected the first mayor of Metro (his opponent was Tax Assessor Clifford Allen; Mayor West did not run), and a new metropolitan legislative council was selected. On April 1, 1963, the Metropolitan Government of Nashville-Davidson County came formally into existence. [37]

GOVERNMENT PRESCRIPTION:
THE NEW SYSTEM

Structural Change

The metropolitan government of Nashville-Davidson County merged the governmental and corporate functions previously held separately by the city of Nashville and Davidson County. The Metro government has a strong mayor-council system. The chief executive is the metropolitan mayor who is elected by the area's voters to a four-year term. His tenure in office is limited to three consecutive terms. The mayor is responsible for the supervision, administration, and control of the executive departments, agencies, boards, and commissions. He appoints department heads subject to council confirmation. In addition, he is authorized to approve or disapprove council ordinances subject to an override by two-thirds of the council. The mayor may also veto line-item budget expenditures, again subject to a two-thirds override by the council (see Figure 1.1). [38]

The legislative branch consists of two parts: the metropolitan council and the urban council. The metropolitan county council is comprised of 40 councilmen and the vice-mayor. Thirty-five of these councilmen are elected from single-member districts of approximately equal population, and five councilmen are elected at large. Councilmen serve for four-year terms. The vice-mayor, who also is elected for a four-year term, is the presiding officer of the council. The three-member urban council's sole and mandatory function is to levy a property tax in the USD that is adequate to finance the budget for urban services. In practice, the metropolitan council establishes the tax rate and the urban council adopts it. [39]

The judicial branch is composed of the metropolitan general sessions court, the county probate court, the quarterly county court, the juvenile court, and the circuit, criminal, and chancery courts. The quarterly county court, formerly the legislative and executive body of Davidson County, was limited in the duties it

FIGURE 1.1 Metropolitan Government of Nashville

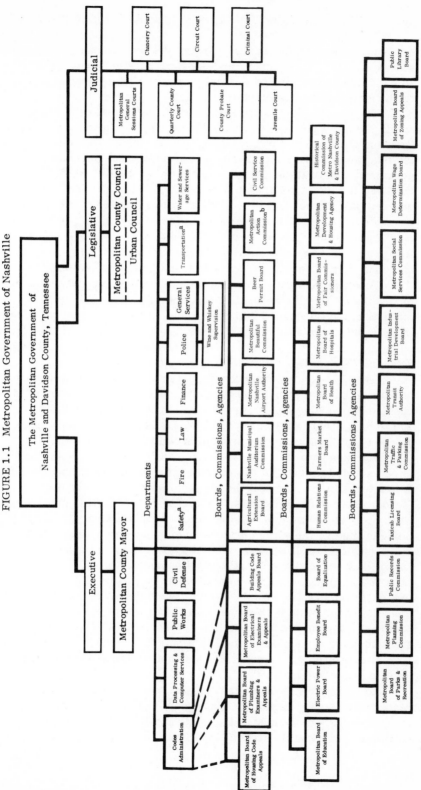

[a]Departments expected to be funded July, 1973.   [b]Expected to be discontinued June 30, 1973.

Source: Metropolitan Government of Nashville.

performs under the new system. Under the new charter, it appoints
notaries public, the coroner, and the ranger. The county court's
16 magistrates are elected for six-year terms while judges serving
on the other courts are elected for eight-year terms. [40]

The charter designates two separate service-tax districts
within the metropolitan government's geographic limits: the general
Services District and the Urban Services District. The GSD comprises
the total area of Davidson County and provides such services as
general administration, police, courts, jails, health, welfare,
schools, transit, and parks and recreation. The USD originally
covered only the old city of Nashville, but, since 1963, it has been
extended to include 140 square miles of territory and 52,000 residents
(see Figure 1.2). The USD provides additional services such as
fire protection, water, sanitary sewers, street lighting, street
cleaning, refuse collection, and additional police protection. [41]

Separate taxes are levied in each district to support the level
of services within the respective district. For example, in 1975 all
citizens of the GSD paid $4.11 per $100 of assessed property valuation,
while residents of the USD paid an additional $1.89 per $100 for the
extra services they received. Thus, GSD residents paid $4.11 per
$100 and USD paid $6 per $100 to Metro government. [42]

The USD may be expanded whenever areas in the GSD need
additional urban services and when the metropolitan government is
capable of providing those services within one year after the
additional USD tax rate is imposed. [43] In 1975, the only services
unique to the USD were fire protection and refuse collection.
Alternate means of financing such as users' fees have allowed services
to be extended to the GSD without enlarging the USD's boundaries. [44]
It is interesting to note that the six incorporated cities of Belle
Meade, Berry Hill, Goodlettsville, Lakewood, Oak Hill, and Forest
Hills continue to exist as they did before consolidation. Their
citizens receive the same services and pay the same taxes as other
residents of the GSD. These cities may become part of the USD
only if they surrender their municipal charters. [45]

Legal changes in the status quo may be proposed in one of
two ways: (1) adoption of a resolution receiving a two-thirds
majority of the council or (2) petition of 20 percent of the
qualified voters of the metropolitan government. The proposed
amendment must then be ratified by a majority of votes cast in a
special referendum. Amendments may not be proposed more than
once in every two years. [46]

Generally considered, the charter specified that ordinances,
resolutions, zoning regulations, property rights, contracts, and
obligations of both the city of Nashville and Davidson County would
remain in force "until revoked, modified, revised or abated" by the

FIGURE 1.2

Services Districts of Metropolitan Government
of Nashville and Davidson County

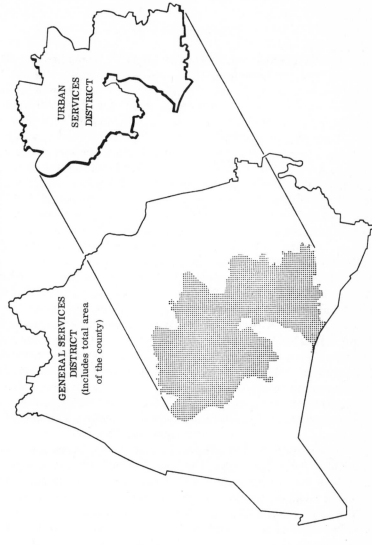

URBAN
SERVICES
DISTRICT

GENERAL SERVICES
DISTRICT
(includes total area
of the county)

Source: James C. Coomer and Charlie B. Tyer, Nashville Metropolitan Government: The First Decade (Knoxville: Bureau of Public Administration, University of Tennessee, 1974), p. 45.

new metropolitan government or its agencies. In addition, if either city or county agencies were abolished, their employees were to be continued as temporary appointees of the appropriate, succeeding metropolitan agency.

Impact of the System

Broadly considered, the major impact of consolidation on the Nashville-Davidson County political system was the eradication of the old county and city governments and the substitution of an entirely new form of government. This eliminated, almost by definition, the old pattern of bickering and buck passing. [47] Beyond this, however, it seems more important to investigate whether Metro has had a favorable effect on the individual citizen. Specifically, the authors sought to examine the following questions: Is responsibility for governmental decisions easier or more difficult to pinpoint now than under the previous system? Has citizen access to government become easier or more difficult since consolidation? Does race or place of residence have any effect on the degree of access?

Daniel Grant indicates that consolidation has probably facilitated "the easier focus of the public spotlight" on the activities of local politicians. He continues, "With only one legislative body and one chief executive, rather than two, the requirements of civic watchfulness are in a sense just one-half as great as they were before Metro."[48] Grant feels that buck passing is certainly possible as, for example, between mayor and council, but such accountability problems do not appear to be as prevalent as they were with the old city-county factionalism. [49] A survey made between 1967 and 1969 asked Metro notables: "What effect has Metro had on the ability of the people to fix responsibility on governmental officials for action or inaction?" Seventeen of the respondents replied that fixing responsibility has been made easier since consolidation. [50]

Opponents of Metro had argued that consolidation would make government less responsible and less accessible because local legislators would represent a larger number of constituents and because a reduction in the number of agencies and departments would mean a corresponding reduction in the number of citizen access points. These assertions have proved to be true to some extent. City councilmen did have smaller districts than the current Metro councilmen. However, the 19 magistrates serving on the quarterly county court were elected at large rather than from single-member districts, and the rural area of the county was over-represented at the expense of the city. Furthermore, the mayor and council are elected for four-year terms rather than the county judges' eight-year term or the magistrates' six. "Thus," Daniel Grant writes,

"it could be argued that as a result of consolidation Metro is much
closer to the stereotyped ideal of grassroots democracy than the old
county government was, but somewhat less close than the old city
government."[51]

In the survey cited above, 14 out of 20 respondents indicated
that Metro had made citizens' access to government easier. "Several
stated that because there is only one government 'it helps the people
know who the responsible official is and eliminates the old city-county
buckpassing'."[52] The same study also reported that the respondents
believed that political access for blacks had become easier since
Metro. Those interviewed noted that there were five black members
on the Metro council compared to three on the old city council and
none on the quarterly court.[53] However, since only two of the 20
respondents were black, these data may only express white perceptions
of blacks' ease of political access. In 1962, Metro council districts
were racially gerrymandered to ensure that at least five seats would
be filled by blacks. In 1970, seven blacks were elected (two from
white districts), although the percentage of black population in the
Nashville-Davidson region remained practically unchanged. Robert
McArthur notes that this has "provided partial refutation to those
who claim that metropolitan consolidation would inevitably result in
dilution of black political influence."[54] On the other hand, others
have pointed out that if consolidation had not occurred, it is
reasonable to assume that the 37.9 percent black minority would
have elected seven or eight blacks to the city council.[55]

McArthur also polled "rural-urban fringe dwellers" to determine
whether Metro had reduced their access to the political system. A
majority, 63.7 percent, agreed that "under Metro it is easier to
know whom to call or see when you have a problem than it was
under separate city and county government." McArthur found that
half of those interviewed felt it was easier to get an attentive hearing
for a problem under Metro and that only 20 percent felt that Metro
made it harder to get a hearing.[56]

Nevertheless, a more recent study by Rogers and Lipsey concluded that residents of the small city of Berry Hill "expressed
higher degrees of satisfaction with . . . the concern of local officials
for the welfare of the community than did respondents of Woodbine—
the community served by a large metropolitan government [Nashville
Metro]."[57] The authors point out that this contradicts the classic
reformist premise that "a decrease in the number of governmental
units . . . and an increase in the size of the governmental unit will
be associated with a greater degree of responsibility on the part of
local officials."[58]

RECORD SINCE CONSOLIDATION

Administrative problems resulting from consolidation were considerable during the first year, beginning with the effort to put together the first budget, a task that involved the merger of city and county accounting systems and a great deal of work for the staffs of the planning commission and legal department concerning organization and functions of merged agencies. "Government by postponment" became the norm as several departments were forced to delay operations in many areas because of pending studies by professional consultants. [59] The merging of two groups of governmental employees was also a difficult undertaking, and as of 1971, Mayor Briley still was receiving complaints from residents of the old county who lacked certain services. Some residents had to pay for independent refuse collection and were without street lighting and adequate fire protection. Many taxpayers outside Nashville complained that they were paying more taxes and receiving no new services, but actually they now were paying for services that they formerly received free.

In spite of these and other similar problems, considerable progress has been made in the Nashville-Davidson County region since consolidation. The supporters of Metro had claimed that consolidation would result in more efficient government because duplication of services would be eliminated and economies of scale would result. In 1964, Mayor Briley reported the following savings, economies, and efficiencies in government:[60]

1. One million dollar savings in school construction through transfer of county students to empty city classrooms.
2. One million dollar savings in construction costs, plus $50,000 annual operating costs by consolidating former city and county sewerage plans . . .
4. Initiated new purchasing policies on the basis of competitive bidding to eliminate favoritism . . .
6. Establishment of a motor pool and fleet purchasing for Metropolitan automobiles . . .
9. Establishment of a Data Processing Unit for increased efficiency in all departments through fast, accurate and up to date records systems.

In a 1962 study, the Tennessee Taxpayers' Association superimposed the Metro government structure on the spending patterns of the old Nashville and Davidson County governments for fiscal year 1960/61. Their analysis indicated that over a ten-year

period, 1966–75, Metro would save taxpayers $18 million. [61] Despite
these projected economies, Metro's budget has continued to rise. In
1962/63 the combined expenditures for the city of Nashville and
Davidson County were $65,764,000, as compared with Metro's first
budget of $70 million for 1963/64. The total budget for Metro's
eleventh fiscal year added up to $216 million—an increase of 210
percent over 1963/64. [62] However, increases in the last decade are
not in themselves surprising, since most major municipalities
experienced sizable increases in their budgets. Grant suggests that,
in part, this increase in expenditures is due to "a kind of civic
revolution of rising expectations" by citizens who demand more
services from Metro than they would have from the old governments. [63]

Another relevant point involves the fact that increases in
expenditures are likely because many government functions are not
subject to economies of scale, since they are labor intensive. Moreover, savings that do result from a reduction of unit costs for
services such as water and sewerage are not large enough to offset
rising costs for other types of services. In addition, it appears that
the most efficient governments serve from 50,000 to 100,000
inhabitants; Metro's population is now 475,500. [64]

The diversification of Metro's revenue base has allowed the
government to meet increasing service demands without resorting to
large hikes in the property tax. In this regard, significant changes
have been made in the areas of sales tax, user's fees, automobile
registration fees, bonds and interest, and property tax.

Sales tax: In 1963 a one-cent sales tax for educational services
was levied. Since then the tax has been raised an additional one-half
cent, which is also used for educational purposes.

User's fees: These have been employed to finance the water,
sewer, electric, and transit services as well as an auditorium.
Water and sewer charges permitted the rapid expansion of sewer
lines while at the same time allowing a reduction in the property
tax.

Automobile registration fees: A $15 registration fee was made
permanent in 1970. This fee was the successor to the unpopular
green sticker tax.

Bonds and interest: Nashville was near its statutory debt limit
before consolidation. Unification not only relieved that problem but
also allowed Metro government to be more effective in investing its
surplus funds. McArthur points out that in the first year of consolidation, Metro earned $400,000 more in interest on its investments
than did the city and county combined in the previous year.

Property tax: In 1960, the city of Nashville's tax rate was
$5.32 per $100. In 1975 the USD's tax rate was $6 per $100. [65] The
Tennessee Taxpayers' Association estimated that if Nashville and

TABLE 1.5

Property Tax Rates

Fiscal Year		Rate
1962/63	County	$2.32
	City	3.00
	Total	5.32
1963/64	GSD	3.70
	USD	2.00
Total for USD residents		5.70
1968/69	GSD	3.50
	USD	1.80
Total for USD residents		5.30
1974/75	GSD	4.11
	USD	1.89
Total for USD residents		6.00

Source: James C. Coomer and Charlie B. Tyer, Nashville Metropolitan Government: The First Decade (Knoxville: Bureau of Public Administration, University of Tennessee, 1974), p. 46.

Davidson County were still separated, the tax rate would be at least $7.[66]

In addition, the tax rate in the GSD has been adjusted in such a way that suburban and rural residents pay for services that they had received free before consolidation.[67] Table 1.5 illustrates how the tax burden has been reallocated between USD and GSD. Moreover, a 1971 Urban Observatory survey indicated that 66 percent of Nashville respondents felt that their local taxes were "about right" or "too low." This attitude seems to be correlated with a rather low property tax rate.[68]

In general, it appears that Metro has reduced the rural-urban service disparity and at the same time has upgraded both the quality and quantity of many services. Since consolidation, the GSD has received an increasing percentage of expenditures for general government services while the USD's share has declined. In 1963-64, the GSD received 71 percent of expenditures for services, compared to 29 percent for the USD. In 1971/72, the GSD's share had increased to 77 percent.[69]

Studies conducted from 1964 to 1971 indicated that the citizen evaluation of Metro was generally favorable. Grant's 1964 survey showed that 71 percent of those polled were satisfied with Metro. [70] A 1971 survey revealed that 92.4 percent of "fringe area" citizens believed that local services as a whole were about the same, somewhat better, or much better than before Metro. [71] A study undertaken by the Urban Observatory of Nashville found that 72 percent of those interviewed felt that local government was better than it had been five or ten years before. The same survey discovered that 71 percent of those polled thought their neighborhoods were getting the same or better services than other neighborhoods in Metro. [72]

Many observers believe that Metro's greatest accomplishments have occurred within its school system. Before consolidation, Davidson County and Nashville supported two competing school systems. The county could not provide the level of school services that Nashville did because county schools and city schools shared the county school funds. Nashville was able to support additional school services by tapping other sources of revenue as well. In 1962/63, the per-pupil expenditure in Nashville was $350 versus $267 per pupil in the rest of the county. Metro supporters claimed that a consolidated government would be better able to provide equal educational opportunities to all county children because it would unify the two school systems.

Since the creation of Metro, teacher salaries have been equalized and upgraded, and, in addition, the pupil-teacher ratio has declined somewhat, particularly in the primary grades. Other significant accomplishments include additional supervisory staff, increased paraprofessional and clerical support, improved methods of teacher recruitment, additional teaching materials and supplies, and expanded vocational, technical, and special education programs. In addition, during Metro's first ten years, 19 new schools were constructed and additions were made to 58 others. Finally, the enlargement of the school system has paid dividends by the increased amounts of funds available from federal and state governments. [73]

Early evaluations of the police department seem to indicate that law enforcement services have also been improved under the consolidated government. Under Metro, the law enforcement agencies were merged and their employees were given permanent civil service status and the benefits of professional training programs. Additionally, many new patrolmen were hired, the number of police cars was doubled, and the number of police zones was increased, all of which contributed to more effective police coverage. As proof of increased law enforcement effectiveness, Metro officials cite a 1965 FBI report that indicated a 7 percent drop in Metro major crime while the national crime rate rose by 5 percent. [74]

Metro also has realized improvements under consolidation in such other areas as data processing, purchasing, a unique solid-waste system that heats and cools part of downtown Nashville, and better cooperation between residents of the central city and outlying areas. When suburbanites started paying taxes for downtown problems, they became interested in solving those problems. [75] Consolidation has eliminated duplication of services and has pinpointed administrative and political responsibility. It has reduced the financial burden of the core city, spread the cost of countywide services throughout the county, and made possible the reasonable projection of long-term tax stability for major downtown property owners.

On the negative side, Coomer and Tyer describe the first year of consolidation as follows:[76]

1. Perhaps because of the over-zealous selling job by the advocates of Metro many citizens of the county came to believe that the Metro form of government could produce needed service twice as fast and twice as cheap as the former governments. When surburban taxes went up and sewers, water and refuse collection did not appear over the weekend, many began to criticize the government.

2. In the reorganization of the two governments, Metro had virtually destroyed civil service, job tenure, and the hiring of new employees by examination and test of ability or experience.

3. In the first six months of Metro there were a number of additions to payrolls with relatively few losses. This meant that instead of having fewer employees, Metro had acquired more since its inception.

4. The Planning Commission was so overloaded with conducting studies that it had little time to develop a comprehensive and much-needed zoning ordinance.

5. During the first year of Metro the mayor and many of his staff had a tendency to explain any failure of the new government, especially the financial difficulties, as being the fault of the "old city" government . . .

Since 1963, other concerns have developed. For example, how would Metro's relationship with the surrounding region, which is rapidly becoming urbanized, develop? Metro participates actively in two regional planning organizations: the Mid-Cumberland Development District (M-C DD) and the Mid-Cumberland Council of Government (M-C COG). McArthur notes that Metro government has shown flexibility on various rural, suburban, and urban issues that have faced the region. This has enhanced Metro's credibility with other communities and agencies within the Mid-Cumberland region. Metro's expertise has been made available to M-C DD and M-C COG to improve their functioning. In addition, other regional organizations have raised their pay scales and benefits to match Metro's.

On the other side of the coin, Metro representatives to M-C COG have advocated more attention to local agencies, which, in essence, means more attention to Metro needs. It is likely that increased competition for highways and for water and sewer development funds will emerge. Both Metro and its surrounding regions will claim that their needs are the greatest needs. "Ironically, Metro may come to behave more and more like the Nashville city government it supplanted in 1962, protecting its interests against the restive suburbs and opposing area-wide controls in many fields."[77]

Difficulties may also develop around Metro's ability to support its increasing rate of expenditure. While it is true that Metro has diversified its revenue base, it still depends on the inelastic and regressive property tax for 44. 8 percent of its income.[78] The second greatest source of revenue—28. 36 percent—is derived from state and federal funding.[79] The amounts and duration of these intergovernmental transfers are unpredictable. Reliance on such funds may hinder the development of other sources of revenue and may also steer spending toward services or programs for which federal and state dollars are available.

Erie, Kirlin, and Rabinovitz have assessed the performance of restructured metropolitan institutions. Several of their conclusions, which are listed below, have been born out by the Nashville experience:[80]

> 1. In general, few scale economies have been associated with reform . . .
> 2. In the short run, the access of minorities is guaranteed, but may in the long run be diluted.
> 3. Performance levels tend to rise, but so do fiscal burdens accompaying increased expenditure.

Erie, Kirlin, and Rabinovitz also suggest other conclusions for which, at least as far as Metro is concerned, supporting data are circumstantial or unavailable:[81]

1. The roles and norms of official decision makers
do not guarantee any substantive conception of the area-
wide interest. All that is guaranteed is a minimal,
procedural definition governing public policy making.
2. The functional emphasis upon tangible goods,
rather than amelioration of social problems, remains
unchanged.
3. By and large, restructuring is associated with
reduced citizen participation in the local electoral
process.
4. The character of citizens' understanding of
attitudes toward the local and metropolitan political
process remains largely unchanged . . .

In another vein, Rogers and Lipsey found that many assumptions
supporting consolidation were disproved in their studies comparing
like communities—Woodbine (a Metro Neighborhood) and Berry Hill.
They suggest that residents of small communities are often satisfied
with the services they receive and therefore will resist consolidation
with a larger governmental unit. Their study leads them to conclude
that local community control over services involving a high degree
of interpersonal relationships such as police services might be
beneficial. [82]

IS THERE A POTENTIAL
FOR BORROWING?

Local governments differ greatly from state to state and from
county to county, and, accordingly, it is impossible to develop one
formula for success that will apply in all instances. As one author
asserts:

Every attempt to solve a metropolitan problem has to
take account of unique features in the particular
community; and each successful effort to provide some
overall metropolitan government has resulted in a
variation in practical experience from place to place,
even among communities in which the leval plans of
government have been quite similar. [83]

The concept of city-county consolidation is not feasible for most
metropolitan areas. Marando points out that consolidation has had a
poor track record—since the 1940s there have been two defeats for
every success. Every successful campaign save one has occurred in
the South, and five of the 12 took place in Virginia. Consolidation,

then, appears to be a southern regional phenomenon. In addition, no
consolidation effort has been successful in metropolitan areas that
extend over more than one county or have populations of over one
million. Nashville had a population numbering only a few hundred
thousand, all contained in a single county. Of the 225 metropolitan
areas in the United States, only about half have roughly comparable
situations. [84] Marando also suggests that "in large metropolitan
areas which are characterized by many political subdivisions . . .
reorganization is extremely difficult if not impossible."[85] In short,
small municipalities that wish to retain their identities and rural
areas that fear higher taxes tend to resist consolidation.

A determining factor for the success of the city-county
consolidation formula seems to be the presence of "unique situational
circumstances." In Nashville, for example, the unique circumstances
included the green sticker tax and annexation proceedings. Other
factors that probably facilitated the adoption of Metro were (1) state
intervention in the form of constitutional amendment and enabling
legislation; (2) a homogeneous white population and a black population
that voted by place (that is, "fringe area," old city) rather than as a
racial bloc; (3) the existence of relatively few political subunits; and
(4) a well-organized, politicized campaign that was fought at the
grass-roots level as well as in the intellectual sphere.

Although the viability of implementing city-county consolidation
in its entirety is limited, it might be useful to analyze some of the
favorable outcomes associated with Metro to see whether they were,
necessarily, the result of this form of structural change. It is
possible that Metro adopted certain approaches that could be
separated from city-county consolidation per se and, thus, conceivably
could be implemented by a different type of governmental structure.

Separate service-tax districts are associated with the gradual
leveling of rural-urban financial and service disparities. Separate
districts, in theory and in practice, ensure that every resident pays
for what he or she receives—those who receive fewer services pay
lower taxes. As the differences between county and city in terms
of types and quality of available services become smaller, the differences between tax rates grow smaller as well. Some analysts
maintain that service differentiation is actually preserved by service
zones. [86] In the case of Metro, services are in fact being expanded,
not only through increased property taxes but by users' and service
fees as well. Hence, the service-tax district approach is not only
useful but probably is transferable as well. It is also an approach
that is not necessarily dependent on city-county consolidation for its
implementation. A two-tier, federated government, for instance,
might be able to incorporate separate service-tax zones within its
existent structure.

A shrinking tax base and increasing service demands forced
Nashville into a progressively more difficult situation. Nashville-
Davidson's solution was to extend the metropolitan limits to include
sufficient financial resources—in terms of both industry and higher-
income suburbanites—to increase significantly its fiscal capabilities.
City-county consolidation is not the only means that can be used to
enlarge the territory of a metropolitan area; both annexation and
federation are alternative methods whose suitability depends on
existing political realities.

Proponents of Metro claimed that consolidated government
would eliminate duplication and the overlapping of services characterized by competing governmental units. In addition, they believed
that economies of scale would allow government to operate more
efficiently and to provide services at a lower unit cost. These
predictions have been fulfilled to a limited extent. But again, as
mentioned above, while city-county consolidation appears to have
resulted in a successful outcome for Nashville, the unitary government approach is not the only one that can achieve such results.
Indeed, the authors believe that, for the most part, the positive
attributes associated with Metro—such as more effective planning
capability, increased professional involvement, and diversified
tax structure—are functions of size and centralization. Size permits
economies of scale and expanded fiscal capability. Centralization
stimulates professional planning and implementation of programs.
Consolidation created a sympathetic environment for rational and
reformist government practices in the Nashville-Davidson region,
but city-county consolidation is not feasible for most urban communities. Accordingly, alternate means of enlarging and centralizing
government structures might be considered.

Finally, despite the fact that many benefits are associated with
Metro, no direct link has been established between structural change
and changes in policy outcome. Improved financial capability may
have made more money available to Metro government, but consolidation has not been connected, empirically, with the decision to
spend this money more wisely. The decision to improve educational
services, for example, may have been an outgrowth of environmental
factors such as income, occupation, or level of education. Analyzing
the effects of political structure on outcomes "is necessary to
determine whether the drastic structural remedy—consolidation—for
dealing with problems in the delivery of urban public goods and
services is warranted."[87]

NOTES

1. Metro Profile, pamphlet published by the Metropolitan
Government of Nashville and Davidson County, n. d. See also

Bertil Hanson, A Report on Politics in Nashville, Part 1 (Cambridge: Joint Center for Urban Studies of MIT and Harvard, 1960), p. 1.

2. U. S. Department of Commerce, Bureau of the Census, United States Census of Population: 1960, Characteristics of the Population, Tennessee (Washington, D. C. : Government Printing Office, 1961); and U. S. Department of Commerce, Bureau of the Census, United States Census of Population: 1970, Characteristics of the Population, Tennessee (Washington, D. C. : Government Printing Office, 1971).

3. Brett W. Hawkins, Nashville Metro: The Politics of City-County Consolidation (Nashville, Tenn.: Vanderbilt University Press, 1966), p. 20.

4. Hanson, op. cit. , part 2, pp. 6-7.

5. Hawkins, op. cit. , p. 22.

6. Ibid. , p. 51.

7. Hanson, op. cit. , part 2, p. 12.

8. Ibid. , p. 15.

9. Ibid. , p. 14.

10. Daniel R. Grant, "Metropolitics and Professional Political Leadership: The Case of Nashville," Annals of the American Academy of Political and Social Science 353 (May 1964): 76.

11. Hanson, op. cit. , part 5, p. 8.

12. James Nathan Miller, "A City Pulls Itself Together," Reader's Digest, July 1967, p. 133.

13. Ibid. , p. 134.

14. Hawkins, op. cit. , pp. 58-67.

15. Ibid.

16. Miller, op. cit. , p. 133.

17. James C. Coomer and Charlie B. Tyer, Nashville Metropolitan Government: The First Decade (Knoxville: Bureau of Public Administration, University of Tennessee, 1974), p. 4.

18. Hawkins, op. cit. , pp. 36-37.

19. Robert E. McArthur, "The Metropolitan Government of Nashville and Davidson County," in Advisory Commission on Intergovernmental Relations, Regional Governance: Promise and Performance (Washington, D. C. : Government Printing Office, 1973), p. 26.

20. Hawkins, op. cit. , pp. 40-41.

21. Ibid.

22. Ibid.

23. Roscoe C. Martin, Metropolitan Transition: Local Government Adaptation to Changing Needs, prepared for the Housing and Home Finance Agency under the Urban Studies and Housing Research Program (Washington D. C. : Housing and Home Finance Agency, 1963), p. 106.

24. Hawkins, op. cit. , p. 45.

25. Martin, op. cit. , pp. 106-10.

26. Hanson, op. cit. , part 5, p. 10.

27. Hawkins, op. cit. , pp. 48-50.

28. Ibid. , p. 51.

29. Ibid. , pp. 56-57.

30. David A. Booth, Metropolitics: The Nashville Consolidation (East Lansing: Institute for Community Development and Services, Michigan State University, 1963), p. 22.

31. McArthur, op. cit. , p. 27.

32. Coomer and Tyer, op. cit. , pp. 14-15.

33. Grant, op. cit. , p. 80.

34. Nashville Banner, June 18, 1962. Reproduced in Hawkins, op. cit. , p. 87.

35. Booth, op. cit. , p. 85.

36. Ibid.

37. Ibid.

38. Charter of the Metropolitan Governments of Nashville and Davidson County, Article 1, Sections 1. 01-1. 02, Article 5, Sections 5. 01-5. 04 (hereafter cited as Metropolitan Charter).

39. Ibid. , Article 3, Section 3. 01, and Article 4, Section 4. 01. See also League of Women Voters of Nashville, Your Metropolitan Government: A Handbook About Nashville and Davidson County, Tennessee (n. p. , 1973).

40. League of Women Voters of Nashville, op. cit. , pp. 36-38.

41. Metropolitan Charter, Article 1, Section 1. 05.

42. Metro Profile, p. 11.

43. Metropolitan Charter, Article 1, Section 1. 04.

44. Coomer and Tyer, op. cit. , p. 29.

45. Metropolitan Charter, Article 18, Section 18.15.

46. Ibid. , Article 19, Section 19. 01.

47. Daniel R. Grant, "A Comparison of Predictions and Experience with Nashville 'Metro'," Urban Affairs Quarterly 1 (September 1965): 38.

48. Ibid. , pp. 38-39.

49. Ibid.

50. Daniel R. Grant, "Political Access Under Metropolitan Government: A Comparative Study of Perceptions by Knowledgeables," in Comparative Urban Research: The Administration and Politics of Cities, ed. Robert T. Daland (Beverly Hills, Calif.: Sage, 1969), p. 269.

51. Grant, "Comparison of Predictions and Experience with Nashville 'Metro'," op. cit. , p. 47.

52. Grant, "Political Access Under Metropolitan Government," op. cit. , p. 258.

53. Ibid. , pp. 263-64.

54. Robert E. McArthur, The Impact of Metropolitan Government on the Rural-Urban Fringe: The Nashville-Davidson County Experience (Washington D. C. : U. S. Department of Agriculture, 1971), pp. 26-27.

55. Steven P. Erie, John J. Kirkin, and Francine P. Rabinovitz, "Can Something Be Done? Propositions on the Performance of Metropolitan Institutions," in Reform of Metropolitan Governments (Baltimore and London: Johns Hopkins University Press, Resources for the Future, 1972), p. 28.

56. McArthur, Impact of Metropolitan Government on the Rural-Urban Fringe, op. cit. , pp. 26-27.

57. Bruce D. Rogers and C. McCurdy Lipsey, "Metropolitan Reform: Citizen Evaluation of Performances in Nashville-Davidson County, Tennessee," Publius 4 (Fall 1974): 19-34.

58. Ibid. , p. 23.

59. Grant, "Metropolitics and Professional Leadership," op. cit. , p. 83.

60. State of Metro Address, April 1, 1964, cited in Coomer and Tyer, op. cit. , pp. 34-35.

61. The Tennessee Taxpayers' Association, A Financial Analysis and Evaluation of the Proposed Metropolitan Government Charter for Nashville and Davidson County (Nashville: Tennessee Taxpayers' Association, 1962), p. 25.

62. McArthur, Impact of Metropolitan Government on the Rural-Urban Fringe, op. cit. , p. 18.

63. Grant, "Comparison of Predictions and Experience with Nashville 'Metro'," op. cit. , p. 40.

64. Erie, Kirlin, and Rabinovitz, op. cit. , pp. 23-24.

65. Coomer and Tyer, op. cit. , pp. 41-50 and McArthur, "The Metropolitan Government of Nashville-Davidson County," op. cit. , pp. 29-30.

66. Tennessee Taxpayers' Association, op. cit. , A Financial Analysis and Evaluation of the Proposed Metropolitan Charter, insert.

67. Coomer and Tyer, op. cit. , p. 46.

68. Urban Observatory Report, "City Taxes and Services: Citizens Speak Out," Nation's Cities 9 (August 1971): 13.

69. Coomer and Tyer, op. cit. , pp. 47-48.

70. Daniel R. Grant, "Opinions Surveyed on Nashville Metro," National Civic Review 54 (July 1965): 375-77.

71. McArthur, Impact of Metropolitan Government on the Urban-Rural Fringe, op. cit. , p. 20.

72. Coomer and Tyer, op. cit. , p. 41.

73. Ibid. , pp. 51-56; and McArthur, The Impact of Metropolitan Government on the Rural-Urban Fringe, op. cit. , pp. 8-9.

74. McArthur, "The Metropolitan Government of Nashville and Davidson County," op. cit., pp. 33-35.

75. "Nashville, A Story of Progress," Forbes (May 15, 1968), p. 57.

76. Coomer and Tyer, op. cit., p. 35.

77. McArthur, "Metropolitan Government of Nashville and Davidson County," op. cit., p. 35.

78. League of Women Voters of Nashville, op. cit., p. 42.

79. Ibid.

80. Erie, Kirlin, and Rabinovitz, op. cit., pp. 36-37.

81. Ibid.

82. Rogers and Lipsey, op. cit., p. 33.

83. Ed Young, "Nashville, Jacksonville, and Indianapolis Examine for Possible Lessons for Future," Nation's Cities, November 1969, pp. 26-41.

84. Miller, op. cit., p. 136.

85. Vincent Marando, "The Politics of Metropolitan Reform," Administration and Society 6 (August 1974): 256.

86. Rogers and Lipsey, op. cit., p. 22.

87. Ibid.

2

THE JACKSONVILLE-DUVAL COUNTY APPROACH

BACKGROUND TO THE MERGER

The city of Jacksonville, Florida, has had a rich and eventful history dating back to the early colonial period when the Spanish and British competed vigorously for control of the Florida peninsula. Situated in the top northeastern section of Florida, the area of Jacksonville was first settled as farmland in 1791. By 1816 there were several permanent settlements in the region, which, by then, had become a stopping-off place on the route toward the West. In 1822 the region was incorporated and named after General Andrew Jackson, who had led the fight to force Spain to cede the Florida territory to the United States. In the same year, the other major political unit of our drama, Duval County, in which Jacksonville is located, was created. Due largely to its warm climate and picturesque landscape along the St. Johns River and the Atlantic Ocean, Jacksonville had become a tourist haven by the middle of the nineteenth century, and from that time forward, despite the interruption of the Civil War period, the city's economy grew increasingly reliant on income from tourism. [1]

Today Jacksonville is perhaps most famous for its port facilities. It is the largest port on the South Atlantic and is located farther west than any other port along the Atlantic seaboard. Duval County is the most populous county in Florida. Since 1900 the number of people in the county has doubled approximately every 20 years. In 1940 the combined population of the city of Jacksonville and Duval County was over 210,000 with some 170,000 in the city and 37,000 in the rest of the county. Since 1965 the county population outside the core city has increased to about 327,000, while the city has declined to under

200,000. Projections have been made to 1980 that indicate the county will continue to increase to 885,000, while the city will remain rather stagnant at 210,000. The 1970 census listed Jacksonville's total population at 528,865.[2] The city is the industrial capital of Florida, with its industries numbering over 500 and running the gamut from lumber, pulp and paper, and fertilizers to canned goods and chemical products. The labor force, which currently exceeds 220,000, has increased at the rate of 4,200 per year since 1960. The community has a balanced employment profile with unemployment seldom exceeding 3 percent.[3]

For a distance of at least 100 miles in all directions, the area surrounding Jacksonville is predominantly rural in character, and there are no urban areas with a population exceeding 75,000. Accordingly, with over 500,000 residents, Jacksonville is the commercial, financial, cultural, medical, and urban center of the region encompassing northeast Florida and southeast Georgia. It also is one of the principal distribution, insurance, and convention centers in the Southeast. The political culture is very much a business-dominated one.[4]

Jacksonville experienced three major setbacks between 1800 and 1901. First, in 1883 a smallpox epidemic in the area significantly curtailed tourism and thus cut off its major source of income. (The smallpox epidemic led to the creation of a Citizen's Health Auxiliary to combat it throughout the county. This was the first example of city-county cooperation.)[5] As a consequence of the epidemic, the city was unable to maintain adequate roads, sidewalks, and streetlights, all of which caused a good deal of citizen unrest. Second, a new state constitution in 1885 forced Jacksonville to annex the densely populated areas adjacent to it, even though the city was clearly incapable of providing services for the additional population. Third, an important turning point occurred in 1901 when a fiery holocaust left the entire city in desolation. The fire broke out in the Cleveland Fire Company and quickly engulfed some 700 acres. When it was all over, 146 blocks of schools, churches, homes, offices, and public buildings were gutted.[6]

The devastating fire set Jacksonville back many years, and as the city struggled to rebuild itself, it became more and more evident that much more was needed than new city buildings. Governmental reform, which hopefully would bring better services and a solid economic base, was also needed, and, accordingly, the city government was substantially revamped in 1917. The system was such a complicated one that it is difficult to conceive of how it could work effectively in the day-to-day operations of a city and county of 200,000 people, which was the approximate population of Jacksonville at that time.

Under the mistaken belief that it would create a system of checks and balances, the 1917 charter provided for both a city council to serve as a legislative body and a city commission to serve as an executive body. The council consisted of nine members elected at large, one of whom was selected to preside over council meetings, and the commission was comprised of five members elected at large, each of whom would head a particular functional area of service. The commission was presided over by a separately elected mayor. [7] Thus, the system established islands of power, and each island was autonomously run. [8] In addition, other elected offices, such as tax assessor, tax collector, recorder, and treasurer, contributed to the fragmentation of governmental services.

Richard Martin in his study of the Jacksonville consolidation observed that "the system has frequently been termed unique by political scientists, and no wonder." The 1917 charter created a "hydra-headed government," intended to produce a model system of checks and balances and to usher in an era of unexcelled good government. In practice, writes Martin, "The system did not work. Over the years, there was a proliferation of elected and appointed officials and of independent boards. At best it was a confusing muddled system. At worst, it encouraged its separate entities to work at cross purposes or collaborate for their own ends to the detriment of the public well-being."[9]

The reform was indeed a curious one. Both the council and the commission were simultaneously in charge of and responsible to the people, and as time progressed, it became nearly impossible to delineate clear-cut lines of responsibility and accountability. The situation was muddled even further because a proliferation of boards and independent commissions were added on an almost annual basis.

The governmental structure of Duval County provided even more problems and greater confusion. The county maintained a traditional governmental system of five county commissioners who were elected at large and served as both formal policy makers and administrators. The voters of the county also elected a sheriff, a tax assessor, a tax collector, and several other officials. Legislative authority rested not with the commission nor with any of the other 69 elected county officials, but, rather, with the state legislative delegation. Until Florida's new constitution went into effect in 1969, local bills pertaining to Duval County could be passed only during a 60-day period every other year. Because of the tradition of the "local bill courtesy" and the fact that for many years Duval County had only one state senator, this latter single person actually possessed veto power over all legislative matters concerning the county. In short, the county government was without the power and authority to meet the problems of an essentially urban and suburban population. [10]

When the city and county governments are considered together, the area of Jacksonville and Duval County was characterized by a maze of duplication, gaps in authority, inefficiency, buck passing, and an inability or unwillingness to cope with emergency problems. Not only were the city and county governments unable to handle their respective problems, but city-county cooperation proved virtually impossible. As Martin points out, as many as four governmental bodies were required to have a voice in any city-county project, these being the city council, the city commission, the county commission, and the Duval legislative delegation. [11] To compound the problems even further, independent local governments began to incorporate in such nearby areas as Neptune Beach, Atlantic Beach, Jacksonville Beach, and Baldwin.

Machine politics prevailed in Jacksonville and was supported by local business and professional leaders with a direct interest in the decisions being made by government employees and by a black voting bloc. Unlike the more regimented model of Daley's Chicago, this "machine" seems to have been a loose coalition of those groups most interested in keeping the local governments responsive to their own interests. The common interests of the entire community tended to be neglected under this system. [12]

In spite of its governmental problems, Jacksonville grew rapidly in the half century from World War I to the mid-1960s. In 1917, the city had a population of 88,000, and by 1950 the figure had risen to over 200,000. However, by the mid-1960s, Jacksonville, like so many other United States cities, was characterized by a shrinking inner-city population as a consequence of the flight to the suburbs. Between 1950 and 1960, Duval County's population increased by almost 800 percent, from approximately 40,000 to 320,000. [13] The county government was totally incapable of handling a demographic shift of this magnitude. An example of the county's ineptitude is evidenced by the fact that 60 percent of all taxable property in Duval County was not even on the tax rolls in 1965. Because of the resultant inadequate supply of funds, the city of Jacksonville was forced to provide many of the county's service functions such as fire protection, garbage collection and disposal, and health. [14] Thus, the city, with its population of 200,000, was providing the bulk of the services for about 500,000 people. The inequities were also reflected in the city's financial patterns. In 1951 the city's budget was $26 million, and the debt was also $26 million. A decade later, the budget was $71 million, and the debt was $100 million. [15] The per capita cost of government rose from $116 in 1950 to $479 in 1965, the highest growth rate in the country. [16]

The decline in the city of Jacksonville's population had dramatic racial, economic, and political implications for the area. In 1965, the black community comprised 41 percent of the city population but only 9 percent of that of the county. This represented since 1950 a 14 percent rise in the city's black population with a concomitant 10 percent decline in the white population. According to the 1966 Local Government Study Commission, Jacksonville ranked third in the nation in the percentage of nonwhite population for cities of over 100, 000. [17] From an economic perspective, Jacksonville experienced a 15 percent decline in the economically productive 20–64 age group. Moreover, the percentage increase of persons over 65 was 36 percent, while for those under 20, the corresponding figure was 17. 5 percent. Thirty-one percent of the inner-city population lived at or below the poverty level, while only 15 percent were in this category in the county. Similarly, only 13 percent of the county's houses were considered in need of repair, but 30 percent of the city's houses were considered in dilapidated condition. Moreover, the city school system had major problems when compared to that of the county. The average number of years of schooling for city dwellers was 9. 5, but in the county, the figure was 11. 5. The condition of the schools in combination with a tradition of politics in educational affairs led to the disaccreditation of every senior high school in the area in 1964. [18]

By 1965 Jacksonville-Duval County was in desperate straits. Its peculiar governmental structure was described by one observer as a "bizarre hodge-podge of overlap and duplication."[19] The city's problems seemed insurmountable. It was losing its productive citizens, and thus its tax base was weakened. Housing and income problems were nearly universal. The city sewer system had completely broken down, and all the raw sewage was being dumped directly into the St. Johns River. The county also was experiencing numerous problems as a consequence of the population growth, with the government being unable to cope with the increased numbers. For example, in spite of the increased population and concomitant wealth, the county's tax base was woefully inadequate because of low property assessment rates and the failure to collect some taxes. (Houses were being assessed at 25–30 percent of their true market value.)[20] In addition, fire and police protection were insufficient and consisted mostly of auxiliary personnel. The county also lacked adequate sewer or septic systems.

THE MOVEMENT TOWARD REFORM

Although the Jacksonville-Duval County region was obviously in need of comprehensive reform, the media, the federal government, minority groups, the general public, and business leaders had all failed to make the appropriate pleas for several reasons. The media felt they could not successfully battle an entrenched city machine.

The federal government had relatively few funds invested in the
Jacksonville area and, therefore, was generally uninterested. The
minorities feared that reform might decrease their rising voting
power, and the general public was fearful of higher taxes should
they make demands for change. For their part, the business leaders
were entrenched in the existing system and, accordingly, were
somewhat alienated by suggestions of reform.

The fact that in Jacksonville reform took place in the mid-
1960s resulted from a combination of unique circumstances. First,
in 1963, a plan to annex 66 square miles and 130,000 people was
voted down by the suburbanites, although favored by the city population. The plan was an attempt to solve the city's drastic fiscal
problems, but the county feared that annexation would bring much
higher taxes since the cost of government had dramatically increased.
In 1964 a similar plan was defeated in the same manner. Soon after
the defeat of this second proposal, the Southern Association of
Colleges and Schools rescinded the accreditation of all 15 of
Jacksonville's high schools. Since the school system had always
been a highly politicized arm of the city government, the blame for
this situation was quickly placed on the governmental system itself.
As often occurs in local government crises, the holders of residual
power, the business and professional leaders, initiated the move
for reform. [21] On January 18, 1965, Claude Yates, a retired
president of Southern Bell Telephone, called a group of leading
businessmen together. Other members of the group were J. J.
Daniel, a wealthy financier and real estate developer; Lex Hestor,
a scholar-administrator (soon to be the first city administrator of
the new government); and Hans Tanzler, the so-called Mr. Clean of
Jacksonville politics. The group drew up what became known as the
Yates manifesto. This was a one-sentence petition calling upon the
local county delegation to introduce an act in the state legislature
that would permit the citizens of Duval County to vote on consolidating
with the city of Jacksonville under one government. Although some
of them were opposed to any form of consolidation, the members of
the Duval County legislative delegation responded to the Yates
manifesto by drafting a bill to create a study commission, and this
bill was duly enacted by the supportive state legislature. [22]

The Local Government Study Commission consisted of 50
members and was given a budget of $60,000, $40,000 of which was
appropriated by the legislature, with the remaining $20,000 to be
raised by the study group itself. No current officeholders or persons
believed to have political ambitions could be members of the
commission. The membership included many business and professional
leaders, four blacks, and five women. A 17-member executive
committee was chosen from within the commission to coordinate the

study. The commission was to begin work on October 1, 1965 and present its final report by March 1, 1967. The commission divided itself into several task forces, which held numerous public meetings and hearings, listened to dozens of arguments pro and con on consolidation, and conducted in-depth studies of other cities such as Tampa, Miami, Nashville, Baton Rouge, and Atlanta. The commission completed its work after 15 months, and the end product was the publication of a plan entitled A Blueprint for Improvement, which called for the consolidation of Jacksonville and Duval County.

Under the terms of the "blueprint," the existing governments of the city and the county and all other governing bodies, except for the authorities, were to be abolished. In their place, there would be created a countywide single level of government of the strong-mayor/council type. An at-large elected mayor was to have full administrative powers, including the appointment of all department heads, and the council was to consist of 21 members, who were to be elected from single-member districts of approximately 25,000 residents and who would serve without compensation. A nonpartisan seven-member school board also would be elected from specific single-member districts. Several of the formerly elected positions such as sheriff, tax collector, tax assessor, and supervisor of elections were abolished, with their functions to be placed under department heads appointed by the mayor. [23]

The plan embodied in the blueprint had to overcome three major hurdles before it was implemented. The first of these involved the drafting of the actual bill to be submitted to the state legislature. For this purpose, the framers of the plan established a group known as the Citizens for Better Government. This group included representatives from the Chamber of Commerce, the County Bar Association, the Duval County Medical Society, the League of Women Voters, the Jacksonville Urban League, the Voters' League of Florida, the media, and most small businesses in the area. The Citizens for Better Government emphasized that consolidation would bring economy, efficiency, responsiveness, and an ability to deal more easily with the region's problems. Taking the opposite viewpoint, the opponents of the plan formed an organization known as Better Government for Duval County. The members of this group included the old city machine politicians, Central Labor Union Affiliates, some suburban leaders, some black leaders, two black newspapers, some members of the legislative delegation, and some right-wing extremist groups. The major arguments of this organization were that consolidation would raise the cost of government and that the wrong mayor could become a dictator. After a great deal of debate, the bill finally was drafted and sent to the legislative delegation at the capital. [24]

It is important to note the role of the black community with
regard to the consolidation movement. Blacks were suffering from
the city's problems more than any other group. They were especially
susceptible to the problems of poor housing, high unemployment,
high crime rates, and practically no representation in the government.
With their numbers approaching a majority in the central city, their
one hope was to gain control of the city through the franchise. Thus,
part of the black community opposed consolidation since it would
reduce black voting power. On the other hand, many blacks realized
that Jacksonville was in such a state of decay that no new businesses
were likely to be attracted to the area to provide them with new
jobs. [25] As one black leader put it: "I might have become the black
mayor, but I would have been only a referee in bankruptcy."[26]
When pledges of better representation in the new government were
made, the majority of the black community was won over to the plan.
This support, however, was almost lost when, during the drafting of
the bill, the legislative districts were rearranged in such a way as
to eradicate a district where a black representative would most
assuredly have been elected. This problem was quickly corrected,
and the black support was regained. [27]

The second major obstacle in the path of consolidation was
securing the passage of an appropriate bill in the state legislature.
The real problem here was to convince the Duval County legislative
delegation to accept the plan since the legislature would in all
likelihood follow the delegation's lead. The members of the delegation decided to go over the plan item by item, making changes
wherever necessary or desirable. Their intention was to water
down the "purist" nature of the consolidation proposal. The problem
had been further complicated by Florida's reapportionment program,
which increased the Duval delegation to 16 members. Six of these
were opposed outright to consolidation, and a seventh began talking
about an alternative reform measure. After a great deal of negotiation
and political in-fighting, the delegation agreed upon a considerably
amended version of the plan, which was submitted to and passed by
the state legislature and signed by the governor on June 27, 1967.
In the final analysis, both the Citizens for Better Government and
the Better Government for Duval County organization worked
diligently to sway the Duval legislators in favor of their side of the
consolidation contest. Although it would appear that the former
group won the battle, the latter group inflicted a number of wounds
in the form of substantial alterations in the original blueprint. [28]

The third and final major problem was convincing the citizens
of Jacksonville and Duval County to accept the consolidation plan in
a referendum. Here again, a large-scale campaign between the two
opposing groups was waged. The arguments of the supporters for

better, more efficient government remained the same as at the outset. The opponents, on the other hand, now began to argue that a larger and more centralized government would reduce the people's power at the polls. Some extremists among the opponents branded the plan as socialistic and a communist plot. During the last several months, however, the opponents had lost a great deal of their clout due to the fact that widespread corruption in the existing government had been exposed. Television station WJXT, which had been investigating wasteful practices in city vehicle purchases, focused its attention on the fact that the city commission was spending $1.3 million a year for insurance, an amount equal to the combined costs of insurance in Miami, Tampa, and St. Petersburg. A grand jury investigation led to the indictment of two city commissioners, four city councilors, the city auditor, and the recreation director on charges of larceny, perjury, and conspiracy. In addition, the tax assessor resigned. [29] This scandal was the key factor in convincing the people to vote in favor of the referendum, which was adopted on August 8, 1967 by a majority in both the city and the county. (One of the amendments that the legislative delegation added included a provision that allowed the four small municipalities of Jacksonville Beach, Atlantic Beach, Neptune Beach, and Baldwin to vote for consolidation and, at the same time, project their own institutions into the new system, which all four did.)[30]

An analysis of the vote is quite revealing. Of the 86,079 votes cast, the city-county consolidation plan polled 54,493 votes in favor, and 29,768 opposed, a victory margin of nearly two to one for the reformers. The densely populated urban fringe areas around Jacksonville supported the referendum by a six-to-one majority. At the other extreme, the lower-income groups in the rural areas of the county supported the measure by the barest of majorities. Along a continuum of increasing support for consolidation were the entire county, the black community, the lower-income groups in the city, the entire city, and the higher-income groups in the city. [31] Thus, there remained a good deal of resistance in the county. Moreover, there is some evidence that at least part of the affirmative vote was cast by those who were desirous of limiting black voting power by enlarging the population base. Other evidence suggests that consolidation was perceived by many voters as a means of benefiting the general populace at the expense of the old-guard machine politicians. [32] Organized labor opposed the consolidation on the grounds that competitive bidding on public works projects would attract outside companies, which would bring with them nonunion workers to compete with dues-paying union members. [33]

The support of the black community for the referendum merits some explanation in that under normal circumstances one would have expected its members to oppose a plan that seemed to threaten the dilution of their power base. As Sloan and French point out, "The fact that black leaders were included in every stage of the consolidation movement in Jacksonville did much to allay their worst fears that the plan was simply a scheme by the white community to dilute the black vote."[34] Whether the inclusion of influential blacks in the planning and implementation of the consolidated government was tokenism or genuine social consciousness is still debatable, but whatever the case, it was a decision that made for good politics. The black community received representation and its members rendered their support.

ORGANIZATIONAL CHANGES
AND THE NATURE OF THE NEW SYSTEM

The new government took over on October 1, 1968. It differed in certain respects from the plan embodied in the original blueprint as a consequence of the concessions made by its proponents in the interest of facilitating its adoption. For example, the blueprint had proposed that the mayor appoint all department heads without the approval of the council, but this was altered to mayoral appointment with council approval; and some department heads, such as the sheriff, the tax assessor, the tax collector, and the supervisor of elections, are elected at large rather than appointed as the blueprint suggested. A seven-member civil service board also is elected at large, and there are several other independently operated boards and authorities such as the school board, the planning board, the Electric Authority, the Hospital Authority, the Transit Authority, and the Port and Airport Authority. Another alteration in the original proposal was a reduction from 21 to 19 in the membership of the city council. Fourteen of the members are elected from single-member districts and the remaining five are elected at large. In order to ensure that no employee would be dischared as a consequence of consolidation, a pension protection program and other benefits for employees were added. Finally, the tax-levying power of the new government was restricted by the imposition of an ad valorem tax limit of 36 mills.[35]

The impact of the new consolidated government has been extensive. All the old overlapping and duplicating jurisdictions have been eliminated. Many, although not all, of the elected offices have been replaced by departmental functions under the control of the mayor. Thus, the organizational structure of the government has been vastly improved. The mayor has considerable administrative and appointive powers and also possesses a veto power over appropriations bills and the budgets of independent agencies and elected officials.

The fiscal structure and policies of the Jacksonville-Duval
County region also have been significantly improved as a result of
consolidation. All areas of government under the new system are
subject to budgetary, auditing, and purchasing controls. Internal
budgetary, planning, and management controls have been implemented,
and a system of independent legislative audits has been instituted to
promote increased efficiency and to identify and correct unsound
fiscal practices. There also has been established a Central Services
Department consisting of purchasing, personnel, data-processing,
legal, communications, and motor pool divisions. All agencies of
the consolidated government are required to utilize the Central
Services Department as a means of effecting economies, developing
greater efficiency, and providing continuity and central administrative
discipline and control over the entire local government. A new
tax arrangement, to be discussed below, has provided a broader
base and increased revenues. The new councilmanic districts have
ensured a more representative system, and, in addition, greater
citizen input has been realized through recommendations of lay boards.
Perhaps the most striking characteristic of the new system is its
business orientation. Mayor Tanzler is fond of referring to the
government as being run just like a business and calling it an
apolitical system. [36] Finally, the consolidated government has tended
to rely on high-quality, professionally oriented personnel at all levels
from the mayor on down to provide economic, workable programs.
They have recruited from Cleveland their administrator of central
services, and from Florida State University their director of data
processing. Jacksonville has paid top salaries for these officials
but has probably saved in the long run as a consequence of their
high degrees of expertise. [37]

Jacksonville in the late 1960s was in a sense going through a
reform period that most American cities had experienced from 1920
to 1950. The pace was very rapid, but many of the issues that
middle-class reformers had raised before in other cities were again
voiced in Jacksonville. Indeed, it is difficult to separate the positive
effects derived from the techniques of sound management practices
from the effects of consolidation as an important political change.

As previously mentioned, the tax structure has been extensively
reformed. In large part, Jacksonville adopted the Nashville model,
which has been discussed in Chapter 1. Property taxes are levied on
an area-wide basis under two categories—an urban services district
(USD) and a general services district (GSD). (At the time, Florida
had a unique tax structure where there was no income or sales tax
and where each person who bought a new house received a $5,000
homestead exemption in figuring property taxes.) The USD, which
includes the old city of Jacksonville and four smaller municipalities

(Jacksonville Beach, Atlantic Beach, Neptune Beach, and Baldwin),
is taxed slightly higher than the GSD, which encompasses the entire
metropolitan area. The GSD provides such services as police and
fire protection, health and welfare, recreation, public works,
housing, and urban development, while the USD provides such
additional services as street lighting, refuse collection and disposal,
street cleaning, and debt service. Any part of the GSD may be
incorporated into the USD if all the services can be feasibly extended
to the new area within one year. This provision of the Jacksonville
charter has quite effectively controlled the growth of the USD. The
differentiated property tax arrangement is intended, of course, to
render the tax system more equitable by linking services to property
taxes paid. The remaining funds derived from the taxes in both the
USD and GSD are expended on services common to both areas,
primarily education. The amount and quality of services has expanded
considerably under the consolidated government in spite of the fact
that tax reductions have occurred during the first three years after
consolidation. The average taxpayer with a $15,000 home had his
taxes decreased by $60 per year between 1969 and 1971, even though
water and sewer charges were increased. The decrease in the mill
rate has been offset, however, in the 1970s by an increase in the
assessment base, which was ordered by the courts. Last, a utility
tax of 10 percent is levied on electricity, gas, water, and telephone
service, and the revenue from the state's gasoline tax is shared by
Jacksonville. [38]

Government spending has increased enormously since consolidation. Expenditures in the year prior to consolidation totaled
$56.2 million. By 1971 the figure had risen to $80.2 million, a $24
million increase. [39] Urban renewal and federally funded programs
accounted for $8 million worth of the increase, and another $16
million was used to upgrade fire and police protection, street
lighting, the child service program, and the Rescue Service System. [40]
In addition, a $131 million sewer and water improvement program
was undertaken. Education, public safety, law enforcement, and public
works account for two-thirds of the total spending, with education
alone accounting for about 51.4 percent of those expenditures over
the first four years of consolidated government. There also was a
15 percent increase in spending for human services over the same
period. Generally, however, the percentage of spending in each
functional area, excluding education, did not differ widely from
preconsolidation days, but the dollar value of the services was far
greater. The budget for fiscal year 1974/75 presents an interesting
overview of the financial system (see Table 2.1). [41]

In some ways, consolidation itself appears to have led to
increased funds and savings. First, the centralized system has

TABLE 2.1

Financial Summary, Jacksonville

Total Budget 1974/75	$ Value	Percent of Budget
City of Jacksonville	135.7	25.6
Independent agencies	243.7	46.1
Duval County School Board	149.9	28.3
Sources of Revenue		Percent of Revenue
Charges for services		47.2
State sources		16.3
Ad valorem taxes		13.2
Fund balance		9.5
State shared revenue		5.0
Federal sources		4.7
Utilities services		3.0
Business licenses and permits		0.5
Fines and forfeits		0.4
Interagency transfers and other sources		0.2
Total		100.0
Receivers of Revenue		Percent of Revenue
Jacksonville Electric Authority		35.4
Duval County School Board		28.3
General services district		16.7
Federal revenue-sharing trust fund		5.0
Duval County Hospital Authority		4.6
Jacksonville Port Authority		4.0
Enterprise funds		3.3
Jacksonville Transportation Authority		1.4
Duval County Beaches Public Hospital Board		0.5
Urban services district		0.5
Jacksonville Area Planning Board		0.2
Federal programs		0.1
Total		100.0

Source: City of Jacksonville, Florida, Financial Summary 1974-1975.

incorporated those persons on the tax rolls who formerly were not being charged. The result was that revenues from property taxes rose from $1.7 billion in 1968 to $2.5 billion in 1971. Second, consolidation brought a larger share of the state's revenue from cigaret taxes, which amounted to $2 million in the first year of consolidation. Third, federal funds, which were practically nonexistent before consolidation, since most city officials had continued the Civil War legacy of mistrusting the federal government, have increased dramatically. In addition, the centralized system has attracted new businesses, which in turn have contributed increased revenues through their payment of corporation taxes. Moreover, the consolidated government's central purchasing system for all departments has been quite effective. For example, the central purchasing of patrol cars resulted in a savings of $500,000, and a coordinated legal division has saved $100,000. A considerable amount of money also has been saved by a coordinated system of validation of municipal bonds. Finally, improved investment practices have led to increased earnings of $800,000, three-quarters of which is directly attributable to better investments.[42]

The proponents have been quick to point out that Jacksonville-Duval County has been improved in many ways under consolidated government. They religiously maintain that many gains have been made in the delivery of services. Utility rates have been equalized throughout the area partly as a consequence of the acquisition of nearly 200 privately owned utility plants. Police and fire protection have been upgraded and their respective departments have been streamlined, resulting in lower insurance rates. The addition of some 200 new policemen in the suburbs has produced a significant reduction in suburban crimes. An improved communications system, the utilization of police helicopters, the establishment of a youth aid division, and the implementation of a Personalized Patrol Vehicle Program, which puts 125 patrol cars on the streets on a 24-hour basis, have all seemed to contribute to better citizen protection. In an effort to reduce burglaries, Operation Identification was launched. Under this program, approximately 10 percent of Jacksonville's 100,000 households had their valuables engraved for easy identification. Nine community crime committees were created to provide a communications link between the police and citizens, and in 1971 the voters approved a $9.5 million bond issue for a police administrative center.[43] In the area of fire protection, volunteers were replaced by full-time firemen in the suburbs, and the city and county fire-fighting services were merged into one regional system. A comprehensive ambulance rescue system, including cardiac arrest teams, has been established. The Emergency Rescue Service makes approximately 20,000 runs a year with, in addition to ambulances, such sophisticated equipment as a fireboat, a rescue boat, and a "Mop Cat" used to combat oil spills.[44]

The sewer system in both the city and the county has been rebuilt since consolidation. This project involved the reconstruction of 133 miles of obsolete and collapsing sewers and the elimination of 72 outfalls pouring millions of gallons of raw sewage daily into the St. Johns River. [45] The city of Jacksonville also has concentrated on cleaning up its neighborhoods. A solid waste disposal program was instituted to better regulate trash removal and to save taxpayers money, and the city adopted a compulsory garbage service for Jacksonville residents. Weed and rat controls were expanded for environmental protection, and the city has picked up twice as many stray animals as before consolidation. [46] Recreation programs have quadrupled in number. Plans were undertaken for the development of ocean-front Kathryn Abbey Hanna Park as one of the major recreational facilities on the Atlantic coast. Another major recreational complex, including the famous Gator Bowl, was to be constructed on the river front. [47] A major street improvement campaign was undertaken in 1971-72. Approximately 70 miles of roads were paved or resurfaced, nearly three miles of safety sidewalks for school children were constructed, and 347 drainage improvement projects were completed. Also in 1971, some 26,000 streetlights were installed in the central city, and in the following year, another 26,000 were installed in the suburbs. [48]

Other achievements under the new governmental arrangements include the creation of a Division of Consumer Affairs, which handles several thousand varied cases per year. The Community Relations Commission set up a 24-hour Rumor Control Center. A new $2 million Health Center was constructed, and ten neighborhood health clinics were opened. A Mental Health Division and a drug abuse program were established. A zoning code has been implemented, which permits better utilization of land resources. A sign control ordinance and new building, electrical, and mechanical codes have been extended throughout the county. A master plan to rejuvenate the downtown area, including the construction of a junior college campus and new housing units with U.S. Department of Housing and Urban Development (HUD) funds, was undertaken, and one of the early results was the attraction of ten new businesses to an industrial park complex. [49] In addition, Westinghouse and Tenneco have jointly sponsored a $250 million program in nuclear research, which created well over 10,000 job opportunities. [50] Newsweek magazine stated in 1973 that the key to Mayor Tanzler's success is his unabashed wooing of industry. Following a $200,000 public relations blitz sponsored by the city and the business community, Jacksonville now boasts $200 million in private development. The Newsweek story observes: "Once accustomed to playing a weak second fiddle to Atlanta as an industrial center, Jacksonville now booms itself as 'The Bold New

City of the South'. The city's biggest catch to date is Offshore Power Systems, a pioneer manufacturer of floating nuclear plants, which has agreed to build its 250 million dollar headquarters in Jacksonville."[51] Two groups known as Jobs for Jacksonville and the National Alliance of Businessmen have been extremely active and fairly successful in securing jobs for the unemployed and the underemployed.[52]

A countywide land-use plan has been adopted, and the last strip of undeveloped oceanfront property has been purchased and is being developed. Countywide traffic engineering has been instituted. An adequately staffed and financed area planning board has also worked to stimulate economic growth. The board's members are appointed by the mayor, and the executive director is part of the mayor's staff. The mayor and the president of the city council are ex-officio members of the board. The planning board must approve all capital investments exceeding $10,000.[53] The new Public Relations Division has facilitated communication among citizens, the government and its employees, and the media, and a Service and Information Center has been established to provide ombudsman services to assist citizens in their dealings with the government.

On the surface, racial relationships in the Jacksonville region have improved since consolidation. In the first elections for the city council, four blacks were elected, including one from an at-large contest, which was an unprecedented phenomenon for this southern city. Unlike the former city government, where blacks were under-represented, their representation on the consolidated council is proportionate to their percentage in the entire Duval County region. However, black representation in the fire department, the law enforcement agencies, the advisory boards, and other areas is little more than token. One study reveals that blacks believe consolidated government is better than the old system but less res-ponsive to their community than to other groups. Blacks, it was felt, now knew who was in charge and were no longer intimidated in expressing their views as they had been prior to the consolidation. However, black leaders also reasoned that making demands does not necessarily mean that they will be met.[54] Currently, there is a good deal of support among blacks for making the sheriff an appointed officer, who would serve directly under the mayor, for two reasons. First, the mayor is considered a strong ally of the black community and thus, probably would appoint a strong supporter of civil rights to the position. Second, the present sheriff, although friendly to blacks, is not powerful enough to prevent the racist practices of some old-regime officials.[55] In general, most of the black community considers itself better off under the new system but also feels too many decisions are made without regard to its welfare. As one black

city councilman put it, "We still have a long way to go, but we have
come a long way too. The white members of the council have learned
a lot. The black members have taught them to feel some empathy
for the poor."56 And as one white council member commented on
race relations in Jacksonville in 1971: "As recently as five years ago,
race relations in Jacksonville were tense and bitter. Today, the
city has become pretty much color blind."57

In general, the black community was involved in the consolidation effort from the outset, participated in the reorganized government
of Jacksonville-Duval County, and has benefited from many of the new
programs. In return the black leadership lent its support to
consolidation despite some major reservations about the slow pace
of the change.

PROBLEMS CONFRONTING JACKSONVILLE

In spite of Jacksonville-Duval County's many accomplishments,
many problems remain to be resolved. Some authorities have been
rather skeptical about the reported savings in Jacksonville. As
Mogulof reports,58

> Certainly no one in Jacksonville's government was
> ready to claim that their central services system
> was any model of efficiency. The promise that
> this system would provide dollar savings was
> used to sell the idea of reorganization. The
> troubled central services system may be suf-
> fering from its residue of personnel who were
> grandfathered into the new structure as the price
> for neutralizing the opposition of municipal
> employees to the reorganization.

The most pressing problem concerns those functional areas that
are not under complete centralized control of the chief executive.
Over two-thirds of the consolidated government funds are spent by
various independent boards, commissions, and authorities representing
these areas. For example, out of every dollar in the 1971 budget,
the school board spent 34.6 cents, the Jacksonville Electric Authority
spent 21 cents, and varying lesser amounts were spent by other such
agencies. Such elected officials as the sheriff, tax collector, tax
assessor, and supervisor of elections are subject to budgetary
control and operate through the Department of Central Services and
the Legal Division, but city council members and several administrators feel that the elected status inhibits the levying of responsibility
and accountability. Another problem results from the fact that the

four small municipalities that are part of the USD perform their own
GSD functions in return for compensation from the consolidated
government under a revenue-sharing scheme. The matter is further
complicated by the fact that these municipalities are legally separate
jurisdictions, thereby fragmenting the system. The reformers and
officials, who have favored a pure consolidation, believe that they
should be incorporated into the consolidated system. The several
authorities (hospital, transportation, port, electric) have thus far
presented only minor coordination problems with government
agencies' recommendations, but the general feeling is that they should
be included in the government as departments. (The authorities
already are under budgetary, appointing, and purchasing control,
and their policies are subject to review.) The school board spends
such a large percentage of locally collected revenues that many
favor mayoral appointment of its members to promote more financial
accountability. The area planning board remains an independent
body, but the consensus is that it should be placed under a regular
department. Finally, the many federal programs (law enforcement,
Regional Planning Council, Community Health Facilities Planning
Council, Manpower Planning Councils, and Community Action
Programs) are not coordinated and thus conflict with local agencies. [59]

In commenting on the type of problems outlined in the preceding
paragraph, an Urban Institute study has observed: "Jacksonville's
price for lacking a consistent willingness and capacity to develop a
central position and for failing to use that position with various
government subunits may be a system dominated by its individual
functions and subunits—which is right back to the problem that
plagues so many urban communities." [60] As Melvin Mogulof, writing
for the Urban Institute, has so aptly put it, in this area as in all
others, Jacksonville, of all the Metros, has stayed clear of conflict.
The city council, acting pragmatically, moves where it sees
opportunities to do "good things" and backs off where the people do
not seem to be ready. This may be commonsense politics, but it
brings no rave reviews from national planners and other such
commentators in the area of metropolitan reform. As Mogulof asks,

> How much longer can the "good" of each independent
> agency be conceived of as adding up to the public good
> for the entire area? And how much longer can the
> consolidated government mute its conflict by not having
> a design by which its own accomplishments and
> relationships can be judged? Jacksonville may continue
> to try to proceed without an overall plan for bargaining
> and accommodation (among/of these diverse interests).

If it does, Jacksonville may be denied the benefits to
be derived from the right kind of conflict. [61]

In many ways, city-county consolidation has been a success in
Jacksonville and certainly has been so regarded by the people of the
area. A public opinion poll conducted by television station WFGA-TV
in February 1969, only five months after consolidation was put into
effect, revealed 64.1 percent public acceptance of the new government.
In a second poll conducted by the same station approximately seven
months later, or one year after consolidation, public acceptance had
increased over 14 percent to 78.8 percent. [62] Other polls conducted
from time to time tended to produce similar results. A survey
administered in October 1969 by television station WJXT-TV was
somewhat less favorable although it demonstrated a 61 percent vote
of confidence. Specifically, 14 percent rated the new system very
good, 25 percent good, 22 percent average, 8 percent poor, 9
percent very poor, and 22 percent had no opinion. [63] Of even more
importance for this business-oriented government is the high level
of support that community leaders exhibit for the consolidation. As
Joan Carver reported in her findings from interviews with community
leaders in Jacksonville, "White community leaders expressed much
enthusiasm for the system and found it highly responsive to all
elements of the community."[64]

The future of the consolidated government in the Jacksonville
area will be determined by its ability to recognize problems and to
take the proper steps to correct them. Any governmental system that
eschews the necessity for change will eventually be doomed to self-
destruction. Jacksonville thus far has stressed economic growth in
construction and service programs, and these undertakings have
been largely successful. In the future, the government must emphasize
social programs by providing for the needs of the lower-income
groups of the region. Apart from a massive low-income housing
project and a few aid programs, usually federally funded, the low-
income groups have taken second place to business interests and
economic growth. These people must be integrated into the system
as a functional and productive unit, rather than being shunted aside
in favor of tall buildings or impressive business ledgers. Moreover,
political centralization of those areas that remain outside the purview
of the consolidated government should be balanced with some
administrative decentralization in order to ensure that all people
are being responded to and treated equitably. In addition, area-wide
planning beyond the consolidated region could be more comprehensive.
Failure to plan and cooperate with the larger area may leave the new
government in the same position that Jacksonville and Duval County
were in prior to consolidation.

As a complete package, it is doubtful that the Jacksonville consolidation experiment could be exported to other metropolitan areas since there were unique circumstances to which Jacksonville had to accommodate itself. There are, however, several aspects of the system, all of which are interrelated, that are adaptable to other areas. First, the central services system of purchasing, budgeting, and personnel management is an effective and economical system for handling these basic governmental functions. A second lesson to be learned is that the hiring of high-quality administrators tends to produce innovative and improved programs and policies. Efficient fiscal management saves dollars and allows greater flexibility. Other urban areas also would benefit by emulating Jacksonville's concerted efforts to upgrade its services to the community.

There are several qualifications that act to limit the utility of the Jacksonville system for most other urban areas. First, most metropolitan areas are in need of some degree of reform, but few are in as drastic a situation as were Jacksonville and Duval County in the 1960s. Fragmentation of the government was seemingly endless, and corruption ran almost rampant in an anachronistic political structure. Second, unlike many urban areas, the Jacksonville metropolitan area is contained almost wholly within one county. Third, overall spending has risen despite the new system's enviable situation of lower taxes. Fourth, Florida's unique tax laws have been very influential in maintaining consolidation. Finally, it should be remembered that the Jacksonville experiment is far from a purely consolidated system. The Jacksonville form of consolidation is not a panacea; it does not solve problems in and of itself. It does, however, seem to provide a reasonably viable means of attacking such problems.

NOTES

1. For a detailed case history of the Jacksonville experience see Richard A. Martin, Consolidation: Jacksonville-Duval County (Jacksonville: Crawford Publishing, 1968), pp. 2-5.

2. John M. DeGrove, "The City of Jacksonville: Consolidation in Action," in Regional Governance: Promise and Performance— Substate Regionalism and the Federal System, Advisory Committee on Intergovernmental Relations (Washington, D.C.: Government Printing Office, May 1973), p. 17.

3. Jacksonville Area Chamber of Commerce, A Profile of Jacksonville (Jacksonville, 1971), p. 3.

4. Ibid., p. 4.

5. See Martin, op. cit.

6. City of Jacksonville, "Early History," A Date with Destiny: October 1968 (Jacksonville, 1968), pp. 5-7.

7. DeGrove, op. cit. , p. 17.

8. Joan Carver, "Responsiveness and Consolidation: A Case Study," Urban Affairs Quarterly 9 (December 1973): 215.

9. Martin, op. cit. , p. 5.

10. Ibid. , p. 30.

11. Ibid. , p. 34.

12. Carver, op. cit. , p. 215.

13. DeGrove, op. cit. , p. 17.

14. Ibid. , p. 18.

15. Jacksonville Chamber of Commerce, op. cit. , p. 4.

16. DeGrove, op. cit. , p. 18.

17. Lee Sloan and Robert French, "Jacksonville-Duval County Consolidation: Black Rule in the Urban South?" Trans-Action 9 (November 1971): 31.

18. DeGrove, op. cit. , pp. 17-18. See also Sloan and French, op. cit. , p. 30.

19. DeGrove, op. cit. , p. 19.

20. See ibid. , p. 18.

21. John Fischer, "Jacksonville: So Different You Can Hardly Believe It," Harpers 243 (July 1971): 21.

22. Martin, op. cit. , p. 10; and for a more analytical treatment of these events see Walter A. Rosenbaum and Gladys M. Krammer, Against Long Odds: The Theory and Practice of Successful Governmental Consolidation (Beverly Hills, Cal. , and London: Sage Professional Papers in Administrative and Policy Studies, 1974).

23. Local Government Study Commission, Blueprint for Improvement (Jacksonville, 1966), see especially pp. 10-17.

24. Martin, op. cit. , p. 19.

25. Sloan and French, op. cit. , pp. 31-32.

26. DeGrove, op. cit. , p. 24.

27. Ibid. , p. 19.

28. Martin, op. cit. , pp. 14-15.

29. Ibid. , pp. 12-13.

30. See DeGrove, op. cit. , pp. 18, 21-23.

31. Ibid. , p. 19.

32. Walter A. Rosenbaum and Thomas A. Henderson "Explaining the Attitude of Community Influentials Toward Government Consolidation: A Reappraisal of Four Hypotheses," Urban Affairs Quarterly 9 (December 1973): 269.

33. Martin, op. cit. , p. 59.

34. Lee Sloan and Robert French, "Race and Governmental Consolidation in Jacksonville," Negro Educational Review, April-July 1970, p. 78.

35. DeGrove, op. cit., p. 19.

36. Hans Tanzler, "Both City, Business Profit from Partnership," Industry Week, January 29, 1973, p. 57.

37. Hans Tanzler, "Business Is Solving a City's Problems," Nation's Business 67 (July 1969): 59.

38. See DeGrove, op. cit., p. 20; Melvin B. Mogulof, Five Metropolitan Governments (Washington, D.C.: Urban Institute, 1972), p. 46; and Carver, op. cit., pp. 232-37.

39. City of Jacksonville, Bold View, Special Report: Two Years of Consolidated Government, March 1971, p. 7.

40. DeGrove, op. cit., p. 21.

41. City of Jacksonville, Florida: Financial Summary 1974-75.

42. DeGrove, op. cit., p. 21.

43. City of Jacksonville, Financial Summary, 1973-74, p. 4.

44. Ibid., p. 10.

45. Hans Tanzler, "Jacksonvillians Like Consolidated City Government," American City 85 (April 1970): 79.

46. Bold View, op. cit., p. 15.

47. City of Jacksonville, Financial Summary, 1973-74, p. 4. See also Lex Hester, "The Jacksonville Story," National Civic Review, February 1970, p. 80.

48. City of Jacksonville, Financial Summary, 1973-74, p. 8.

49. Hester, op. cit., p. 80.

50. "Shakeup in Jacksonville," Newsweek, August 13, 1973, p. 61.

51. Ibid., p. 61.

52. Tanzler, "Both City, Business Profit," op. cit.

53. Carver, op. cit., p. 228.

54. Ibid., p. 244.

55. DeGrove, op. cit., p. 24.

56. Fischer, op. cit., p. 20.

57. Ibid., pp. 20, 21, and 24.

58. Mogulof, op. cit., p. 58.

59. DeGrove, op. cit., pp. 21-23.

60. Mogulof, op. cit., p. 90.

61. Ibid., pp. 89-90.

62. Jacksonville Journal, May 1970.

63. Ibid., p. 15.

64. Carver, op. cit., p. 221.

3

THE INDIANAPOLIS-MARION COUNTY APPROACH

DEMOGRAPHIC AND STRUCTURAL CHARACTERISTICS

Indianapolis was settled in 1820 and incorporated in 1847.[1] It is the largest city in the state of Indiana and has served as the state capital since 1825. Geographically, it is located directly in the center of Marion County, and Marion County is situated directly in the center of the state.

Prior to consolidation, the 1960 census ranked Indianapolis 26th among the nation's cities, with a population of 476,258 and an area of 82 square miles.[2] Twenty-one percent of the city and 14 percent of the county population were nonwhite and less than 2 percent were foreign born.[3] Today the population is over 800,000, which makes it the ninth largest city in the United States and the largest city, since the turn of the century, to consolidate with the county within which it is located. In recent decades, population growth has been greater in the suburban areas than in the city itself, and the city's share of the county's assessed property valuation dropped from 77 percent in 1950 to 60 percent in 1966.[4]

Indianapolis is not only Indiana's most populous city but also the state's most prosperous city. The railroad and the automobile saved the city from an isolated existence. The White River, on the banks of which the city was originally founded as a small forest village, proved to be nonnavigable, and a planned canal system was lost in the Panic of 1837. However, the emergence of the railroads provided the vital transportation links with the rest of the state and nation. Situated between the agricultural areas of the Midwest and the South and the industrialized areas of the North and Northeast,

Indianapolis has become a transportation hub. In the language of its
Chamber of Commerce, Indianapolis is the "Crossroads of America."
Today the metropolitan area is served by several railroads and
seven major arteries of the interstate highway system running north,
south, east, and west.

This important transportation network has attracted industry,
and today the city boasts a diversified industrial economy. Ford,
Chrysler, and Chevrolet are among the city's largest employers, a
list that also includes Detroit Diesel Allison Division (General Motors),
Western Electric, Eli Lilly, RCA, and International Harvester.
Other major industries include pharmaceuticals, metal fabrication,
electronics, heavy machinery, and food processing. In addition,
more than 70 insurance companies maintain their headquarters in
Indianapolis, and the city is an important corn, grain, and livestock
market, with the largest stockyards east of Chicago. [5]

Indianapolis is rapidly becoming a highly respected educational
and research center. The new Indianapolis Center for Advanced
Research draws upon the resources of the Indiana University School
of Medicine and the Purdue University of Engineering and serves as
a catalyst for research interests of local industry. The Holcomb
Research Institute and the Regenstrief Institute for Health Care are
making major contributions to the scientific advancement of the entire
nation. Other forms of advanced study are carried on at the campus
of Indiana University-Purdue University at Indianapolis (IUPUI).
Additional educational opportunities are available at Indiana Central
College, Marion College, Indiana Vocational Technical College, and
Butler University.

Indianapolis has been plagued with most of the social ills and
forces that have affected many American cities. While the region's
central city has seen its population increase by 2 percent from 1960
to 1970, the rest of Marion County's population has risen 40 percent.
Racially, Marion County remains white, while the inner city has
become increasingly black. The county's black population in 1960
was 14 percent, approximately the national average, while Center
Township, which is the core of Indianapolis, had a black population
of 27 percent. In 1970, the black population of Marion County
increased to 17 percent while that of Center Township climbed to
39 percent. [6]

Both the Republican and Democratic parties are strong and
active in Marion County and Indianapolis politics. Typically, the
Democrats have been stronger in the city of Indianapolis, while the
Republicans have enjoyed greater success in the suburbs and the
county at large. Most elections, however, produce no large majority
for either party. As York Willbern has commented:[7]

Local government in Indiana tends to be highly partisan. The two major parties compete vigorously for local office, and long tenure in office by either of the parties is the exception rather than the rule in most of the more populated counties and cities. The spoils system governs the appointment and tenure of many, perhaps most, employees of the general governmental units. The schools and some of the other special purpose units have some degree of exemption from partisanship and the spoils system, and there are also elements of professionalism and tenure in some areas of general governmental employment.

The Indiana constitution is a major determinant influencing the structure of local government in Indiana. It provides that all 92 counties shall elect the following administrative officials: clerk, recorder, auditor, coroner, treasurer, surveyor, and sheriff. As a result of their constitutional status, these offices cannot be abolished without an appropriate constitutional amendment. Moreover, the constitution is so specific with reference to the details of local government that "home rule," in the traditional sense, does not exist for municipalities. For example, local government indebtedness cannot exceed 2 percent of the assessed property valuation. In 1969 the taxable property for all of Marion County was $1.8 million. For a population of 800,000, a $36 million ceiling is pitifully inadequate. [8]

THE MOVEMENT TOWARD CONSOLIDATION

Prior to consolidation, Marion County, which completely surrounded Indianapolis, had approximately 60 governments within its boundaries. In addition to the county government and the government of the city of Indianapolis, there were nine townships (of which the only significant function was that of administering relief to the poor), 22 cities and towns, 11 school districts, and 16 other special service districts. None of the suburban municipalities had a population of 20,000, and only three had over 10,000 inhabitants.

The maze of special service districts contributed to inefficient and unresponsive government. As Roul Tunley explained:[9]

For example, one stretch of highway, which badly needed widening to handle commuter traffic, went untouched for six years while five agencies with street-paving jurisdictions—the Board of Public Works, the Department of Public Safety, the Marion

County Board of Commissioners, the Mass Transportation Authority of Greater Indianapolis, and the
Department of Public Parks—argued over who should
do the job. Other agencies, with similar disputes,
took the same path—and the public was always the
loser.

The government of the city of Indianapolis prior to the reorganization can best be described as an example of the strong-mayor plan.
The mayor and nine councilmen were elected at large, but the latter
were required to live in districts. Marion County was governed by
a county council and a county commission. Three county commissioners
had limited legislative power and the traditional custody of county
property. The county council, composed of five members, had some
control over the budget, but little additional authority.
The successful governmental reorganization in the Indianapolis-
Marion County region can be attributed to several unique factors.
First, the reorganization did not require approval by referendum.
In Indiana, all the structures, powers, and processes of local
government are prescribed by the constitution or by state law. The
referendum is, of course, the hurdle that has defeated many
reorganization attempts in other states. Indianapolis was confronted
with no such obstacle. Second, the municipal elections of 1967 and
the state elections of 1968 resulted in complete Republican domination
of state and local government. The governorship, the state legislature,
and the governments of Marion County and Indianapolis were all
controlled by the Republican party. These were rare circumstances
indeed for a state with a fairly competitive two-party system. Third,
and perhaps most important, the proponents of reorganization
demonstrated considerable skill in working around areas of potential
conflict through numerous compromises. The philosophy pursued by
Unigov proponents was that "half a loaf is better than none. "
The three factors mentioned above transcended all other factors
because of their salience. The absence of any one of them probably
would have defeated the reorganization proposal. Nevertheless,
there were other factors that were extremely important, if not
indispensable. Not the least of these was the dynamic leadership and
tireless advocacy of Mayor Richard Lugar, whose prominent role
will be described below. Another significant factor lay in the fact
that Indianapolis was both the capital and the only "first-class" city
in the state. This not only provided a wealth of legal and administrative
expertise in the region but also afforded Indianapolis a considerable
advantage vis-a-vis the state legislature. The Indiana General Assembly
maintains a Committee on Affairs of Marion County, which is composed
predominantly of Marion County representatives. When the Unigov

proposal, as it came to be dubbed, was introduced in the Assembly in 1969, it was quickly reported on favorably by this committee. The situation in the general assembly was akin to "a type of home rule, since the Assembly ordinarily deferred to the wishes of the delegation with regard to items applying to the county only."[10]

Indianapolis was also psychologically prepared for consolidation. Piecemeal consolidation had been taking place for decades— governmental reorganization had been considered in Indianapolis as early as 1925. However, the first significant steps in this direction did not occur until the period following World War II. As the metropolitan area population increasingly spilled over Indianapolis city limits in the post-World War II years, the Marion County government was unable to accommodate the expansion effectively. The traditional structure of three county commissioners, a five-member county council, and numerous other elective officials with narrowly defined and limited duties was poorly suited to the greatly expanding responsibilities. Moreover, the persons migrating to the suburbs demanded services that were beyond the geographic authority of the city to provide.[11]

These pressures evoked a slow, but steady, progression of legislation, which eventually led to metropolitan reorganization and city-county consolidation. After World War II, the first step was the expansion of the sewer and sanitation district beyond the city limits. In 1947, the library service and its supporting tax base were extended countywide, and in 1951, the Indiana General Assembly created a countywide corporation with jurisdiction over hospitals and public health facilities within the region. In 1953, eventual city-county consolidation was foreshadowed by the creation of a corporation that constructed and operated a joint city-county office building in Indianapolis. In 1955, a countywide planning, zoning, and subdivision control commission was established, followed in 1961 by countywide structures dealing with airports and parks and recreation. A Metropolitan Thoroughfare Authority was created in 1963, and, two years later, in 1965, a countywide corporation was formed to construct a convention and exhibition center. Studies of possible school district and police consolidations, in 1959 and 1967, respectively, indicated that these proposals were politically infeasible, and the efforts were dropped.[12]

The sporadic efforts described above did somewhat extend municipal services and also helped to ease the indebtedness restrictions imposed by the state constitution, but they did nothing to foster cooperation or integration across functional lines. By the mid-1960s, there was a clear need, as expressed in the classic reform ideology, to bring order out of the chaos of numerous, diverse, and autonomous special-service districts. The mayor, the city council, and various county officials exercised only partial, vague, and often overlapping powers. [13] As with most metropolitan areas in the United States, public policy formulation and implementation constituted a fragmented process involving many different political actors and governmental units.

When the Democrats swept to victory in Indianapolis in 1964, they succeeded in passing a number of bills that increased the mayor's control over the functional agencies. After the Republican electoral debacle, a group led by L. Keith Buben, a young lawyer, bucked the regular Republican organization and formed a new structure called the Republican Action Committee. This faction succeeded in winning control of the regular Republican organization in 1966. In 1967, the Republicans reversed the Democrat's previous sweep and elected Richard Lugar Indianapolis's first Republican mayor in 16 years and won a majority on the city council and a majority of the county offices. In the state elections of 1968, the Republicans elected Governor Edgar Whitcomb and captured majority control of both houses of the state legislature. The Republicans now had a golden opportunity to reorganize the government structure, and Mayor Lugar was quick to take advantage of it. [14]

Richard Lugar came to the mayor's office with an impressive background. His fellow classmates both in high school and at Denison University had recognized his leadership abilities and elected him their class president. He was a Rhodes Scholar, and as a U.S. navy officer, he had been selected for the key assignment of intelligence briefer to the chief of naval operations. [15]

Lugar soon earned the respect and confidence of the citizens of Indianapolis. In 1969, the National League of Cities expressed a similar confidence when they elected him their vice-president, over New York Mayor John Lindsay. The following year, he was elected to the presidency of the league, quite an accomplishment for a Republican in a Democratic-dominated organization. [16]

Although Lugar had not discussed reorganization in his 1967 mayoralty campaign, soon after taking office he became intrigued with the concept and its possibilities. He was much impressed by the reorganizations in Nashville and Jacksonville, and, of course, he was very much aware of the piecemeal changes that had studded Indianapolis's recent history. In addition, he was influenced by the fact that the Greater Indianapolis Progress Committee, a group of business and civic leaders that had been put together by the former Democratic mayor, John Barton, suggested aiming toward reorganization. Finally, Mayor Lugar, soon after taking office, encountered considerable frustration in his administrative efforts as a consequence of the dispersed power structure and overlapping responsibilities of city, county, and special district governments with which he had

to work. Even more than his predecessor, Lugar realized that a
thorough reorganization of municipal government should be seriously
pursued. According to Willbern, [17]

> In describing these frustrations then and later, he
> frequently used the example of the development of
> the Eagle Creek reservoir in northwestern Marion
> County, a major stream impoundment which required
> changes in roads, land uses, health and sanitation
> facilities, and governmental services of many kinds.
> As chief executive of the central city, there were
> many ways in which he was necessarily interested
> in this development, but responsibility for action
> was divided among agencies over which he had
> limited influence.

In early 1968, Mayor Lugar began a series of meetings on the
topic of reorganization with key community and government leaders
from both Indianapolis and Marion County. In frequent attendance at
these private informal meetings were such influential individuals as
Thomas C. Hasbrook, president of the Indianapolis City Council;
Beurt SerVass, president of the Marion County Council; L. Keith
Buben, county Republican chairman; John Burkhart, president of
the College Life Insurance Company and president of the Capital
Improvement Board; John Walls, deputy mayor and chief staff
officer of the Greater Indianapolis Progress Committee (GIPC);
Charles Whistler, lawyer and president of the County Planning
Commission; Carl Dortch, chief executive of the Indianapolis Chamber
of Commerce; Dr. Lawrence Borst, veterinarian and state senator;
and Dr. Ned Lamkin, physician and state representative. As their
titles suggest, these individuals represented important business,
professional, political, and governmental interests of the region. The
group was characterized by close personal relationships, a spirit of
enthusiasm for the idea of governmental reorganization, and, perhaps
even more significantly, a common Republican political affiliation.
Several of these persons were members of the original Republican
Action Committee. [18]

There eventually emerged from these meetings a commonly
agreed-upon general model of governmental reorganization. The
group then requested attorney Lewis C. Bose to assume responsibility
for the technical preparation of a reorganization bill for introduction
into the Indiana Legislature during the forthcoming 1969 session. It
was imperative that the proposed bill be acted upon by the 1969
legislature if the Republicans were to take advantage of the rare
opportunity afforded by their control over all levels of government.

Bose accepted the task even though the legislative deadline was only
a few short months away. He quickly put together a staff of ten of
the state's most competent constitutional lawyers and set to work. [19]

The reorganization issue now for the first time became widely
publicized, and the list of those asked to join in its support was
expanded to include key Democrats, black leaders, the League of
Women Voters, and additional business leaders and prominent
citizens. This enlarged group became known as the Mayor's Task
Force on Improved Governmental Structure. It held its first formal
meeting on November 27, 1968, with Hosbrook and SerVaas serving
as cochairmen. With less than a month and a half remaining before
the convening of the state legislature, the major elements of the
reorganization package had been formulated. The members of the
task force were confident that the opposition, expected primarily from
Democrats and blacks, would have little time to organize effectively
against the measure. The entire public debate on the reorganization
proposal, now christened "Unigov," took place in the space of just
four months from November 1968 to March 1969, when the measure
was signed into law by the governor. [20]

Opposition to Unigov developed primarily on three fronts.
First, some Democrats recognized that the Republicans would
benefit greatly from the proposed reorganization since the mayor's
electoral constituency would shift from the Democratic-biased city
to the Republican-biased county. Second, some blacks believed that
the proposal was discriminatory in that it would effectively eliminate
the growing possibility of the election of a black mayor by setting
back the percentage of black voters in the consolidated city to the
level attained 20 years earlier in the city. This problem ultimately
was taken to the courts for resolution. Finally, many persons in
suburban and rural Marion County simply did not want to become
part of any city, especially one that many of them had recently chosen
to leave. The strength of these opposition groups was greatly diluted,
however, due to the mixed feelings of their members. For example,
many Democrats recognized the need for reorganization and, indeed,
had themselves begun to move in that direction in their own previous
administration. For their part, the blacks knew that their attainment
of the mayor's office in the existing governmental system might well
be an empty victory if that office was an ineffective one within a
chaotic power and responsibility structure. Most black leaders
conceded that Unigov appeared to be a realistic approach to the
resolution of many of the region's problems. [21]

With most members of the task force firmly in support of it,
the Unigov proposal was formally released to the general public on
December 19, 1968. Mayor Lugar and the Marion County Republican
delegation now initiated an intense campaign to secure legislative

support. Lugar had campaigned in 1968 on behalf of various
Republican legislative candidates throughout the state, and he now
solicited their backing of the Unigov bill during the upcoming general
assembly. [22] Speaking before the annual convention of the National
Association of Counties in 1970, Lugar frankly admitted, "I used the
tools that were at hand, and they were political loyalties."[23] One
tool that was not employed was the referendum, which was discounted
by the supporters because they felt that its use might have the
unfortunate result of racial and sociological polarization. Moreover,
the Republican strength at the time was in the state legislature and
the state house, and not necessarily among the electorate. However,
a poll that was taken among the affected population indicated 63 percent
in favor and 37 percent opposed to the Unigov proposal. [24] The
Chamber of Commerce, the League of Women Voters, and the mass
media, including the influential Indianapolis Star and Indianapolis
News, as well as other important forces, either backed the proposal
or were silently neutral toward it.

When the 1969 legislative assembly convened in January, the
Unigov bill was quickly referred to and reported out of the locally
dominated Affairs of Marion County Committee. So well had the
lawyers prepared the bill that only a few technical amendments
were added by the senate. Some opposition was voiced by the
Association of Indiana Counties and a few officials of Marion County
and small towns. Circuit Court Judge John Niblack and Prosecutor
Noble Pearcy attempted to obtain a two-year delay for further study
prior to enactment. In addition, a Republican senator expressed the
objections of a sizable number of suburban conservatives. The
opponents were few in number, however, and on February 15, with
the nearly unanimous support of the Republicans of the Marion County
delegation, the bill passed the senate by a vote of 28 to 16. In the
house, Speaker Otis Bowen, a Republican whose hopes for the
gubernatorial nomination had been thwarted by the Marion County
Republican leaders, delayed consideration of the bill until the last
possible day, but nevertheless, it was adopted by a vote of 66 to 29
on March 5. Amendments offered were successfully defeated by the
bill's proponents. Their argument was that a referendum was not
required and would only increase the delay and expense involved. [25]
Their real feelings were probably more accurately expressed by
Lugar before the National Association of Counties annual convention
in 1970 when he stated, "to throw an issue which has tested the
wisdom of the best constitutional lawyers in the state to persons
who have not the slightest idea about what government was before or
after is not wise."[26]

When Indiana Governor Edgar D. Whitcomb signed the
Consolidated First-Class Cities and Counties Act, Chapter 173 of

the Indiana Acts of 1969 into law on March 13, 1969, Unigov became
the first major city-county consolidation to be enacted without a
referendum since 1898, when New York City was created. [27] Suddenly,
without anyone outside Indiana really noticing it, Indianapolis had
become the nation's eleventh largest city. (See Figure 3.1.)

THE PROCESS OF REORGANIZATION

The Unigov bill that was submitted to the state legislature was
lengthy and sweeping in scope. In Mayor Lugar's words, "We drew
up a bill of some tens of thousands of words that repealed successfully
everything that occurred in Marion County from 1851 on, in terms of
either the county or the city. "[28] The 86-page document drew heavily
on the city-county consolidation experiences of Jacksonville, Florida
and Nashville, Tennessee, but due to the peculiar circumstances
from which it arose, Unigov is quite unique.

Administratively, the principle goal of the reformers and,
indeed, the achievement of the Unigov act, was to centralize control
of the formerly separate and autonomous agencies and service
districts. These were merged into six departments, the directors of
which were appointed by the mayor. These are the Departments of
Administration, Metropolitan Development, Public Works, Transportation, Safety, and Parks and Recreation.* As would be expected,
the mayor, who is elected for a four-year term, is much stronger
under the reorganization and serves, in fact, as a spokesman for
both the city and the county. He also appoints two deputy mayors
who assist him. [29] Five of the six departments maintain departmental
boards within their organizational structures. Thus, there exist
boards of public works, transportation, safety, parks and recreation,

---

*The Department of Administration includes the following
divisions: personnel, finance, purchasing, records, citizens' affairs,
and legal. The creation of legal division, which merged the separate
legal offices that had been serving the individual agencies of Marion
County, was considered an important accomplishment. The Departmen
of Public Works inherited the powers and responsibilities of the Board
of Sanitary Commissioners, the County Drainage Board, the Department of Flood Control, the Indianapolis Board of Public Works, the
City Market, and the Air Pollution Agency. The Department of
Transportation assumed the responsibilities formerly held by the
county commissioners, the Mass Transportation Authority, the Park
Board, the Safety Board, the County Highway Department, the County
Surveyor, and the Board of Public Works. The scheme is similar
with respect to the remaining three departments.

FIGURE 3.1

Indianapolis–Marion County, Indiana:
Units of Government

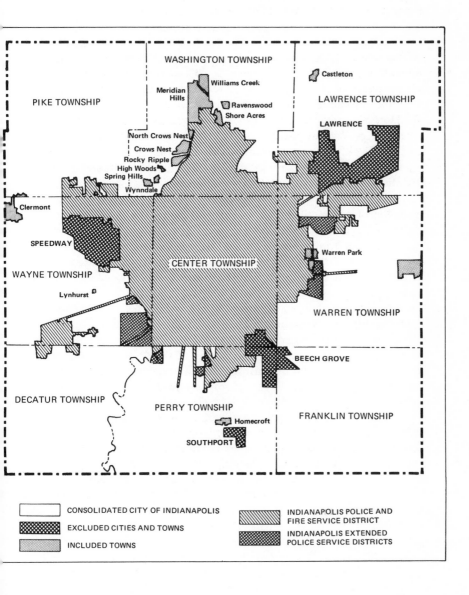

Source: Consolidated Cities and Counties Act, Chapter 173, Indiana Acts of 1969.

and a fifth board, which is somewhat different from the Metropolitan Development Commission (MDC). Only the Department of Administration has no corresponding board.

All the boards, except for the MDC, consist of five members, of whom two are appointed by the mayor and two by the council. The fifth member is the corresponding department director who serves as the board's presiding officer. The boards are authorized to receive the budgets of their respective departments before they are submitted to the city-county council. They also are empowered to sell property of the departments, to approve all contracts for purchase of capital equipment and facilities, and to purchase real estate. The MDC is comprised of nine members. Four are appointed by the mayor, three by the council, and two by the county commissioners. There still exists a county commission, which is made up of the county auditor, assessor, and treasurer. Initially, the MDC shared with the mayor the appointment of the directorship of its corresponding department, the Department of Metropolitan Development, but this power was later modified by amendment, with the result that the mayor now possesses this power exclusively. The MDC serves as a planning and a zoning board as well as a redevelopment commission. [30]

The new city-county council centralizes the legislative and deliberative functions previously held by the old city council, county council, county commission, and various boards and commissions of the old autonomous agencies and service districts. There are a total of 29 council members; four are elected at large and the other 25 are elected from single-member districts. The Unigov Act authorized the council to determine the boundaries of the districts. The act also required the council to establish a standing committee for each of the executive departments and permitted other committees to be created as the need might arise. These committees posses the powers to investigate, subpoena, and audit their parallel departments. The council is, of course, the major legislative body for Unigov and is empowered to enact legislation concerning all affairs of the consolidated city. In addition, the council confirms many of the mayor's appointees, makes some appointments itself, levies taxes, and determines appropriations. The new budgetary powers are described by Lawrence and Turnbull as follows:[31]

> The budgetary powers of the council have been substantially increased under Unigov compared with those given the previous city and county councils. The council has the exclusive power to adopt budgets, levy general or special taxes, and make appropriations for the consolidated city and any of its departments. The council's fiscal

authority extends to many of the independent agencies and boards and to the offices of all the "constitutional" officers of the consolidated government whose powers and duties have not been changed by consolidation. Thus, the council has the power to review and modify the operating budgets and the tax levies of the airport board, the health and hospital board, and the library board, but it has no power with respect to any bonds that may be issued by those boards. It also has the power to review the budgets of the welfare board, the election board, voter registration officials, municipal courts, court clerks, juvenile centers, the cooperative extension service and all township assessors.

The merging of Indianapolis's former special districts into one of the six new administrative departments has greatly enhanced the authority of the mayor. (See Figure 3. 2.) Currently, the mayor possesses complete appointment power with regard to all department directorships. As noted earlier, the mayor also controls three of the five appointments to the department boards. In addition, he possesses the power of a line-item veto, which can be overridden only by a two-thirds vote of the entire city-county council. [32]
An interesting limitation is that a council member may not participate in activities concerning a service district that does not encompass at least 50 percent of the district he or she represents. The reason for this requires a description of the geography of the reorganized government. Not all of the services furnished by the new government are extended throughout the entire 379. 4-square-mile area involved in the consolidation. In fact, most service districts cover areas approximately similar to those they served prior to the reorganization. Specifically, the Fire Service District of the Department of Safety has the same boundaries as the old city. Fire protection outside this area is generally furnished by volunteer fire departments. The Department of Safety's Police Service District is slightly larger, with police protection outside the area provided by town marshals, other municipal police departments, and the county sheriff's department. The Department of Metropolitan Development's Housing Authority extends five miles beyond the old city limits. The Library District serves all of Marion County except for two small municipalities. All other services encompass the entire area of the consolidated city. Each service is funded by a tax levied by the council upon the valuation of the property within the area covered by the particular service. Thus, there are still a number of tax base areas overlapping one another. Although the Unigov act authorized a tax to be levied upon the entire consolidated city base to support

FIGURE 3.2

Unigov Organization Chart:
Consolidated Government for Indianapolis–Marion County

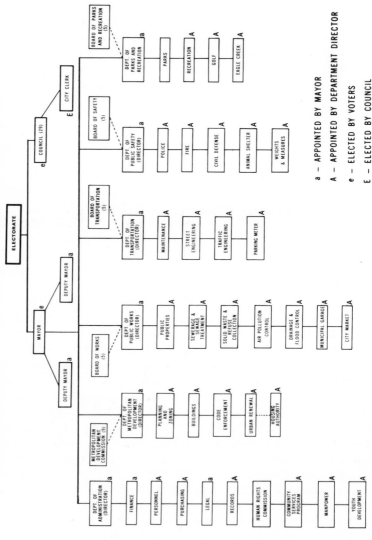

Source: Indianapolis–Marion County, Indiana.

the general government, the only one yet levied is that which supports the organs of government such as the mayor, the council, and the Department of Administration. Correspondingly, the general focus of the consolidated city-county government has not been expanded to include the entire area of its jurisdiction. 33

One of the reasons for the somewhat limited focus of the new government is probably the continued existence of about 60 governments within Marion County even after consolidation. As a matter of fact, there has been little change in the number of governments operating in the region due to Unigov. At least part of the reason for this can be traced back to the dynamics of the political situation that led to Unigov. The Indiana state constitution is quite detailed in its mention of county government and of Indianapolis as the only first-class city in the state. A complete consolidation of Indianapolis and Marion County would have required a constitutional amendment, which is a lengthy process involving approval of consecutive Indiana Legislative Assemblies, which meet only once every two years. In addition, a popular referendum would also have been required. With the Republicans' hopes for reorganization tied to the passage of the measure by the Republican-controlled 1969 legislature, a constitutional amendment was not feasible. The Unigov measure was thus prepared as a compromise measure that avoided any constitutional conflict. 34 Accordingly, Indianapolis, Marion County, nine townships, three incorporated cities, and numerous organized towns legally continued to exist after the enactment of Unigov. The three cities, Lawrence, Speedway, and Beech Grove, as well as the town of Southport, were excluded from the consolidation as a means of avoiding conflict with conservative suburbanites who opposed consolidation. The residents of these four municipalities elect their own mayor and city council and vote for the consolidated Indianapolis mayor and council to whom the residents are subject when they act as the area-wide county government. The rest of the county government and townships are somewhat less active. The county sheriff, auditor, treasurer, reporter, coroner, surveyor, and assessor remain as independent elected officials. The auditor, treasurer, and assessor also carry out those functions of the preconsolidation county commission that were not transferred to the mayor or council. The townships perform only a poorly defined "poor relief" function and tax assessment under the supervision of the county tax assessor. These functions are discharged by elected township trustees. 35

A number of other governmental units also were little changed by consolidation. For example, no alterations were attempted in the judicial system or in the 11 school districts of Marion County. The school districts were left untouched in order to avert a public outcry from the traditionally intensely loyal and supportive school district

citizens. In addition, several autonomous agencies continued to
exist under Unigov although their independence has been reduced in
certain cases by the mayor's appointive authority and the council's
budgetary powers. These agencies include the Airport Authority,
the Health and Hospital Corporation, the County Board of Public
Welfare, the County Home, the City-County Building Authority, and
the Capital Improvement Board. [36]

As should be evident at this point, Unigov is far from being a
complete or perfect consolidation. The structural change did not
greatly reduce the total number of governmental agencies operating
in Marion County nor did it greatly expand the jurisdiction of many of
these agencies. It did, however, simplify the procedures for future
progress in such areas. By way of example, service districts may
be expanded by approval of the voters of the affected areas. Moreover, landowners in the excluded areas may join the consolidated
city at any time as long as their property adjoins the existing
boundary. The excluded cities may join the Unigov system upon
approval of 51 percent of their voters. The consolidated city itself,
on the other hand, is not permitted to annex additional areas either
within Marion County or adjoining it. [37]

As a means of firmly establishing Unigov's legal validity, its
proponents challenged it in court. Its validity was upheld by the
Indiana Supreme Court on January 26, 1971, and later challenges in
federal courts had the same results. [38]

Unigov became effective on January 1, 1970. However, as a
transitional measure, an interim city-county council composed of the
members of the existing city and county councils was activated on
June 30, 1969 in order to prepare the consolidated city's 1970
budget. [39] On January 1 of the following year, Indianapolis Mayor
Lugar became the first mayor of the consolidated city. The
Indianapolis City Council and the Marion County Council officially
merged to form the city-county council. In conformity with the
provisions of the Unigov Act, the new council—prior to the first
postconsolidation election of November 1971—created 25 councilmanic
electoral districts of approximately equal population and configuration
subject only to natural boundaries. [40]

The 1971 election was considered by many to be, for all
practical purposes, a referendum since it provided the general electorate with its first real opportunity to express its feelings about
Unigov. The Republican Unigov forces won an overwhelming victory
even though the Democrats swept most other municipal elections
throughout the state. Mayor Lugar increased his winning margin
from the 9,000 votes of his 1967 victory to some 54,000. [41] Also
significant was the fact that 28 to 30 percent of the black vote went
to the Republican Lugar. Representing some 17 percent of the

consolidated city's electorate, blacks elected five councilmen—
approximately 18 percent of the 29-member council. Prior to
consolidation, blacks comprised 27 percent of the old city population,
but there was only one black councilman—approximately 11 percent
of the then nine-member council. The increase in black representation
can be attributed to the fact that there were more single-member
districts under Unigov. [42] From the perspective of the black community,
the guarantee of single-member districts, which meant more black
councilmen, was a good tradeoff in exchange for the enlarged scope
of the metropolitan government, which diluted the percentage of
blacks in the total city-county population. Unigov's first elected
officials took office on January 1, 1972. The new system was now
a reality, and only time would prove its success or failure.

Several amendments to the Unigov Act were effected in 1971
and 1972. These included amendments to increase the mayor's
appointment authority and to give him the powers of the previous
county commissioners, to change certain aspects of the police
personnel system, to extend the tax base of the redevelopment
district, and to increase to at least 58 percent the portion of a
single-council-member district that must be encompassed by a
service district to allow a councilman to engage in activities concerning that service district. [43]

At the same time that Unigov was being considered by the 1969
general assembly, those who believed that centralized countywide
governmental structures should be balanced by formal, small,
local institutions, introduced a "Minigov" bill. This bill required
the MDC to prepare a plan for the subdivision of the consolidated
city into communities of 5,000 or more. Each community would
decide by referendum whether to establish a community council.
Each such council would receive its authority and funding from the
city-county council, and the latter would be required to consult with
the local councils concerning any planning or zoning actions affecting
their communities. The Unigov proponents lacked enthusiasm for the
Minigov proposal, and accordingly, it languished until it eventually
was passed in 1972, becoming effective on July 1 of that year. However, the approved law allowed the "minigovs" to do only such things
as the council saw fit. They seemed destined to perform the role of
the advisory neighborhood association. [44]

Although the Indianapolis SMSA includes seven other counties in
addition to Marion County, these were not seriously considered for
inclusion under Unigov, which, of course, was the creation of the
Marion County legislative delegation. Only three specialized and
relatively obscure associations encompass these outer counties. They
are the Comprehensive Health Planning Council of Central Indiana,

the Indiana Criminal Justice Planning Region Number Five, and the Hoosier Hearland Association of Soil and Water Conservation. [45]

THE RESULTS OF REORGANIZATION

Although Unigov has existed for less than a decade, some significant trends and events can be attributed to the consolidation apart from the facts that Indianapolis's population was increased from about 450,000 to approximately 800,000 and the city's territory was expanded from approximately 82 square miles to an area of over 400 square miles. First, as was indicated earlier, Unigov as a term is meaningless from the viewpoint of complete consolidation of all local government functions within Marion County. However, it does have substantial meaning from the perspective of unifying administrative control under a vastly stronger mayor and new city-county council. Mayor Lugar likened the executive function of Unigov to a private corporation. Speaking before the 1970 Convention of the National Association of Counties, he described "the Mayor as president of the corporation . . . with a deputy mayor as nominated by him, and six vice-presidents of the corporation or directors of county wide agencies . . . . Each can be terminated if he does not serve well. So can anybody in our entire government, all the way down, from top to bottom."[46] It is not surprising that Republican party and business leaders would favor such a business model, which would in their view solve the problems of local government. They have subscribed to this general view for many years. The notion of running local government as a business can be traced back to the reform movement of the 1920s, which challenged the delivery of local services by boss-run political machines. Similarly, the city-county council has been compared to the board of directors of a corporation since it formulates policy, passes laws, and budgets the city's money. Since the mayor and his six department directors carry out the policies and laws and implement the budget in a coordinated effort, some observers have reasoned that the confusion, frustration, and wastefulness of the dispersed and overlapping units of the former governmental structure have been eliminated. [47]

The unified voice of the new government and the concomitant sounder fiscal climate have attracted a great deal of new industry and construction. Tens of thousands of new jobs and millions of dollars of new construction have been attributed to the Lugar administration and the Unigov system. [48] One building contractor credited the increase in construction to the fact that under Unigov there is only one government and one simplified building code with which to do business rather than more than dozen structures and codes, as was previously the case. [49]

Indianapolis has enjoyed its greatest period of economic growth under Unigov in spite of the existence of inflationary and recessionary pressures. The business index has doubled since 1967; the downtown retail sales have reversed their previous decline; the unemployment rate has been significantly below the national average; and, in 1974, the National Council on Municipal Performance singled out Indianapolis as the city with the healthiest economy in the nation. This assessment was based on per capita income, equality of income, extent of poverty, economic stability, and availability of jobs. In the same year, Indianapolis ranked sixth among the nation's cities in the total value of building permits issued. [50]

Similarly, physical services have been improved and expanded under Unigov. The Department of Transportation, which consolidates all the transportation functions of the previous city, county, parks district, Mass Transportation Authority, and Metropolitan Thoroughfare Authority, has resurfaced a yearly average of 112 miles of roads, compared to only 16 miles per year county-wide prior to consolidation. [51] Before Unigov was created, there were few parks and other recreational areas developed outside the central city, and in Indianapolis itself, no new swimming pools or other recreational facilities were constructed for a period of 25 years. During the period between 1969 and 1973, the Unigov Department of Parks and Recreation purchased 450 acres of land to be used for recreational purposes and has built six new swimming pools and supervised 47 additional summer playgrounds. The Department of Public Works has presided over a 33 percent reduction of pollution and the removal of over 10,000 abandoned cars. Although it would be quite difficult to prove that Unigov was the primary cause, in 1973 the Department of Public Safety could boast a substantially decreased crime rate and the best safety record in the country for cities of comparable size. [52]

Combining the functions of planning, zoning, building inspection, code enforcement, urban renewal, and housing, the MDC is one of the nation's most comprehensive planning and development units. It has completed 1,026 low-income and 250 elderly housing units and removed 597 condemned buildings. Largely because of the multifarious responsibilities of this department, Indianapolis became the first city to receive federal funding for a unified planning program. The department receives about $15 million annually in federal funds, and, in 1971, it was the largest recipient of approximately 20 cities awarded grants for Planned Variations to supplement the Model Cities Program. Indianapolis was one of the 25 cities that the Office of Management and Budget permitted to submit integrated federal grant applications, thereby resulting in a great reduction of red tape for the city. During the Nixon and Ford administrations, Unigov and Mayor Lugar's unique role as one of the few large-city Republican

mayors greatly improved the position of Indianapolis relative to the
federal government by putting the city in the forefront of most
federally funded urban programs. [53]

One final aspect of the MDC that should be noted is the fact
that a small tax levied on the entire consolidated city base to fund
the city's share of the urban renewal program is one of the few
examples of resource reallocation under Unigov. In this case, all
the region's taxpayers are financing improvements confined to the
core city. [54] Overall, however, there is a reluctance on the part of
the suburban communities to increase their financial contributions
for the payment of services to the core city. Resource redistribution
may be easier in a legal sense, but politically, the suburbanites
now appear to be in a stronger position to resist these changes than
they were prior to reform.

Another benefit that has been attributed to Unigov has been the
saving of money, principally by means of the implementation of
economies of scale. A streamlining of city-county insurance policies
has saved $150,000 annually since 1970 even though the total
coverage has been increased. The consolidated Legal Division of
the Department of Administration has saved approximately $129,000
per year in legal fees, and the Department of Administration as a
whole has realized approximately $84,000 per year through centralized
purchasing. Consolidation also has enabled the city to centralize its
investments, with the interest yield increasing from $581,000 to
$3,160,000. A study of trash collection for the entire Unigov region
indicated that this service could be accomplished with 60 trucks
instead of the previous 80 by changing the routes. This involved a
savings of $360,000 a year in wages alone. In all, a savings of
about $2 million per year has been credited to a reduction of some
230 employees through consolidation functions. [55] It is, of course,
rather difficult to separate improvements related only to Unigov
from improvements related to good management techniques.

As has already been noted, one of the most significant outcomes
of Unigov has been the change in the relative strength of the two
major political parties. Tangential to this change has been the
diminished political influence of the black community. Prior to
consolidation, the blacks were approaching a majority of the then
dominant Democratic party. Unigov both destroyed that dominance
and significantly diluted the overall black percentage of the total
population, which grew from 480,000 to 792,299, with the increase
being nearly all white. Marion County Republican Chairman L. Keith
Buben estimates that about 85,000 of the increase were Republicans. [56]
Many others, including Marion County Democratic Chairman William
Schreiber, believed that the dilution of black political power was a
conscious goal of the Unigov proponents. He argued, "Consolidation

in Indianapolis has had its predicted effects. If they have not
consolidated government, Republicans have consolidated their
political grip in City Hall . . . . And while blacks finally approximate
the percentage of the population on the City Council, the real prize
of executive branch control [the Mayor's office] has been placed
beyond reach. "[57]

In a panel discussion of York Willbern's article "Unigov, Local
Government Reorganization in Indianapolis," held at Shaw College
on January 24, 1973, two of the panelists tended to agree with
Schreiber. Panelist Raymond Lahti observed: "I think that this
Unigov indicates just another example of where the white power
structure absolutely flubbed it up in seizing a marvelous occasion to
do something meaningful about some real problems in the metropolitan area. They just missed the opportunity, in my opinion. "[58]
Panelist Conrad Mallet stated, " . . . if you attempt to unify the
powerful and the powerless under one organizational framework, the
powerful will gain power, and the powerless will lose proportionately
more power, certainly under this Unigov plan, that did happen. "[59]
Only the future can determine whether these critics of Unigov were
correct. However, as Carl Dortch, executive vice-president of the
Indianapolis Chamber of Commerce, wrote, [60]

> Unigov is a fresh start. To many of us, with all
> its limitations, our new consolidated city concept
> is a worthy experiment. It has its appeal in the
> businessman's perception of pinpointing responsi-
> bility—knowing who's boss or where the buck stops.
> Perhaps, too, it testifies to the concern of one
> community to a basic dilemma of American life—is
> the city or, for that matter, the county as we know it
> today, worth saving? We believe it is.

POSSIBILITIES OF REPLICATION

There are valuable lessons to be learned from the Unigov
experience, but as a recipe for reorganization of other metropolitan
areas, it has definite limitations. Unigov was created for the unique
political, governmental, and constitutional factors existing in
Marion County in 1969. The accumulated frustrations with numerous
governmental units and autonomous special service districts,
Indianapolis's unique status as the only first-class city receiving
direct legislative attention, the rare Republican victories at all
levels of government in 1968, the strong leadership of Mayor Lugar
and other key Republicans, and the Indiana state constitution's
declared authority over local governmental forms and offices all had

a tremendous impact upon the many choices and compromises that resulted in the Unigov approach. The chance that the Unigov structure would appropriately fit circumstances elsewhere is quite remote.[61]

There are certain aspects of the Unigov experience, however, that could have wide applicability. First, no referendum was held with regard to Unigov, the feeling being that the average citizen has so little interest in, or understanding of, local governmental forms that a referendum is both meaningless and irrelevant. In Indianapolis, reorganization was considered to be the responsibility of the political leadership with legal assistance. Second, reorganization was considered to be a political process, with the emphasis placed on political feasibility and political loyalties. Mayor Lugar stated to the National Association of Counties in 1970: "One of the reasons city-county consolidation has not occurred more frequently during this century is that a keen sense of practical politics may have been missing from the process."[62] The political expertise of the Unigov proponents was demonstrated by the manner in which they established realistic goals, stressed the positive features of their proposal, effected necessary compromises, and circumvented areas of potential conflict. As has been seen, the state government of Indiana played an active role in the Indianapolis consolidation, and this would appear to be an essential and desirable avenue to be pursued by other metropolitan regions contemplating similar reorganizations. State governments possess greater authority and resources than local governments, and they usually can perform in a more objective manner than the latter, hopefully transcending the political conflict of a region seeking reorganization. Although such transcendence was not the case in Indiana, an activist role by a state government can very definitely yield positive results.

Finally, the way in which the new Unigov system has kept the lines of communication open with the public is something that should be imitated by other areas that have undergone reorganization. By creating neighborhood governmental units (Minigovs), and by establishing a telephone complaint system connecting citizens directly to an appropriate administrative department, the leaders of Unigov have begun to enhance citizen responsiveness and to reinforce a sense of community identity.

The record of Unigov since its inception demonstrates that a compromise, incomplete consolidation, can benefit its citizens, provided strong leadership is present, without seriously alienating the opposition or polarizing the community in general. To date, the record of the new system has been impressive in spite of its limitations. It remains to be seen, however, if Unigov will prove itself capable of responding to the changing political circumstances and the citizen demands of the future.

NOTES

1. "United States: The Cities," Reader's Digest 1972 Almanac and Yearbook, (Pleasantville, N. Y. : Reader's Digest Association, 1973), p. 272.

2. York Willbern, "Unigov: Local Government Reorganization in Indianapolis," in The Regionalist Papers, ed. Kent Mathewson (Detroit: Metropolitan Fund, 1975), p. 207.

3. Ibid. , p. 208.

4. Ibid. , p. 209.

5. "United States: The Cities," op. cit. , p. 272.

6. Willbern, op. cit. , p. 208.

7. Ibid. , pp. 208-9.

8. See David M. Lawrence and H. Rutherford Turnbull, III, "Unigov, City-County Consolidation in Indianapolis," Popular Government, November 1972, p. 19.

9. Roul Tunley, "The City That Married its Suburbs," Kiwanis Magazine, December 1972, p. 3.

10. Willbern, op. cit. , p. 218. We are also in debt to the work of James Owne on the political history, background, and enactment of the Unigov bill.

11. Willbern, op. cit. , p. 210.

12. Ibid. , pp. 209-10.

13. Ibid. , p. 210.

14. Ibid. , p. 211.

15. "Self-Help and the Cities," Nation's Business 59 (June 1971): 23.

16. Ibid. , p. 24.

17. Willbern, op. cit. , p. 212.

18. Ibid. , p. 213.

19. Ibid. , pp. 213-14.

20. Ibid. , p. 214.

21. "Three Mayors Review Their Governments," Nation's Cities 7 (November 1969): 32-40.

22. "Self-Help and the Cities," op. cit. , 24.

23. "City-County Consolidations, Separations, and Federations," American County 35 (November 1970): 31.

24. Ibid. , p. 17.

25. Willbern, op. cit. , p. 217.

26. "City-County Consolidations, Separations, and Federations," op. cit. , p. 17.

27. Joseph Zimmerman, "Indiana Consolidates," American City 85 (January 1970): 76.

28. "Three Mayors Review Their Governments," op. cit. , p. 29.

29. Willbern, op. cit. , pp. 221-22.

30. Lawrence and Turnbull, op. cit. , pp. 20-23.

31. Ibid.

32. Ibid. , p. 20.

33. Willbern, op. cit. , pp. 219-22.

34. Ibid. , p. 215.

35. Ibid. , pp. 215-16.

36. Ibid.

37. Zimmerman, op. cit. , p. 76. See also "Three Mayors Review Their Governments," op. cit. , p. 29.

38. Willbern, op. cit. , p. 218; and Dortch v. Lugar, 24 Ind. Dec. 357, 266 N. E. , 2d ed. (1971).

39. Zimmerman, op. cit. , p. 76.

40. "Consolidated Government for Indianapolis as Provided by Chapter 173, Indiana Acts 1969," anonymous unpublished synopsis, pp. 2-3.

41. Roul Tunley, "The City That Married Its Suburbs," Reader's Digest, May 1973, p. 6.

42. For a discussion of the negative implications of Unigov from the perspective of the Democratic party, see William Schreiber, "Indianapolis-Marion County Consolidation, How Did It Happen?" unpublished manuscript, pp. 9-33.

43. Willbern, op. cit. , p. 223.

44. Ibid. , p. 224.

45. Ibid. , p. 223.

46. "City-County Consolidations, Separations, and Federations," op. cit. , p. 17.

47. "Questions Most Frequently Asked About Unigov," unpublished paper prepared by the Indianapolis Mayor's Office, p. 1.

48. "City-County Consolidations, Separations, and Federations," op. cit. , p. 17.

49. Tunley, op. cit. , p. 5.

50. The Record Speaks for Itself, Indianapolis-Marion County Republican Central Committee, pp. 2-3.

51. Ibid. , p. 5. See also League of Women Voters of Indianapolis, Unigov: What It Is—What It Isn't (Indianapolis: Chamber of Commerce, 1972), p. 11.

52. "Questions Most Frequently Asked About Unigov," op. cit. , pp. 7-11.

53. Ibid. , pp. 7-8. See also Willbern, op. cit. , pp. 221-22.

54. Willbern, op. cit. , p. 226.

55. "Questions Most Frequently Asked About Unigov," op. cit. , pp. 7-11 and Tunley, Kiwanis, op. cit. , pp. 4-5.

56. William Schreiber, op. cit. , p. V.

57. Ibid., p. 35.

58. "Panel Discussion of Regionalist Paper #10," Regionalist Papers, op. cit., p. 233.

59. Ibid., p. 234.

60. Carl R. Dortch, "Consolidated City-County Government Indianapolis-Marion County, Indiana Style," unpublished manuscript, p. 3.

61. Willbern, op. cit., pp. 218-19.

62. "City-County Consolidations, Separations and Federations," op. cit., p. 17.

CHAPTER

4

THE MIAMI-DADE COUNTY APPROACH: COMPREHENSIVE URBAN COUNTY PLAN

HISTORICAL BACKGROUND

Dade County, located in the southeast section of Florida, has a territorial expanse of approximately 2,300 square miles, which encompasses all of the Miami area and stretches westward to the Everglades. Constant population growth in the county began with the completion of the Florida East Coast Railroad in 1896. Construction of the railroad was started after a severe frost during the winter months of 1894–95 destroyed northern Florida's citrus industry. In 1897 the railroad was extended to Homestead and later to Key West. With the completion of the railroad, the economic development of Dade County began in earnest. The agricultural industry, which had hitherto been limited in Miami and the surrounding region, experienced a major boom as a consequence of the expert services provided by the railroad. Also associated with the railroad was a steady increase in revenues derived from the tourist industry. The tourist industry continued to flourish over the years until the point was reached early in the 1950s when the revenues from tourism surpassed those received from the agricultural/citrus industry. [1]

Historically, Dade County experienced a series of municipal incorporations by the core city and its surrounding suburbs. The city of Miami was incorporated in 1896, Homestead in 1913, Florida City in 1914, Miami Beach in 1915, Coral Gables in 1925, and Opa Locka and Miami Springs in 1926. In 1920 Dade County had a population of only 42,000, but the real estate boom of the 1920s added 100,000 more residents. In 1960 the population had increased to 935,000, almost triple what it was at the end of World War II, and in 1970 it was 1,267,792. Thus, the growth of Dade County over

the last few decades has been nearly astronomical, making it one of
the fastest-expanding metropolitan areas in the country. By 1960
Dade County was comprised of 26 municipalities and the surrounding
unincorporated areas, with a total land area of 2,257 square miles.

The population patterns of Miami and its suburbs are not typical
of other metropolitan areas in the United States. In greater Miami,
the population has been constantly growing (28 percent between 1960
and 1970), not as a consequence of spillover from the central city,
but rather from in-migration from all over the United States. [2] There
also has been a large influx of Latin Americans into the Miami area.
Of Dade County's permanent residents, 34 percent are of Spanish
descent, and the county recently has been declared a bilingual and
bicultural area. [3] As Longbrake and Nichols have written, "Of the
total county growth in the last decade nearly 76 percent was
attributed to net migration and the remainder to natural increase.
About seventy percent of the net migrants during the 1960s were
Cuban refugees. "[4]

Florida's "Old South" is made up of those counties located in
the northern and western sectors of the state. Prior to the Civil
War, these areas were traditionally conservative in economic matters.
However, by the 1880s and 1890s there had been sufficient change
to foster support for the Populist party and the National Farmers'
Alliance, but this turn to economic liberalism did not alter north
and west Florida's extreme conservatism in racial questions. Today
economic conservatism prevails in south Florida along the eastern
coast and also amidst the resort communities along the western shore.
The great wealth in these regions, revolving around vast citrus
groves, huge cattle ranches, large truck farms, and the presence
of many affluent Northerners, helps explain the economic conservatism.
Due to a large white population, southern Florida is far less concerned
than northern and western Florida with racial problems. [5]

Traditionally, northern and western Florida has supported
economically liberal candidates while southern Florida has tended
toward more conservative politicians. Since the end of Reconstruction
in 1876, the Democratic party, with its conservative and liberal
factions, has been dominant in the state. Since roughly 1948, the
trend within the Democratic party has been toward the center, with
much of the power concentrated in the hands of moderate conservatives. The Republican party, however, has been steadily increasing
its impact on Florida politics. Since 1876, there have been five
presidential elections in which Florida gave a majority of its vote to
the Republican candidate. In 1954 Congressman William Cramer
became the first Republican elected to Congress from Florida since
Reconstruction, and he was reelected three times. In 1961 there were
only seven Republicans in the state legislature (one in the senate

THE MIAMI-DADE COUNTY APPROACH

and six in the house) out of a total membership of 133 members. The
party historically has been split and disorganized at both the state
and local levels. [6]

V. O. Key's chapter in his classic Southern Politics, entitled
"Every Man for Himself," reflects the disorganization of both major
parties in Florida. [7] Although the Democrats constitute the dominant
political force in the state, they are far from being a unified,
centralized, political unit, and this is even more true of the
Republicans. Among the factors contributing to this lack of
organizational sophistication are long distances between the major
geographical areas of the state, heavy urbanization in certain regions,
the migration from other states of persons with differing values
and ideas, and the state's multifaceted economy. In combination,
these factors have militated against solidified, stable, political party
organizations.

When the cities in the Dade County region were first established,
the call for their creation revolved around several factors such as the
desire to obtain inexpensive land, the imperialistic instincts of land
promoters, the hope of dodging zoning restrictions, and the desire to
procure liquor licenses and other such fringe benefits. As the cities
developed, they took on quite separate individualized identities due
to their diverse interests and needs. The end result was the political
fragmentation of the Dade County region. The four largest cities
in the county exemplify best this municipal diversification. First
and foremost is the core city of Miami. With a population of 291,688
in 1960, it was the central and largest municipality in Dade County,
representing approximately 31 percent of the total population. The
general inclination in the city of Miami was against governmental
change, an attitude promoted primarily by the black population,
which had succeeded in establishing satisfactory working relationships
with the local authorities (it had even managed to secure a separate
black police force and court within the city). The black segment of
the city's population feared that consolidation might disrupt the spirit
of cooperation then in existence. [8]

The second major city, Hialeah, had a population of 66,792 in
1960. This municipality possessed an industrial character, and the
majority of its citizens were typically lower middle class. With a
Tammany-like political atmosphere, Hialeah had developed a quality
of brotherhood among its population, which set it apart from the other
cities in the area. The third largest city, Miami Beach, had a
1960 population of 63,145. Dominated by its Jewish citizenry, Miami
Beach had a provincial character and was opposed to any new,
questionable system of government. The city possessed the finest
educational system in Dade County, and this fact contributed substantially to its resistance to consolidation. Finally, the city of Coral

Gables, with a 1960 population of 34,793, was the most affluent of
the region's leading municipalities. This high-income community
boasted a high level of governmental services and, accordingly, was
little interested in change. [9]

Thus, each of the four major municipalities identified above
possessed a unique character. Due to the lack of political leadership
and organized factions, the most influential forces within these
communities were the specialized interests that were represented
on a multiplicity of boards and commissions. These city governments
were headed by council-manager arrangements, which paralleled the
collegial executive at the state level. The remaining 22 municipalities
in the Dade County region at the time of consolidation were North
Miami, North Miami Beach, Miami Springs, South Miami, Opa
Locka, Homestead, Miami Shores, West Miami, Florida City, Bay
Harbor Islands, Surfside, Biscayne Park, Virginia Gardens, El
Portal, North Bay Village, Bal Harbour, Sweetwater, Golden Beach,
Hialeah Gardens, Medley, Pennsuco, and Indian Creek. [10]

THE MOVEMENT TOWARD REFORM

Before Metro came into existence, the government of Dade
County was a conglomeration of officials elected under a commission
form of government. Voters in Dade County elected 39 county officers,
including five county commissioners, ten heads of independent
departments, 14 judges, five constables, and five justices of the
peace. These officials were not usually associated with one political
party or another. They normally ran for office independently on the
basis of personality and past political experience. [11] Although the
Dade County region was deficient in many governmental organizational
areas, its one advantage, from the perspective of potential consolidation, was the relatively low number of local units. At the time of
consolidation in 1957, it had only 31 such units compared to the 18
other similar metropolitan regions in the country, which averaged
more than 120 each. However, any one of these 31 entities was
nearly autonomous in every respect, whereas in the nation's other
metropolitan areas, there often has been a higher degree of
cooperation.

Prior to the creation of the Miami Metro, there was no effective
countywide agency responsible for long-range regional planning in
such areas as economic development, welfare, recreation, and the
physical environment. Local planning boards did exist, but these
were generally unproductive due to such factors as poorly trained
technical staffs, inadequate financial support, and the inability on
the part of both local governmental officials and the general public
to understand the nature of an adequate planning function. In an

attempt to correct these deficiencies, the Dade County Coordinating
Planning Council was created in 1944, but the council failed to
realize its objectives, primarily because it was unable to rise above
the fragmented local interests. Most decisions were made on the
basis of the needs of the moment as perceived in the various local
communities. [12]

The needs of the unincorporated areas of Dade County, consisting of one-third of the total population, constituted a particularly
serious problem before the comprehensive urban county experiment.
In order to procure essential services, which they were unable to
provide themselves, for their rapidly growing populations, these
unincorporated areas frequently entered into contracts with more
governmentally advanced municipalities. For example, the city of
Miami sold water to a private utility as well as to the cities of
Hialeah, Miami Springs, West Miami, and Miami Beach. Miami
Beach in turn provided services to its own residents as well as to
the neighboring communities. Another service provided by the city
of Miami to neighboring communities was police communications
and training. This consisted primarily of providing economies of
scale for these communities and making available the facilities of
the Miami police academy, which is considered to be among the best
in the nation. In addition, fire-fighting services were provided
by Miami and other cities to various small towns and unincorporated
areas, although here agreements were not formalized until 1957,
with the creation of a "sliding zone" or "belt" system for emergency
response beyond the normal established municipal boundary lines.
The major problem with these agreements was that the major cities
were burdened with the lion's share of the expenses for the services
provided to the smaller areas, but they were without the power to
extract revenues for these services.

In addition to the largely informal cooperative agreements
described in the preceding paragraph, there also developed, beginning
in the early 1940s, several formal agreements. As a matter of fact,
no single functional consolidation measure ever failed to be adopted,
whether it was presented at the polls or to the legislature. In 1943,
a countywide health department was established and the Dade County
Port Authority was created in 1945, replacing a two-year-old
Greater Port Authority under city jurisdiction. [13] Also in 1945, ten
school districts were consolidated into one county school system under
the authority of a County Board of Public Instruction, which was
given the power to levy, subject to the approval of the voters, a
countywide property tax of up to ten mills. At the time of the consolidation, there were 28 separate school bank accounts throughout
the county. All of the districts within Dade County were in favor of
the merger, with the exception of Miami Beach whose educational

standards, as mentioned earlier, surpassed the minimum standards existent in the other areas of the county. Moreover, with only 7 percent of the county population, Miami Beach was paying 20 percent of the tax burden. [14]

In 1949 jurisdiction over the principal public hospital in the Miami region, Jackson Memorial, was transferred from the city of Miami to Dade County. Prior to the transfer, Miami bore the entire cost of maintaining the hospital, estimated to be $600,000 in 1947 and $1 million in 1948, even though the facilities were being utilized by people throughout the county. Nevertheless, Miami government officials were reluctant to give the hospital over to the county without receiving compensation for the city's past investments. Due to a diarrhea epidemic at Jackson Memorial in the early part of 1948, during which several infants died, a special committee was created by the Miami government to investigate the causes of the epidemic and conditions pertaining to the hospital in general. The findings of the committee indicated inadequate funds and facilities. The Miami City Commission, by a three-to-two vote on June 2, 1948, approved the transfer of the hospital to the county, with the new arrangements to take effect on January 1, 1949. [15]

Although each of the functional consolidations described above was ultimately approved, it was not without, in each case, considerable opposition. During each debate, sides were taken and lines were drawn that were to remain intact right through the major consolidation effort that was to occur in the mid-1950s. Aligned over the years on the side of further cooperative efforts were the central city's business-men, the Miami Chamber of Commerce, the majority of the residents in the unincorporated areas, the League of Women Voters, two leading daily newspapers (the Miami Herald and the Miami News), and the Dade County delegation to the state legislature. Among those rallying against even functional consolidation were numerous city officials and workers who were understandably worried over the future status of their positions and jobs. Also in opposition were various business groups in the smaller communities, the newspaper the Miami Beach Sun, the League of Municipalities, and numerous ad hoc citizen committees.

Although the forces against functional consolidation ultimately lost on each occasion, they never failed to win whenever the issue turned to the broader concept of consolidating general-purpose governmental units. Several such attempts were made between 1945 and 1957, and all resulted in defeat. In 1945 the mayor of the city of Miami, Leonard K. Thomson, suggested a consolidation proposal whereby the county and all of its cities would be combined into a single city and county of Miami. The plan was voted down in the state senate. [16] Dade County voters in 1948 rejected an amendment to the

Florida constitution that called for the merger of Dade County, the city of Miami, and the four small communities of North Bay Village, Virginia Gardens, West Miami, and Flagler City. The vote was 23,513 for and 27,821 against, a negative margin of 8.4 percent. [17] The closest vote occurred in a referendum in 1953 calling for the abolition of the core city of Miami and the transfer of its functions to the county. This time the margin was only 908 votes, or 1.7 percent in a total vote of 54,292. The closeness of this referendum election led to the creation by the city of Miami on July 1, 1953 of the Metropolitan Miami Municipal Board (3M Board) to study the feasibility of governmental reorganization. The city of Miami selected 11 members of the board, the Dade League of Municipalities selected eight, and the Board of Public Instruction chose one. [18] Also in 1953, the Dade County delegates concluded an informal agreement among themselves to stymie creation of any additional cities within the county through special legislative acts. This agreement, in conjunction with the delegation's success four years earlier in having adopted by the state legislature a measure prohibiting any subsequent incorporation into the county of an unincorporated area under the general laws of Florida, served to obviate possible additional opposition to Metro from newly incorporated, autonomous units of government. [19]

The 3M Board hired the Public Administration Services (PAS) of Chicago to assist it in its study of regional government possibilities. The principal recommendation from PAS was for a two-tiered or federated form of metropolitan government for the Dade County region. The city level would be responsible for local functions, the minimum standards of which would be set by the county. The other level would be that of a reorganized and enlarged county government, which would be responsible for such regional functions as water, sewage, solid waste disposal, transportation, traffic, and overall metropolitan planning. [20] The PAS recommendations were generally accepted by the 3M Board, which proceeded to draft an amendment to the Florida constitution designed to give home rule to Dade County. The state legislature approved the proposed amendment in June 1955, and two months later, the legislature created a Metro charter board and appointed its 19 members. This board was replaced over a year later, in August 1956, by a 17-member board appointed by the governor as a consequence of the question being raised of the legality of the legislature's both establishing an agency, in this case, the charter board, and appointing its members. [21]

The proposed home rule amendment was placed before the Florida electorate on November 6, 1956 and was adopted by a margin

of over two to one. * The amendment served as the constitutional
foundation for the anticipated consolidation. Basically, it freed Dade
County and its cities from dependence on the state legislature for
the enactment of local laws. It also permitted the county's voters to
create a metropolitan government, provided that such a government
would not involve any conflicts between the state and the county.
Worthy of note is the fact that during the amendment election campaign,
no effort was made to inform the voters of all the implications of
home rule. For example, the powers granted by the state through
home rule were not enumerated, and, accordingly, the voters were
largely unaware of the freedom given to the county in forming a
metropolitan government. Moreover, the voters were not apprised
of the fact that the amendment did not grant new taxing powers to
whatever consolidated government might be established. Thus, the
revenue for the operations of the new government would have to be
derived from existing tax sources.

Following the acceptance of the amendment by the electorate,
the charter board addressed itself to its task of drafting a home rule
charter authorizing a metropolitan system. The board at this juncture
was confronted with two major related problems—the most appropriate distribution of powers between the county and the city governments
and the extent of the limitations that should be placed on the power
and authority of the county. The board completed its work in the
spring of the following year, and on April 15, 1957 the 19 members
affixed their signatures to the final version of the charter they had
decided upon. Prior to the referendum election, the Dade County
League of Municipalities created a special committee of its own to
study the proposed charter to determine whether or not the league
should endorse it. Two months before the election, the special committee returned a negative report. The members of the committee
then met with the charter board members in order to seek a provision
for municipal autonomy. Following its failure to secure this con-
cession, the special committee recommended that the league oppose
the charter. In spite of this opposition, the charter was approved
on May 21, 1957 by a slim margin with only 26 percent of the county's
voters going to the polls. The official tally was 44,404 for the charter
and 42,620 opposed, a difference of only 1,784. [23]

THE NATURE OF THE NEW SYSTEM

The charter approved by the Dade County voters, in addition to
providing home rule powers, established a two-tier governmental

*The statewide vote was 322,839 (69.9 percent) for and 138,430
(30 percent) against. The vote in Dade County was 86,612 (71.5 percent) for and 34,437 (28.4 percent) against. [22]

structure that essentially reorganized the former limited county government into a countywide metropolitan governmental system capable of performing most municipal-type functions on an area-wide basis, but leaving to the individual municipalities the performance of those services not requiring coordination. [24] Daniel Paul, the lawyer for the second charter board, went so far as to maintain that the charter in actuality created a central government strong enough to take over eventually every function of the cities. [25] Nevertheless, the charter at the time of its enactment did have a definite division-of-powers provision even though it was heavily weighted toward the county government. In fact, inclusion of this division of powers provision probably enabled the charter to squeak through the referendum election. Anticonsolidationists had come to the realization that some form of more centralized government probably was inevitable, and the proposed system, though far from ideal, was preferable, as far as they were concerned, to the outright eradication of the municipalities.

The powers of the county government under the terms of the charter can be separated into four distinct categories: municipal-type functions, responsibilities in unincorporated areas, responsibilities for setting minimum standards, and elastic powers. The major powers included in the category of municipal-type functions were as follows:[26]

1. building and regulation of roads, bridges, tunnels, and parking facilities;
2. construction and operation of air, water, rail, bus, and port transportation systems;
3. traffic control and maintenance of central facilities for records, training, and communications for fire and police;
4. police and fire protection;
5. preparation and implementation of comprehensive, county development plans;
6. maintenance of hospitals and uniform health and welfare programs;
7. provision and maintenance of parks, playgrounds, libraries, museums, and other recreational and cultural facilities and programs;
8. establishment and administration of housing, slum clearance, urban renewal, air pollution control, flood and beach erosion control, and drainage programs;
9. regulation of water supply and sewage and solid waste disposal;

10. establishment and enforcement of building zoning
    and codes and business regulations;
11. levying and collecting taxes and special assessments,
    borrowing and expending of money, and issuing
    bonds, revenue certificates, and other obligations
    of indebtedness as provided by law.

The specific responsibilities of the county government with
respect to the unincorporated areas included, in addition to the above
powers, which applied to all areas, licensing and regulation of
taxis, limousines, and all other rental cars and establishment and
enforcement of regulations for the sale of alcoholic beverages. In
the minimum standards category, the county government was
empowered to set such standards for all governmental units for
performance of any service or function provided that these standards
were not discriminatory among areas. Should a governmental unit
fail to comply with such standards, the county government was
empowered to "take over and perform regulate, or grant franchises
to operate any such service."[27] Finally, and most broadly, the
elastic provisions of the charter authorized the county government
to "exercise all powers and privileges granted to municipalities,
counties and county officers by the Constitution and laws of the state,
and all powers not prohibited by the Constitution or by this Charter,"
to "adopt such ordinances and resolutions as may be required in the
exercise of its powers . . ." and to "perform any other acts consistent with laws which are required or which are in the common interest
of the people of the county."[28]

The fact that the county government was to be the dominant
partner in the new metropolitan relationships was clearly evidenced
by the implied-powers article and "supremacy clause" cited below:

> No enumeration of powers in this Charter shall be
> deemed exclusive or restrictive and the foregoing
> powers shall be deemed to include all implied powers
> necessary and proper to carrying out such powers.
> All of these powers may be exercised in the incor-
> porated or unincorporated areas, subject to the
> procedures herein provided in certain cases relating
> to municipalities.[29]

> This Charter and the ordinances adopted hereunder
> shall in cases of conflict supercede all municipal
> charters and ordinances, except as herein provided,
> and where authorized by the Constitution, shall in

cases of conflict supersede all special and general
laws of the state. 30

Although the division-of-powers principle was strongly weighted
on the side of the county government, the individual municipalities
were given certain protections and prerogatives. Thus, the county
could not abolish an incorporated municipality without the express
permission of its voters nor could the county arbitrarily rearrange
municipal boundaries. Municipalities retained the right to change
their respective charters provided the provisions did not conflict
with the county charter. Each city could exceed county minimum
standards for zoning, and, subject to county standards, each city
could regulate taxis and other rental vehicles, determine hours for
the sale of alcoholic beverages, and provide for fire and police
protection. In response to the concern for job security and civil
service protection of municipal and county workers affected by the
governmental change, the charter board arranged for the placement
of any surplus employees as top priority on the county employment
list. In addition, these workers were not to lose their accumulated
civil service rights nor pension benefits. 31

A Board of County Commissioners was designated under the
terms of the charter to serve as the legislative and governing body
of the county and to oversee the entire metropolitan system. Initially,
the board consisted of 11 members—five commissioners elected by
the voters of the county at large (but each of whom was required to
be a resident of a different county commission district), five commissioners elected from each county commission district only by the
voters of the district, and one commissioner elected from each
city within the county possessing a population of 60,000 or more. 32
In 1963 the charter was amended to reduce the membership of the
board to nine commissioners with eight to be elected by the voters
of the county at large subject to the requirement that each commissioner must reside in a different county commission district, of
which now there were eight. The ninth member, who was to serve
as the mayor and chairman of the board, also was to be elected by a
countywide vote. All commissioners, including the mayor, were to
serve four-year terms. 33

Under the terms of the charter, the elective status of the
assessor, tax collector, surveyor, purchasing agent, and county
supervisor was abolished. To administer the new county government,
the charter provided for the appointment of a county manager by the
board of commissioners. The manager was to be responsible for
administering all county governmental units and for implementing
board policies throughout the region. Four departments—finance,

personnel, planning, and law—were established under the manager
with the proviso that the manager was free to create any additional
departments that he concluded were necessary for efficient
administration. [34] The charter also established a metropolitan
court, the judges of which were to be appointed by the Board of
Commissioners to serve six-year terms. The jurisdiction of the
court was to apply to all cases arising under ordinances adopted by
the board. [35]

RECORD OF PERFORMANCE

Upon the establishment of Metro, several ordinances were
adopted by the Board of County Commissioners in such areas as
public works, traffic control, building, and zoning. The quick
drafting and passage of these ordinances irritated many localists,
mostly municipal officials and employees and former county officeholders, who had not as yet become accustomed to the consolidation
itself. These critics argued that the new Metro should concentrate
on developing programs to raise the level of services in the unincorporated areas and to improve the efficiency of the existing
regional machinery instead of immediately enacting complicated and
comprehensive ordinances. The supporters of the ordinances were
quick to retort that city officials would have fought each and every
step of the way no matter how slowly the county moved toward
centralization. The opposition did indeed wage bitter attacks on
Metro at every opportunity, and the end result was numerous lawsuits
and amendment referendums.

One of the earliest suits brought against Metro revolved around
the new traffic code, which transferred jurisdiction over traffic
violations from the municipalities to the metropolitan court. Miami
Shores went to court to challenge the county commissioners' right
to curtail the exercise of a city's power under its municipal charter.
In its decision of June 27, 1958, the circuit court dismissed the
Miami Shores grievance and upheld the power of the county commission by ruling that the minicipalities must enforce the Metro traffic
code, which had been lawfully enacted under the home rule charter
and, therefore, superseded and nullified all municipal traffic
ordinances and codes in Dade County. This decision was upheld by the
Florida Supreme Court on December 17, 1958. [36] The decision not
only gave teeth to the county commission but also served as a precedent
for future litigation against the county commission's authority. [37]

A second type of challenge took the form of an attempted local
autonomy amendment to the home rule charter. Resentful of what
they felt was a usurpation of their powers, Miami and other municipalities, working through the Dade League of Municipalities, drew

up an amendment to the charter, which stipulated that "neither the political autonomy nor the right of self government or self determination of any of the municipalities of Dade shall be infringed upon . . . and [that] they [the municipalities] shall maintain their continuous right to exercise all powers . . . ."[38] The Dade League of Municipalities expended $32,000 on a campaign to persuade the county's voters to support the amendment, and the Coral Gables commissioners approved the mailing, at public expense, of "vote yes" letters to their constituents. Anti-local-autonomy forces included the Miami-Dade Chamber of Commerce, the League of Women Voters, and a citizens' "Vote No" Committee. The referendum election was held on September 30, 1958, and the autonomy amendment was defeated by a vote of 60 percent against and 40 percent for. (The vote totals were 74,420 against and 48,893 for.)[39]

A stronger challenge to Metro occurred four years later in 1961. This took the form of the so-called McLeod amendment, which proposed no fewer than 37 changes in the charter. If adopted, the amendment would have eradicated the council-manager form of government and virtually ended Metro's control over such area-wide functions as sewage, water supply, transportation, traffic, and central planning.[40] The amendment, however, was defeated in a referendum election held on October 17, 1961 by a 4 percent margin of 52 to 48 percent. (The vote was 105,097 against and 97,170 for.)[41] A more recent attempt to alter the charter occurred in 1972. Two years earlier, the Board of County Commissioners created the Dade County Metropolitan Study Commission, which ultimately made four major recommendations. The recommendations were to change the system to a strong mayor form of government with the election of most county commissioners by district, to establish an ombudsman, to create service districts in the unincorporated areas, and to create a Metro zoning review board.[42] The first proposal, to change to a strong mayor form of government, brought varied reactions. Edward Sofen supported the change in an editorial in the Miami Herald in which he stressed the point that the county needed a single person citizens would look to and hold responsible for the proper administration of county government. Opponents countered that such a person would become a "boss mayor" with extensive patronage powers that would bring an end to professional administration in the county. The strong mayor proposal as well as the other three changes were defeated.[43] Miami Metro provides an example of how metropolitan government can breed extended conflict, even where it is successfully implemented. From the outset, Miami has been a case study of how not to reform, and many of the political wounds remain open today.

In spite of the various attempts to alter Metro, the system has survived and has registered a number of impressive accomplishments, not the least of which has been, in the words of Bollens and Schmandt, "the integration of a formerly haphazard administrative organization, installation of modern management practices by standardizing procedures and developing a full battery of auxiliary services such as data processing, record handling, and internal auditing, and staffing the departments with professionals."[44] At the end of his 3.5-year term as Metro's first county manager, O.W. Campbell noted several areas of progress: "a reduction and coordination of county departments, new budget practices, water and sewer improvements, transit, a seaport, uniform traffic planning and law enforcement, and a thorough reassessment to lighten the burden on industrial and commercial taxpayers."[45]

In 1972 Dade County successfully passed one of the largest general obligation capital improvement bond issues ever approved in the United States at the local government level. The $553.1 million "Decade of Progress" program will generate more than $2 billion of improvements in Dade County through 1982 with the inclusion of state and federal funds. The program is being implemented through the Decade of Progress Office under the county manager.[46] In the same year, the county commissioners gave final approval to a countywide water and sewer system to be operated by a semiautonomou board formed by merging a county agency and the 21-year-old Water Board created by the state legislature to manage these services for the city of Miami.[47] Also in 1972, Metro inaugurated the South Dade Governmental Center as a means of making county services more accessible to the people of that area. The center provides offices for public works, pollution control, traffic and transportation, water and sewer, and housing and urban development. These several operations are coordinated by a special assistant to the manager who is stationed in the South Dade facility.[48] In 1974 the Department of Human Resources was established, replacing the Office of Human Resources. This department oversees the management and coordination of federal, state, and local programs throughout the county, which in 1975 totaled approximately $38 million.[49]

Responsibility for physical development of the Dade County area is divided between the county and the municipalities. The municipalities administer zoning ordinances within their jurisdiction and Metro handles zoning in unincorporated areas. Police communications also is a divided responsibility. Fire protection is provided by the county in the unincorporated areas and in 13 cities at the request of these cities. Garbage collection is provided in the unincorporated area by the county and in the cities by the city governments. More than 30 years in the making, Miami's new port facility, called Dodge

Island, has become a year-round base for nine cruise ships sailing to such vacation ports as Nassau, Freeport, San Juan, St. Thomas, and Kingston. The construction of the port facility cost approximately $22 million, which was raised through taxes and revenue bonds. Port Director Irvin J. Stephens estimates that the facility will service some 700,000 passengers yearly by 1980. [50] Metropolitan Dade County maintains an extensive park system, which includes golf courses, oceanfront beaches, nature preserves, a zoo, a county auditorium, and a central stadium. The county also manages several neighborhood parks throughout the unincorporated areas and provides recreation programs at these facilities. The cities maintain their own parks, playgrounds, and recreational programs.

The most important new policy issue to arise under the 1974/75 county budget was the establishment of a municipal service area for the unincorporated areas. The annual budget now is prepared in two major parts—one representing countywide responsibilities and the other representing the unincorporated areas. The countywide portion of the budget allocates funds for major metropolitan services for all residents, regardless of where they live. The budget is funded mainly through general property-tax revenues, federal grants, state and federal revenue sharing, and special fees. The municipal service area portion is for local services to the unincorporated areas and is supported by its own special property tax. [51]

Metro, like other urban governments, relies heavily on state financial assistance. The state of Florida shares revenue derived from motor fuel and cigarette taxes with localities. In 1974 Dade County received $3 million as its percentage of Florida's $.08 gasoline tax and another $2 million from state cigarette taxes. Metro has been quite successful in attracting federal funds, but controversy exists regarding future federal assistance. There are those within the Metro bureaucracy who feel that increased reliance on federal funds could be detrimental. Funds with "strings attached" prevent local authorities from controlling where money is to be spent. Federal and local priorities often do not coincide and the absence of longevity in federal assistance frequently causes serious problems, such as rising expectations that cannot always be met.

Metro taxes on a countywide basis. In 1975 the value of the county's taxable real estate and personal property was $18.9 billion. The tax base is steadily increasing partly as a result of services transferred to county control. For example, Metro obtained control of the Coral Gables bus systems and the Miami Shores and Sweetwater fire departments in 1975. [52] The municipalities are finding it increasingly difficult to maintain autonomy in providing the various services traditionally performed at the local level, and as a result, they have acquiesced in the takeovers by the county. A Miami Shores

official summarized the dilemma of the cities in the following words:
"There is an anti-Metro feeling in the Shores which made it difficult
to give up the fire department. But it was too big of a financial
burden for a small city like this."[53] It is difficult to gauge precisely
the impact that Metro has had on the efficiency of governmental
operations. During the last decade, inflation has caused major
increases in all municipal and county budgets. In addition,
metropolitan reforms often seem to stimulate indirectly a degree
of activism that demands new programs for the major problems
of any metropolis. However, there is evidence that in Dade County,
due largely to the formation of Metro, "the rate of increase in
expenditures has been substantially reduced."[54]

Although Metro appears better off financially than most of the
municipalities in Dade County, it has experienced fiscal difficulties
of its own. In February 1975, the county manager instituted a four-
day work week for some county employees to help weather an $8
million revenue shortage. The county's share of state revenues that
year was reduced by $4 million, and local building permit revenue
was down $2 million from what had been projected. Due to
retaliatory work slowdowns by departments whose personnel had been
cut, County Manager Ray Goode was forced to reinstitute full work
weeks at a faster pace than originally anticipated.

Metro's problems go beyond its financial dilemmas. Citizens
have frequently complained that county government is out of touch
with the people. After taking office in October 1970, Goode discovered that Metro was receiving approximately 30,000 public complaints yearly. Upon his recommendation, a major public relations
effort employing 100 people and operating under a budget of $2
million annually was instituted. A large part of this effort was the
creation of a new department entitled Citizens' Information Services
(CIS) to deal with citizen complaints on a daily basis. [55]

Several of the problems confronting the government of Dade
County revolve around the region's varied population, which includes
numerous blacks, Cubans, migrant laborers, and retirees. [56] Blacks
represent approximately 15 percent of the Dade County population.
The number of black-operated businesses has increased significantly
since the late 1960s, but they are relatively small in size, and they
suffer from such factors as high unemployment rates and limited
purchasing power among blacks and rising insurance rates and credit
discrimination resulting, in part, from the high crime rate within
the black community. Almost 30 percent of Dade County's population
is of Cuban extraction. Of the 83,000 Cuban householders in Miami
alone, 88 percent speak Spanish at home. The Cuban immigrants
have not only taken many jobs from the native citizens, but, in
addition, they have placed a considerable burden on the educational

system. Today Spanish is the primary language in several of the area's schools. However, unlike the penniless immigrants from Europe who entered the United States in the nineteenth century, many of the Cubans who emigrated in the 1960s to escape the Castro regime in their homeland brought considerable wealth along with them. In Miami and Miami Beach many of the downtown shops, which were previously run by Jewish proprietors, are now owned and operated by Cubans.

The migrant labor force, which is comprised mainly of Mexican-Americans and blacks, has presented problems of its own that have taxed the Metro budget heavily. By way of example, in 1973 a typhoid epidemic struck the South Dade Labor Camp, and although fortunately there were no deaths, 218 persons became seriously ill. More than $850,000 was spent to alleviate the problem, but little was accomplished in eliminating the rats, seeping sewage, inadequate water supply, and general filth. In 1970 there were approximately 146,000 retired persons residing in the metropolitan Miami area, which amounted to a 91 percent increase in this segment of the population since 1960. This substantial increase in the number of senior citizens was accompanied by increased demands for more and better services in such areas as health care, public transportation, and public housing. In addition, the spiraling inflation rates over the past several years have made it much more difficult for many of these senior citizens to maintain a satisfactory standard of living, given their limited incomes derived primarily from pensions and social security benefits.

The urban county approach will probably encounter future problems in Miami as the growth of the region extends beyond the boundaries of Dade County. As of 1970, the Census Bureau still included Dade County as the only county of the SMSA. However, more recent growth patterns and projections suggest that this South Florida metropolitan area now embraces at least two other adjoining counties. Mogulof writes of this problem:[57]

> If Miami-Dade growth is overflowing presently
> defined metropolitan boundaries, this indicates
> graphically the major shortcoming of the urban
> county approach. If Dade County is to remain a
> governing form capable of acting throughout the
> real metropolitan area, it may require state
> action to expand Dade County lines at the expense
> of neighboring counties with Dade County. In that
> case, the attractiveness of the urban county, on
> the basis that it does not tamper with existing
> political boundaries, would vanish.

Although two decades have passed since the metropolitan consolidation was initiated in the Dade County region, the system is far from being universally accepted. Local autonomy dies hard. It is still a controversial issue in Miami, and as Miami's Mayor Maurice Ferre has stated, "Metro should face a basic fact, it is not going to get rid of Miami, Hialeah, Coral Gables, and Miami Beach."[58] As Edward Sofen has commented, critics like Ferre often see Metro as a monster bent on seducing the municipalities.[59] Even Dan Paul, who was the initiator of the original Metro charter, has expressed the belief that Metro's ultimate goal is to abolish all municipalities in Dade County.[60] Criticisms such as these would appear to be unfounded. Admittedly, the trend would appear to be toward more consolidation in the Dade County region, but this shifting of governmental responsibilities will undoubtedly occur in the future, as it has in the past, in those areas where the municipalities have found it either necessary or desirable to shed services that have become too costly.

Those who argue for secession and complete local autonomy cannot really ignore the economic and technological arguments that favor a centralized system. The smaller unit governments are poorly equipped to take advantage of economies of scale and technological innovations and, thus, find it more difficult to respond to the needs of their citizens.[61] The Miami Metro was organized to take advantage of the desirable aspects of both centralization and decentralization through a sharing of power between two levels of government. The system may not have provided neatness and symmetry, but it has succeeded in eliminating some costly replication of services while preserving local governmental units, and it has been reasonably successful in dealing with the many complex issues confronting metropolitan Dade County. Governmental officials throughout Dade County agree that some basic services should continue to be provided by municipal governments. Even County Manager Goode agrees that local police patrols and garbage collection can be provided efficiently at the local level, while Metro should provide such area-wide services as health care, transportation, public housing, environmental pollution control, and tax assessment and collection. Such a system would afford economies of scale, area-wide planning, and equities in finance. Opposition and criticism continue to exist and problems remain to be resolved, but Miami Metro has survived, although the movement toward the "promised land" of metropolitan government seems more akin to the 40 years of wandering in the wilderness by the Jews. Parris Glendening's analysis indicates that the conflict in Dade County between the pro-Metro and anti-Metro forces has not decreased with the formation of the new system, but instead has increased.[62] This conflict has not been an

internal bureaucratic secret as the Dade County Metropolitan Study
Commission concluded in 1971 that "the relationships between
municipalities of Dade County, the unincorporated areas of the
county, and the metro government represent the most important
and troublesome problem areas faced by Dade County today."63

NOTES

1. For an excellent review of the growth and development of
the Miami region, see David B. Longbrake and Woodrow W. Nichols,
Jr., Sunshine and Shadows in Metropolitan Miami (Cambridge, Mass.:
Ballinger, 1976), pp. 14-17.
2. Dade County Government Publication, June 7, 1975.
3. Miami Herald, June 6, 1974.
4. Longbrake and Nichols, op. cit., p. 7.
5. Edward Sofen, The Miami Metropolitan Experiment
(Bloomington: Indiana University Press, 1963), p. 3.
6. Ibid., pp. 4-5.
7. V. O. Key, Jr., Southern Politics (New York: Knopf, 1955),
chap. 5.
8. Sofen, op. cit., p. 13.
9. Ibid., p. 14.
10. Ibid., p. 15.
11. Ibid., p. 9.
12. Ibid., pp. 19-20.
13. Aileen Lotz, "Metropolitan Dade County," in Regional
Governance: Promise and Performance—Substate Regionalism and
the Federal System, vol. 2: Case Studies, Advisory Commission
for Intergovernmental Relations (Washington, D.C.: Government
Printing Office, 1973), p. 6.
14. Sofen, op. cit., p. 22.
15. Ibid., pp. 24-25.
16. Ibid., p. 30.
17. Ibid., pp. 31-32.
18. Ibid., pp. 32-35.
19. Ibid., pp. 37-40.
20. Ibid., p. 38.
21. Ibid., pp. 40-41.
22. Ibid., pp. 44-45.
23. Ibid., pp. 68-69.
24. Dade County Government Publication, June 7, 1975.
25. Sofen, op. cit., p. 49.
26. Metropolitan Dade County, Florida, Charter, Article I,
Section 1.01 A.
27. Ibid., A (18).

28. Ibid. , A (21, 22, 23).

29. Ibid. , B.

30. Ibid. , Article VIII, Section 8. 04.

31. Ibid. , Articles IV and V.

32. Ibid. , Article I, Sections 1. 03 and 1. 04.

33. Sofen, op. cit. , p. 61.

34. Metropolitan Dade County, Florida, Charter, Article III.

35. Ibid. , Article VI.

36. Sofen, op. cit. , pp. 227-30.

37. Several of these cases are treated in Joseph Metzger, "Metro and Its Judicial History," University of Miami Law Review 15 (Spring 1961).

38. Sofen, op. cit. , p. 97.

39. See Appendix D in ibid. , p. 278.

40. Ibid. , p. 165.

41. See Appendix D in ibid. , p. 279.

42. Dade County Metropolitan Study Commission, Final Report and Recommendations, June 1971, p. 5.

43. See Miami Herald, June 29, 1971, p. 18A and March 15, 1972, p. 6B.

44. John C. Bollens and Henry J. Schmandt, The Metropolis, Its People, Politics, and Economic Life (New York: Harper & Row, 1975), pp. 277-78.

45. Business Week Magazine (February 18, 1961): 102.

46. Metro Government Model for Action, Dade County, Florida, Office of County Manager, November 1975, p. 5.

47. Miami Herald, December 28, 1972, p. 16A.

48. Metro Government Model for Action, op. cit. , p. 7.

49. Ibid. , p. 5.

50. Dade County Government Publication, June 7, 1975, p. 9.

51. Miami Herald, July 16, 1975, pp. 4A, 5A, 6.

52. Miami Herald, November 17, 1975.

53. Miami Herald, October 20, 1975, p. 6.

54. Parris Glendening, "The Metropolitan Dade County Government: An Examination of Reform," Tallahassee, Florida State University, Ph. D. diss. , 1967, p. 154.

55. Miami Herald, June 5, 1972, p. 7.

56. For a discussion of the impact of these groups, see Longbrake and Nichols, op. cit. , pp. 47-57.

57. Melvin B. Mogulof, Five Metropolitan Governments (Washington, D. C. : Urban Institute, 1972), p. 9.

58. Miami Herald, October 20, 1975, p. 6.

59. Comments of Edward Sofen in an interview with Paul Boudreau, December 1975 in Miami.

60. Ibid.

61. See <u>Reshaping Government in Metropolitan Areas</u>
(New York: Committee for Economic Development, 1970), pp.
16-19.

62. Glendening, op. cit., p. 181.

63. Dade County Metropolitan Study Commission, <u>Final Report
and Recommendations</u>, June 1971, p. 43.

CHAPTER

5

THE TORONTO
APPROACH:
FEDERATION

BACKGROUND

The metropolitan Toronto area is situated on the northern shores of Lake Ontario in the Canadian province of Ontario, which is the most populous and wealthy of Canada's ten provinces. Toronto is a word of Indian origin signifying "place of meeting." The region was originally settled by the French, but they surrendered their claims to this and all Canadian territory to the British under the terms of the Treaty of Paris, which terminated the French and Indian War in 1763. Due to its advantageous geographic location in the Great Lakes region, Toronto became an important center for the fur trade in its early history, and as more and more people began moving into the region, it developed into a thriving commercial and governmental center. In 1787 the British government purchased the territory from the Mississauaga Indians, and six years later, in 1793, the site was selected as the capital of the newly created province of Upper Canada (present-day Ontario). The lieutenant-governor of the province, John Graves Simcoe, named the site York, in honor of the Duke of York, but the name was changed back to Toronto in 1834, when the area was incorporated as a city.

Today Toronto is second only to Montreal among Canada's largest urban areas, with a population of nearly 2.7 million, which represents approximately one-tenth of all of Canada's people. The period immediately following World War II marked the beginning of an unprecedented population growth in the Toronto area, brought about primarily by the heavy influx of immigrants from the war-ravaged countries of Europe. The largest single immigrant group to establish Toronto as its home was the Italians, followed by the

Germans, the Poles, and the Ukrainians. During the years 1945-46, the population in what is today metropolitan Toronto increased by over 400,000. This rapid immigration from Europe substantially changed the population mix of Toronto from a predominantly British population to a population containing sizable percentages of different nationalities. The enormous population increase experienced in the immediate postwar period ultimately tapered off as the conditions in Europe improved, but, nonetheless, the growth rate has continued to be impressive. Between 1951 and 1971, metropolitan Toronto's population grew at an average annual rate of 4.3 percent. Growth was more rapid in the first ten years of the period, but even between 1961 and 1971 the region was growing more rapidly than the province and the nation. [1]

Prior to the governmental reorganization that took place in 1953, the 240-square-mile Toronto metropolitan area contained 13 municipal jurisdictions that stretched out from Lake Ontario in three concentric rings. At the core was the city of Toronto, which experienced a slight decrease in population (2 percent) from 1945 to 1953. During the period, there occurred the typical exodus of business firms and middle-class citizens from the central city to the outlying districts and a steady in-migration of lower-income families. Next, there was an inner ring of nine suburban communities, which were the township of York, the towns of Weston, Mimico, New Toronto, and Leaside, the village of Forest Hill, the township of East York, and the villages of Swansea and Long Branch. These communities experienced an increase in population during the postwar years, but in absolute terms the numbers were slight. These small municipalities, which were relatively well developed, sprang up after the city of Toronto had ceased annexation movements around 1912. An outer ring of three larger suburban communities, Etobicoke to the west of Toronto, North York to the north, and Scarborough to the east, experienced a phenomenal growth rate of over 200 percent in the eight years following 1945. This tremendous population increase understandably generated rising concerns over water supplies, sewers and sewage disposal, housing, and other municipal functions. Thus, although the population of the Toronto metropolitan area has continued to increase at an impressive rate, central-city Toronto, like other North American cities, has been losing population to its suburbs. In 1951 the city included almost two-thirds of the total population for the metropolitan area, but 20 years later, in 1971, the figure had dwindled to just over a third. Nevertheless, while the city's share of the metropolitan population has been declining, the city's actual population has been increasing, which is unlike the situation in many large North American cities. [2]

Toronto is the hub of the Canadian transportation system. Its harbor is one of the most important on the Great Lakes and admits seagoing vessels from the St. Lawrence Seaway. The city is the center of Ontario's provincial highway system and also is serviced by the country's Trans-Canadian Highway. Two railroads, several steamship lines, and Canadian, U.S., and European airlines service the city as well. This excellent transportation system has contributed significantly to Toronto's role as the busiest and most prosperous financial, commercial, and industrial center in both the province and the country at large. It serves as the headquarters for four of the ten chartered banks in Canada, and the Toronto Stock Exchange is the largest market for mining shares in the world. Also located in Toronto is the headquarters for Eaton's and Simpson's, Canada's largest department store and mail order house. The region's major industries are meat packing, textiles, printing and publishing, machinery, electrical products, furniture, food products, rubber goods, and sheet metal products. In all, there are nearly 6,000 industrial establishments in the Toronto region, and the area represents approximately a third of the nation's purchasing power. [3] Economic activity in metropolitan Toronto has increased at the phenomenal rate of 62 percent over the last ten years. Approximately 100 new manufacturing plants are constructed each year within a radius of 100 miles. This impressive economic growth has led to a unique trend in residential patterns, which paralleled the trend in business activity. Blue-collar workers are becoming increasingly suburbanized, while managerial and office personnel are moving into the central city. [4]

The government of the city of Toronto prior to the reorganization was of the mayor/board-of-control/council type. Although this form of government was experimented with in Winnipeg, Manitoba from 1907 to 1918, and in London, England, from 1917 to 1918, today it is pretty much unique to the province of Ontario. The Toronto City Council was comprised of a mayor, four controllers, and aldermen. The mayor and the controllers were elected at large, and the aldermen were elected by wards. The city was divided into nine wards of unequal populations, with each ward represented on the council by two aldermen. This governmental scheme represented neither the people nor their interests with any degree of effectiveness. The mayor and the controllers constituted the board of control, which performed as the governing body for the council. The primary function of the board was to make recommendations and proposals concerning any matter of government to the entire council. Although the council, as a whole, had to approve the recommendations, it required a two-thirds majority to override any board recommendation. This meant that 16 out of 18 aldermen had to vote against a board proposal to veto it while only seven aldermen needed to vote affirmatively for a proposal for it to be approved. [5]

Historically, the city of Toronto has had a strong planning tradition. The Toronto City Planning Board, appointed by the city council in accordance with the provisions of the Planning Act of 1946, was charged with the obligation of preparing an official plan that would outline capital improvements for a period of 30 years. The city and county also appointed the Toronto and York Planning Board, which served the city of Toronto and the 12 municipalities that later incorporated into Metro. The membership of this board was somewhat arbitrary. Five of the nine members were also represented on the Toronto City Planning Board. However, there also existed a broader advisory committee comprised of one representative from each municipality, which had to approve any proposal or policy recommendation. [6]

The city of Toronto had long pursued a policy of annexation. The trend was that communities would emerge on the outskirts of the city, and if they prospered economically, they could look forward to being annexed by Toronto. In 1928, Toronto formally announced a nonannexation policy. The three communities that had been anticipating annexation at that time were later incorporated. These communities grew in size and established economic bases independent of the city. [7]

After World War II, Toronto's problems began to multiply as a consequence of the large influx of foreign immigrants into the central city and the migration of many middle- and upper-class persons from the inner city to the suburbs. New industries tended to locate in the suburbs rather than in the central city, while the established city industries also joined in the flight to the outlying areas to escape the high tax rate in Toronto. [8]

The city of Toronto began to experience considerable difficulty in financing its increasing needs in such areas as urban renewal, public assistance, and public housing at a time when the city's tax revenues were falling while its tax rate, already among the highest in Canada, was rising. The three rapidly developing, outer-ring suburbs of Etobicoke, North York, and Scarborough were also having their troubles. For these communities, the problem was their inability to meet the service and capital construction needs of their burgeoning populations. These outer-ring suburbs lacked sewers, water mains, reservoirs, roads, bridges, and schools. By 1950 the outstanding capital debts in these communities had reached such heights that they had difficulty borrowing operating funds. Sandwiched in between central Toronto and the three outer-ring suburbs were the contented smaller suburbs. Benefiting from the use of inner-city hospitals, libraries, and parks without taxation, these communities

had no need to expand facilities and enjoyed relatively low tax rates
and favorable industrial-residential ratios. [9]

REFORM IS SOUGHT

Beginning in the 1930s, several studies dealing with metropolitan problems in the Toronto region were conducted, but none of these resulted in significant governmental alteration. One of the earliest studies was conducted by Professor A. Plumptre of the University of Toronto for the Ontario Department of Municipal Affairs in 1935. Three years later, the Province of Ontario established the Committee for the Study of Municipal and Related Problems in Toronto and Its Neighboring Municipalities. In 1945 the Bureau of Municipal Research published a white paper entitled "Where Are Toronto and Its Metropolitan Area Heading?" The paper favored amalgamation as the best means of resolving metropolitan problems and recommended the borough system as a second possibility. From 1949 to 1951 the Committee on Metropolitan Problems of the Civic Advisory Council issued a series of reports emphasizing the economic and social interdependence of the city of Toronto and the surrounding municipalities. [10]

The movement toward the governmental reorganization that eventually took place began in 1946 when the town of Mimico requested the Ontario Municipal Board (OMB) to create an area for joint administration of municipal services. The OMB had been created in the 1930s with the purpose of controlling the borrowing practices and debts of the province's municipalities, many of which were then technically bankrupt. The OMB evolved into a provincial, quasi-judicial body with extensive powers over municipal governments, including the power to mandate changes in municipal boundaries or municipal governmental structures. The OMB was responsible to the provincial government for the effective operation of municipal government in Ontario. [11]

In 1947 the province of Ontario established the Toronto and Surburban Planning Board. The board was charged with studying the problems of the burgeoning population that affected the region as a whole. Some of the specific areas investigated by the board were sewage disposal, water supply, education, and public transportation. The board, subsequently renamed the Toronto and York Planning Board, issued a report in 1949 recommending the progressive amalgamation of the region's 13 municipalities. [12]

Hearings before the OMB on the Toronto question began in 1950. By this time several other communities had joined Mimico in the request for a joint administrative district, while others supported the retention of the status quo. The city of Toronto, for

all practical purposes, performed the role of complainant before the
OMB by attempting to prove the existing governments in the surrounding
communities were inadequate and to convince the board that
amalgamation was the proper solution. In short, Toronto's petition
called for the city's annexation of the financially sound, inner-
lying suburbs, but not the less developed, outer three suburbs. The
hearings before the OMB were long and detailed, with 85 witnesses
appearing in nearly a year of testimony. Neither the Mimico nor
the Toronto petition was particularly appealing to Lorne Cumming,
the chairman of the OMB, who ultimately presented his own compromise
solution, which called for the creation of a metropolitan federation.
The Cumming report was submitted to the Ontario provincial legislature
on January 20, 1953. [13] In part, the findings concluded:[14]

> The most promising avenue of approach to a solution
> of this question is clearly indicated in the political
> history of our own nation, and in the fact that many
> of the fundamental principles so wisely applied in
> the federation of the British North American Provinces
> can be profitably adapted in the organization of a
> suitable form of local government in this area . . . .
> the board had carefully avoided any unnecessary
> reductions of the existing powers of the local
> authorities . . . . it [OMB] has not hesitated to
> assign to the central authority definite responsibility
> for the functions and services considered vitally
> necessary to the continued growth and development
> of the entire area as an urban community.

In February 1953, the Cumming report of the OMB was introduced into the Ontario legislature as Bill 80, or the Municipality of
Metropolitan Toronto Act. The bill was presented by the prime
minister of Ontario, Leslie Frost, and in this way, the full support
for the Toronto reorganization by the provincial government was
demonstrated. The bill was adopted by the legislature on April 15,
1953 and went into effect on July 1, 1953. North America now had
its first urban federation. [15]
      Several points should be noted by way of explaining why the
federation approach was deemed the most appropriate alternative
for the Toronto reorganization. First, it was recognized by its
supporters as being the only viable scheme for the region. Lorne
Cumming and the OMB considered federation to be the course of
least political resistance, with the added advantage of relatively
easy implementation and the promise of administrative and operational effectiveness. [16] The history of governments has revealed that

when major reorganization inclined toward centralization is
contemplated, federation often is the only politically feasible course.
There are several reasons for this. Governments, like individuals,
tend to have strong instincts for self-preservation and generally do
not condone any action that might severely restrict their sphere of
influence. However, in theory, federation can offer real benefits to
communities without drastically affecting local autonomy and,
accordingly, can prove appealing to those who are looking for
cooperative benefits without the loss of local independence. In
addition, the transition from many local autonomous units to any
form of centralized government is an arduous task that requires
many years of experience to perfect, often in the costly manner of
trial and error. Federation can offer the advantage of a relatively
smooth transition period by making available to the metropolitan
government the governmental expertise already existent at the local
level. Federation also tends to keep the government close to the
people. Individuals traditionally have identified themselves with their
towns, and they may become more politically alienated should they be
deprived of their local governmental structures.

More directly related to the acceptance of federation for the
Toronto region was the fact that Cumming, who, as mentioned
earlier, proposed the federation compromise, possessed considerable
influence with Prime Minister Frost. In short, whatever Cumming
suggested was bound to carry weight with the prime minister. [17]
Finally, it should be pointed out that home rule traditions are not
nearly as strong in Canada as they are in the United States. The
political culture in Canada has evolved in such a manner as to accept
strong provincial influence over municipalities. Provincial governments are routinely in the forefront of any significant planning involving
changes in municipal governments, and it is fully expected that the
provincial governments will assume this dominant role. Voters in
the Toronto metropolitan area did not vote on any of the reorganization
proposals. The Ontario legislature simply adopted Bill 80, and that
was all there was to it. This, of course, is a far cry from the
situation in the United States, where the vast majority of metropolitan
governmental reorganizations go to referendums after being passed
by the state legislatures, a requirement that has resulted in many
reorganization defeats.

CREATION OF METRO

The Metropolitan Toronto Act created a two-tier, federative
system of government for the metropolitan Toronto region. In many
ways, this type of government was similar to that which exists at the
federal-provincial level. As noted in an earlier chapter, in the

two-tier approach there are two levels of government with
extensive interactions between them. Legally, the individual municipalities comprising the first lower-level tier and the second
metropolitan-wide tier exist as separate units. In practice, however,
the two tiers much cooperate with each other for the federative
approach to produce the intended results.

Under the terms of the 1953 act for the Toronto region, a
metropolitan council was created to serve as both the executive body
of Metro and the legislative body representative of each of the 13
municipalities. In the words of the Cumming report, "there is, at
the present time, a serious cleavage between the city and the suburbs
. . . and undoubtedly this will continue until a better spirit of
metropolitan unity is achieved, by giving equal representation to
the major divisions of the metropolitan population, notwithstanding
the theoretical advantages of representation by population."[18] In
accordance with this principle, the metropolitan council was comprised of a total of 25 members, 12 from the city of Toronto, one
from each of the 12 suburbs, and an independent chairman, who was
to be appointed for the first two years by the provincial government
and thereafter to be elected by the council. The representatives
from the suburbs were to be the respective mayors, or reeves as
they were called, while the city's delegation consisted of the mayor,
two controllers, and an alderman from each of the nine city wards.[19]
Thus, metro council members actually serve on two councils—the
metropolitan council and their individual municipal councils. This
dual role can at times be difficult, especially on issues that clearly
benefit Metro but benefit only slightly a particular municipality.

At the urging of Cumming, Prime Minister Frost appointed
Frederick Gardiner as the first chairman. Gardiner, a former
mayor of the wealthy, residential area of Forest Hill and a well-
known lawyer, was recognized by both Cumming and Frost as a
person who would provide aggressive, creative leadership in the
early stages of Metro's development. In this they were not to be
disappointed, and Gardiner continued to serve as chairman for the
first eight years of the federation. The chairmanship of the metropolitan council was assigned little formal power under the terms of
the Metropolitan Toronto Act, being limited to such functions as presiding
at meetings, interpreting the rules of procedure, and casting a vote
only in the case of a tie. However, unlike the members of the council,
the chairman is a full-time official who can devote his total time and
energy to Metro matters and thereby acquire a considerable edge
over his council colleagues. Under the dynamic direction of Frederick
Gardiner, who was often referred to affectionately as "Big Daddy,"
the chairmanship became in practice, in spite of its formal limitations,

the most influential component in the new governmental system.
Frank Smallwood writes of Gardiner:[20]

> As a former Reeve of wealthy, suburban Forest Hill
> and as a successful lawyer of considerably personal
> means, Gardiner provided the Metro program with
> a symbolic aura of prestige, integrity, and honesty
> . . . and a sense of personal drive, self confidence,
> and determination. As the former Vice-president of
> the Ontario Conservative Association, he was on very
> close terms with the then-Provincial Premier, Leslie
> Frost, and the personal liaison he established between
> Metro and the Province government was so close as to
> be characterized as a "Family Compact." Finally,
> and of most telling significance, Gardiner possessed
> an understanding of, and a willingness to utilize,
> his potentially explosive council from flying apart.

A practical example of the manner in which Gardiner succeeded
in increasing his overall influence pertains to Metro's executive
committee. Nowhere in the Metropolitan Toronto Act is there a
provision for such a committee. However, Chairman Gardiner
concluded that he could more effectively work with, and, indeed,
more easily influence, a smaller group such as an executive committee
than the entire council. Accordingly, he tactfully introduced the
idea to the council. The council saw merit in the proposal and
adopted a procedural bylaw that established a seven-member
executive committee as an integral part of the metropolitan council.
The members of the new structure were to be chosen by the entire
council, and it was to possess all the powers exercised by boards of
control in municipal governments. More specifically, the committee
was empowered to prepare budgets, nominate department heads,
nominate candidates for positions on independent boards, award
contracts, and perform several other administrative actions that
were legally the responsibility of the metro council. Thus, Gardiner
obtained a mechanism that was much more efficient for policy
implementation than was the 25-member council, and in Chairman
Gardiner's skillful hands, the executive committee was employed to
increase the unity and cohesiveness of the metropolitan government,
while diminishing the parochialism. For all practical purposes,
"the Executive Committee became the de-facto head of the
administration, and Gardiner became the informal head of the
Executive Committee."[21]
    Gardiner's influence was also very much present on the
administrative side of the new Metro. The council gave him full

authority to recruit department heads and staff, and Gardiner
proceeded to acquire the best available public administrators. Policy
initiation and definition were begun by these administrators, but
the council action was always handled and controlled by Gardiner.
He ultimately decided what was to be brought before the council,
when it was to be presented, and in what form. During the early
period of the new system, Gardiner's decision to limit the council
agenda to generally noncontroversial items greatly aided in uniting
the members into a single group. What went to the council for action
during the first years of Metro were in large measure substantial capital outlay programs, mainly in the areas of transportation, water
supply, and sewage disposal. This pattern reflected Gardiner's philosophy that if Metro were to succeed, it needed immediate tangible or
physical achievements that the citizens could see and with which
they could identify. [22]

Concerning the division of powers between the two tiers of
the federation, only public transportation became a fully Metro
function. For the most part, the metropolitan government dealt with
the more critical regional problems, while such matters as police,
fire, public health, and public welfare were left primarily in the
preserve of the 13 municipalities. A system of shared responsibilities
was set up in such areas as street construction, road maintenance,
traffic control, public assistance, zoning, and planning. In education,
a federal-type scheme of Metro subsidies to the municipalities with
local school boards was combined with a Metropolitan Educational
Board that was given area-wide discretion with regard to capital
school costs. [23]

Metro's most important powers were in the area of public
finance, which reflected the Cumming report and the Ontario
legislature's perception of the most serious problems to be resolved
in the Toronto region. Regional problems of highest priority were
seen as revolving around the inability of the suburbs to borrow funds
at reasonable rates. Among other things, this resulted in the
inadequacy of suburban water and sewer facilities. In the early
1950s, the outlying suburbs frequently suffered for weeks during dry
spells when limitations were encouraged on water consumption.
Other critical areas were transportation—the need for the construction
of more expressways to accommodate the increased use of the
automobile—and school construction, especially in the outer-ring
cities. Metro was given the power to cope with these problems by
receiving the authority to do all of the borrowing for all of the
municipalities and independent boards in the region, thereby obtaining
an extremely favorable interest rate. Metro also secured the power
to apportion its revenue needs among the 13 communities, utilizing

a formula whereby each municipality's share was based upon a total
assessment area. [24]

In 1957, the structure of the metropolitan government was
altered slightly as a consequence of a formal review conducted by a
royal commission of inquiry chaired by OMB Chairman Cumming.
Under the recommendations of the commission's report, the police
departments of the 13 municipalities were consolidated under the
Metropolitan Board of Commissioners of Police. The Metropolitan
Toronto Region Conservation Authority was created and given
exclusive jurisdiction over air pollution control facilities and all
streams and rivers in the Toronto area entering Lake Ontario. Metro
also was given the responsibility for issuing business and corporate
licenses, while the area municipalities retained control over dog
licenses, marriage licenses, and building bylaws. [25]

PROBLEMS UNDER THE ORIGINAL METRO

The modest reorganization in 1957 did not really address what
eventually became a serious hindrance to Metro's ability to deal with
area-wide problems—namely, the representational formula under the
1953 act for the metropolitan council. Unfortunately, this formula,
which gave one representative to each community, except for the
city of Toronto, tended over time to result in an overemphasis
within the council on parochial interests. Council deliberations
frequently turned into bargaining sessions for local demands.
Councilors who, as it will be recalled, were municipal mayors,
councilors, or aldermen, often found it difficult to overcome their
inclinations toward narrow local interests, and the end result was
the sacrificing of a broad philosophy of representive judgment. This
drift toward parochialism was further compounded by rapid population
growth, which created gross inequities in representation on the
council. Smaller communities increasingly took a defensive attitude
in their approach to Metro's problems, especially in the controversial
welfare and school expenditure area. [26]

The 1953 Cumming report stressed local autonomy for all 13
communities involved in the metropolitan experiment, thereby making
possible a variety of service levels from community to community
under the federal principle. Although Metro attempted to deal with
particularly pressing problems on an area-wide basis, certain
financial inequities that had existed prior to 1953 had deteriorated 10
years later. Metro's relative share of service costs simply could not
keep pace with the increasing burdens of the local municipalities.
As a consequence of the disparities in economic capacities, the gap
between the communities in specific service performance widened as
time progressed. Moreover, no real equalization of the basic

resource base (tax assessment base) of various communities had taken place since Metro's beginning.

The nature of the growing inequities can be seen most easily by analyzing the expenditure patterns in certain specific areas such as welfare and education. The inner city of Toronto, like most urban centers, tended to attract a large number of welfare cases. In the early 1960s, the transfer of payments for welfare cost to Toronto from Metro was roughly 25 percent below what the city actually needed to meet the increasing welfare demand. Since Toronto was providing the most complete welfare program in the region, its costs rose rapidly as more and more indigents moved into the city. Although each municipality was required to pay certain welfare costs and maintain their own programs, discretion as to the amounts expended was left up to the local councils, with the result being wide and serious disparities. [27]

Similar disparities existed in the area of education. Although the Metropolitan Toronto School Board was established to coordinate school capital expenditures, pupil expenditures remained in the preserve of the 13 local school boards. Fluctuations were inevitable since economic development and growth were unequal throughout the area. With the passing of time, Metro began to carry a relatively declining proportion of the cost for certain "key" shared services due to the fact that its capital expenditure program neared maturity in the early 1960s. [28]

Thus, as Metro entered the 1960s, the situation was becoming one of growing inequity, frustration, and indecisiveness. The wealthier communities were getting richer but were reluctant to share their revenues, while the less fortunate communities balked at assuming increased responsibilities. Smallwood succinctly captured the general tone of the problems when he wrote:[29]

> Under Gardiner, Metro had been inclined to operate
> more as a business than as a governmental organi-
> zation . . . . Ten years cumulative experience
> indicates that the Metropolitan Council has been
> consistently aggressive in attacking "hard core"
> problems where results are concrete and obvious,
> and considerably less assertive in meeting some
> of the "softer" more socially-oriented issues where
> results are usually less tangible and more controversial
> . . . such fields as public housing, planning, welfare,
> and education.

THE 1967 REORGANIZATION

In 1961 a new report on metropolitan problems in the Toronto area was published by George E. Gathercole, deputy minister of economics of the province of Ontario and a close adviser to the prime minister. This report, known as the Gathercole report, recommended preserving the essence of the federated structure but with certain alterations in the second tier of the government. The report concluded that the consolidation of the 13 existing municipalities into four or five boroughs would provide more equalized services throughout the region. The Gathercole report was essentially a preliminary data-collection instrument that focused on the administrative procedures and practices within the entire Metro government. It included the budgets and other financial documents for all 13 communities, present and future staffing requirements, and a multiplicity of other relevant facts necessary for any logical governmental revision. [30]

Early in 1963, the city of Toronto formally requested the OMB to begin hearings on the city's request for total amalgamation of the metropolitan Toronto district. Temporarily suspending the OMB's reviewing powers, the provincial government decided instead on the appointment of a royal commission. In June 1965, after two years of study and evaluation, the commission, which was chaired by Dr. H. Carl Goldenberg, issued its findings. On the basis of these findings, the Ontario legislature in 1967 enacted Bill 81-A, "An Act to Amend the Municipality of Metropolitan Toronto Act." Although Bill 81 did not accept the Goldenberg report's recommendations in toto, the reorganizational principles were essentially the same. * Under the terms of the revision, the two-tier federation was retained, but a greater centralization was effected by means of consolidating the 13 communities into only six, these being the city of Toronto and the five boroughs, as they were to be called, of East York, Etobicoke, North York, Scarborough, and York. The specifics of the merger were as follows: the joining of the old city of Toronto with Forest Hill and Swansea to form the new city of Toronto; the combining of Etobicoke, Long Branch, New Toronto, and Mimico into the borough of Etobicoke; the combining of York and Weston into the borough of York; and the joining of East York and Leaside into the Borough of East York. The townships of North York and Scarborough were

---

*The major difference between the Goldenberg commission report and the provisions of Bill 81 was the recommendation that the 13 municipalities be merged into four rather than the six ultimately decided upon.

FIGURE 5.1

Municipality of Metropolitan Toronto

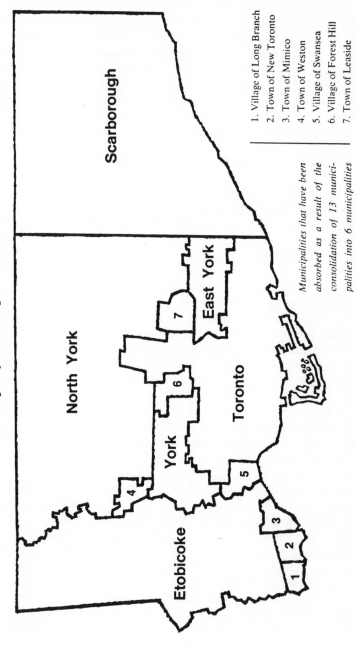

1. Village of Long Branch
2. Town of New Toronto
3. Town of Mimico
4. Town of Weston
5. Village of Swansea
6. Village of Forest Hill
7. Town of Leaside

Municipalities that have been absorbed as a result of the consolidation of 13 municipalities into 6 municipalities

Source: The Municipality of Metropolitan Toronto; and Committee for Economic Development, Reshaping Local Government in Metropolitan Areas (New York: the Committee, 1970), p. 81.

simply renamed as boroughs, with the retention of the same boundaries. [31] See Figure 5.1 for greater details on these changes.

The revision also altered the composition of the metropolitan council by aligning representation in accordance with current population in the newly formed six districts, thereby relieving the previous metro council's grave malapportionment problem. The new council consisted of a total of 33 members, including the chairman, who was to be elected by the entire council. The city of Toronto was to continue to be represented by 12 members, roughly 40 percent of the total, while each of the new boroughs was to be represented by a number calculated by dividing the respective borough's population by 12. [32]

Contrary to the recommendations of the Goldenberg commission, the new representational formula retained the principle of selecting the members of the council indirectly through their election to the local councils. Specifically, metropolitan council members may gain their seats by any one of three election methods. As noted earlier, certain officials such as mayors and controllers become metro council members solely by virtue of their municipal offices. Others are selected for the metro council as a consequence of their margins of victory in their municipal elections—for example, ward aldermen who receive the greatest number of votes. Finally, a member may be elected to his or her municipal council and then be chosen by that group to be a delegate to the metropolitan council. The number and the method of selection for members of the metropolitan council are amended among the various units as their populations shift, in the interest of maintaining an equitable balance. [33]

This complex system for determining the membership of the metropolitan council has several effects on the local electorates. First, an individual usually does not know whom he or she is electing to the metro council. A vote for a particular candidate for a municipal office may or may not also elect that candidate to the metropolitan council. Thus, voters cannot really discriminate among candidates whom they might prefer for one council but not for the other. Moreover, this method of election means in practice that there is little emphasis on metropolitan issues in municipal elections. The candidates as well as the voters do not know who will become metro council members, and, accordingly, they do not generally campaign on metropolitan issues. [34]

The Metro Executive Committee, which hitherto existed as a procedural bylaw of the metropolitan council, became, under Bill 81-A, a formal structure of the revised federation. Because of the actual power exercised by this committee, a more equitable representational scheme was adopted. The membership was increased from seven to

11 members (it was later increased to 14), representing the Metro chairman, the six mayors (the mayors of Toronto and the five boroughs), and the four members of the Toronto Board of Control. Its responsibilities are similar to those of a municipal board of control: staff departments of Metro report to a chief administrative officer, who, in turn, reports to the executive committee. [35]

The 1967 reorganization also granted more authority to the metropolitan government in those service areas where it was felt that greater efficiency could be obtained through increased centralization. For example, the public welfare function became solely the responsibility of the metro council in the interest of providing for the needs of all the region's welfare recipients in a more equitable fashion. Urban renewal, waste disposal, ambulance services, and the juvenile and family court system also were relegated to Metro to be administered in an integrated manner. To correct the problem of the widening disparities in the burden of school costs, the Metropolitan Toronto School Board was given the added responsibilities of reviewing all operating budgets of the area's schools, distributing grants for school purposes, and levying taxes to finance school operations. School funds were to be allocated by Metro in accordance with variations in local requirements. The metropolitan government assumed responsibility for all outstanding school debts as of December 31, 1966. An improved appeal procedure was established providing for the OMB to settle disputes between the municipalities and Metro with regard to both capital costs and current operating costs. [36]

The metropolitan system of school boards is quite complex. The Metropolitan Toronto School Board is made up of the six chairmen of the municipal school boards plus trustees from each municipality. The Metropolitan Toronto School Board directly operates programs only for the retarded and disabled. As previously noted, its main responsibility involves the reviewing of budgets and the coordination of education among the several municipalities. [37] There also is a system of publicly supported Catholic schools in the Toronto region, which is governed by the Metropolitan Separate School Board. Trustees on this board are elected from districts devised especially for this purpose from combinations of wards. Voters who identify themselves as separate-school supporters elect these trustees to operate schools for students through grade ten. Separate-school supporters also elect representatives to the municipal boards of education. These latter representatives, however, vote only on issues relating to secondary education. [38]

Like the area municipalities, the metropolitan government appoints certain special-purpose bodies. Examples of such bodies are the Metropolitan Library Board, the Toronto Transit Commission, the Metropolitan Board of Commissioners of Police, and the Metropolitan Licensing Commission. In addition, there are appointed boards of management such as the Canadian National Exhibition Association and the Board of the Civic Garden Centre. Metro also has some power to appoint and fund promotional bodies such as the Convention and Tourist Bureau and the Industrial Board. [39]

One potential problem in a federated government is lack of coordination between the levels or tiers. In the Toronto system, day-to-day coordination between constituent units is accomplished by the civic employees or departmental liaison arrangements. The Provincial-Municipal Liaison Committee, the Toronto-Centered Coordinating Committee, the Metropolitan Toronto Technical Transportation Advisory Committee, and the Toronto Area Transit Operating Authority have all been established to promote provincial-municipal coordination. At every third meeting of the Provincial-Municipal Liaison Committee, a federal representative is present to facilitate federal-provincial-municipal control. [40]

THE METROPOLITAN DELIVERY OF SERVICES

The preceding sections outlined the organization of legislative and executive powers and the responsibility for education in metropolitan Toronto. A more thorough understanding of how the governmental system actually operates can be gained by examining the manner in which specific services are delivered by the civic departments and special purpose agencies. Further services are provided by the superior levels of government—the provincial and the national. The provincial and federal governments also may participate in funding and regulating services that they do not directly provide.

A description of all local and Metro services is not attempted here. Rather, the aim is to present a general overview of the two-tiered government and the way it interacts with the superior governments. A detailed description of the functional division of powers following the 1967 reorganization appears in Figure 5. 2.

Public Safety

The area of public safety provides an interesting example of Metro's flexibility in delivering services at either the municipal or metropolitan level, whichever seems most appropriate. Since 1957, police protection throughout the region has been provided by a unified Metropolitan Toronto Police Force. The chief of police reports to the Board of Commissioners of Police rather than to an elected body. This arrangement may well help free the chief from political interference, but it also may make the position less responsive to the

FIGURE 5.2

Distribution of Responsibility

Finance and Taxation		Water Supply		Health	
Assessment of property	M	Purification, pumping and trunk distribution system	M	Public health services	A
Courts of revision	MA			Chronic and convalescent hospital	M
Taxation of property	A	Local distribution	A	Hospital grants	A
Debenture borrowing	M	Collection of water bills	A	Ambulance services	M
Local improvement charges	A	Sewage Disposal		Police and Fire Protection	
Planning		Sanitary trunk system and disposal plants	M		
Official plans	MA			Police	M
Subdivision approval	MA	Connecting systems	A	Fire	A
Zoning	A	Storm drainage	MA	Administration of Justice	
Recreation/ Community Services		Garbage Collection and Disposal			
				Magistrates' courts	M
Regional parks	M	Collection	A	Court house and jail	M
Local parks	A	Disposal sites	M	Juvenile and family court	M
Recreation programs	A	Air Pollution		Coroner's office	M
Community centres/ arenas	A	Air pollution control	M	Registry and land titles offices	M
Municipal golf courses	M				
Municipal zoo	M	Public Education		Licensing and Inspection	
Regional libraries	M				
Local libraries	MA	Operation of school system	A	Business licensing	M
Grants to cultural societies	MA	School sites, attendance areas, building programs	M	Dog licensing and pound	A
Road Construction/ Maintenance				Marriage licenses	A
				Buildings by-laws	A
Expressways	M	Operating and capital costs	M	Civil Defense	
Arterial roads	M	Housing			
Local roads	A			Emergency measures	M
Bridges and grade separations	MA	Low rental family housing	M	Other Municipal Services	
Snow removal	MA	Elderly person housing	M		
Street cleaning	MA	Moderate rental family housing	A	Collection of fines	MA
Sidewalks	A			Collection of vital statistics	A
Traffic Control		Welfare		Distribution of hydro power	A
Traffic regulations	MA			Harbor	A
Cross-walks	MA	Welfare assistance	M	Island airport	A
Traffic lights	M	Hospitalization of indigents	M	Municipal parking lots	A
Street lighting	A			Preparation of voters' lists and administration of civic elections	A
Pavement markings	MA	Assistance to Children's Aid Societies	M		
Public Transit					
Toronto Transit Comm.	M	Homes for the aged	M	Redevelopment	MA

Note: M = Municipality of Metropolitan Toronto;
　　　A = area municipalities

Source: Committee for Economic Development, Reshaping Government in Metropolitan Areas (New York: CED, 1970), p. 83; and Richard P. Baine and Lynn McMurray, Toronto: An Urban Study (Toronto: Clarke, Irwin, 1972), p. 102.

electorate. There is some feeling that the unified police is too centralized and too distant from the people, but, nevertheless, the force has a reputation for effectiveness in the performance of its metropolitan-wide duties. [41]

In contrast to the police situation, fire protection has remained at the municipal level. Each borough has its own fire department, which reports to the metropolitan council. While some efficiencies might result from a unified fire department, the fire chiefs agree that unification is not desirable at this time. [42]

Planning

The role of Metro in planning has never been sufficiently delineated, nor are the unique planning interests of each level of government clear. The Metropolitan Planning Board originally had jurisdiction over an area much larger than that of the present Metro. The original area was reduced to Metro's boundaries, and the planning boards were turned over to the metropolitan council. The council is required to submit an official plan to the province, and once the plan is approved, it is binding on the public sector. A draft metropolitan plan was drawn up in 1959, and a more formal plan was prepared, but not accepted as official, in 1966. A new, revised Metropolitan Toronto Official Plan was initiated in 1976. [43]

Members of the Metropolitan Toronto and Region Conservation Authority (MTRCA) are appointed by both an area council and the metropolitan council to promote conservation and management of natural resources. Metro has assumed the responsibility for flood plains and conservation areas used as parks. Metro and MTRCA work closely together and have exercised their powers jointly to acquire land. MTRCA is an example of a body that represents an area within Ontario that is larger than metropolitan Toronto. The jurisdiction was created because of a need for the management of resources based on geographic rather than political boundaries. [44]

Physical Services

The physical services area illustrates a logical division of duites whereby the levels of government are involved in different aspects of the same service. The two tiers share responsibilities in water supply, sewage, and refuse collection and disposal. Electric power distribution, on the other hand, does not involve the metropolitan government.

When Metro was initially formed, it became the owner of all water treatment plants, pumping stations, reservoirs, and trunk mains. The area municipalities, however, distribute the water to the consumers. Capital expenses requiring borrowing must be approved by both Metro and the OMB, a process that can cause delays adversely affecting construction schedules. The metropolitan council sells water to the individual localities at a rate per thousand gallons, which enables the system to be self-sustaining. Customer rates thus vary among the boroughs, where most customers are metered. Similarly, the Metro government provides sewer trunks and sewage treatment, but the area municipalities provide local sewer and customer services. [45]

With regard to solid waste, collection is managed by the local units while disposal is performed by Metro. This represents a changed situation from when Metro was first formed, at which time the boroughs were charged with both collection and disposal. Difficulty in finding sufficient space for sanitary landfill led to the delegation of the disposal function to Metro. Initially, the metropolitan government was empowered to locate disposal sites within the Metropolitan Planning Area, which was larger than Metro itself. Locating landfill sites is becoming more difficult since the planning area no longer includes outside areas and since citizens are increasingly reluctant to have disposal facilities situated near them. The lack of disposal sites has also led to rising costs for the municipalities in the transportation of waste. Overall, a serious problem is developing in solid waste disposal. Several innovative solutions are being examined, but it is possible that provincial assistance will be needed. [46]

Electricity is distributed by six municipal utilities. The Hydro-Electric Commission of Ontario is the bulk generation and transmission authority and provides electricity to the municipalities at cost. Ontario Hydro also regulates the municipal utilities. The development of a metropolitan-wide unified distribution system would be difficult, at least in the short run, due to technical operating differences among the localities, and no metropolitan role appears imminent. [47]

Social Services

The fields of social services have had varied histories in Ontario, which probably affect current trends in their development. For example, education traditionally has been largely a local concern, but recently it has become more and more centralized, as has been previously mentioned. Health, welfare, and recreation all started in the private sector. Today, however, health services are a public endeavor involving all levels of government, welfare is particularly a federal responsibility, and recreation is increasingly a responsibility of local government.

When the Toronto metropolitan government was instituted, education was the only social service delegated to it. This was done in the interest of equalizing educational quality and cost burdens throughout the region. However, the increased dependence on provincial grants, mandated spending ceilings, and other financing complexities are now generating growing concern that there has been a loss of local control.

Both the federal and provincial governments play major roles in health care policy formulation and financing. The Public Health Act, however, is administrated by municipal boards of health. There is no metropolitan board of health, though such an agency was recommended by the Goldenberg commission in its review of the Metro government. The commission suggested that the city of Toronto should provide metropolitan-wide health services on a fee-for-service basis rather than set up an additional service delivery department. (Public support of separate schools is provided for in the Canadian Constitution, the "British North American Act.")[48]

The province provides and regulates social welfare services and also provides funds to the municipalities and voluntary agencies. Federal welfare programs operate both through the distribution of funds to the provinces and directly to individuals. Local welfare services were amalgamated at the metropolitan level in the 1967 reorganization, at least partly to equalize the financial burden that had fallen most heavily on the city of Toronto. The Metropolitan Commissioner of Social Services now reports to a metro council committee. [49]

Recreation is an area in which dual systems have developed. Each municipality has a recreation department, as does the metropolitan government. The municipal departments are primarily involved with active recreation requiring specialized facilities, whereas the metropolitan department is more involved with passive recreation requiring open space. Both levels of government operate parks. [50]

Transportation

Transportation in the Toronto region is provided in part by each level of government. The responsibility is divided among the province, the metropolitan government, and the municipalities. King's Highways linking population centers, major connecting arterials, and local streets are the respective domains of the three levels. [51] Public transit is supplied by the Toronto Transit Commission, which is funded by the metropolitan and provincial governments and customer fares. The province pays 75 percent of capital costs and subsidizes 50 percent of the operating losses up to a ceiling. [52] The Toronto

Transit Commission is a public agency consisting of five commissioners appointed by the metro council. [53]

The federal government also is involved in transportation. The federal Ministry of Transport constructs, operates, and regulates aviation, marine, and some railway transportation facilities. Supplementing the local, metropolitan, provincial, and federal roles in transportation is the Toronto Area Transit Operating Authority (TATOA). The authority includes the Toronto transportation chairman and the chairmen of adjacent Regional Peel and Regional York. TATOA provides interregional transit, coordinates service, and disseminates information. Coordinating committees have been established from time to time to link all the various levels of transportation service and regulation. Some of these committees have lasted only a short time, while others have existed since the inception of Metro. [54]

Housing

Housing is another area in which all levels of government are actors. The federal government is involved in provision of housing, mostly by means of financing; the province both finances and regulates; the municipalities are chiefly regulatory; and the metropolitan government is involved the least. However, the province, Metro, and municipalities are becoming more and more involved in public housing and land banking. Housing density and location are greatly affected by development controls such as zoning and building codes at the municipal level, and the provision of such services as sewers, roads, and schools is a task shared by municipal and metropolitan levels. [55]

Finance

Important to an understanding of the metropolitan Toronto form of government is at least a brief examination of the financial base and the trends in financing. An advantage of the metropolitan structure is that all debentures are joint obligations of Metro and the area municipalities, and the borrowing power of Metro rests on the combined assets of all the municipalities. [56] Metropolitan government also decreases the importance of municipal differences in assessment per capita because metropolitan services are provided equally throughout the region. [57] This means that an exodus of middle- and upper-income citizens from the central city to the outer boroughs would not leave the city strapped by a decreasing tax ability and increasing service demands.

Taxation is not, however, a wholly metropolitan function. Mill rates vary from one municipality to another, with each municipality including rates for municipal general purposes, metropolitan general purposes, education, and transit construction. The municipalities may add up to an extra 1.5 mills for schools and other special local improvement charges. In 1973, of all local taxes, 73.1 percent went to the metropolitan level of government, including 46.5 percent for schools. The metropolitan council, the Metropolitan School Board, and the Metropolitan Separate School Board all prepare budgets and set municipal levies, but collection of taxes is performed by the municipalities. [58]

Metro is in fairly good shape financially, but there are questions about the future. In 1973, metropolitan debt (including the debt for all municipalities) was 3.42 percent of equalized assessment, down from 5.09 percent in 1968. [59] Metro also has a relatively good ratio of commercial and industrial to residential assessment. The proportion of tax-exempt property, however, increased by about 1 percent of total assessment between 1967 and 1973. [60] Metropolitan finances have become increasingly dependent on provincial grants, the total amount of which increased 91.3 percent between 1968 and 1973. [61]

The most disturbing financial problem confronting metropolitan Toronto was stated in a royal commission report in 1975 as follows: "the main overriding fact to emerge is that assessment growth, the traditional source of increased municipal revenue, is not keeping pace with the rate of increase of municipal expenditures."[62] Average annual assessment growth between 1967 and 1973 for Metro was 3.8 percent, but the average annual growth in tax needs during the same period was 8.59 percent. The dramatic increase in provincial grants allowed Metro to limit average annual tax increases to between 2 and 6 percent, but, should this provincial support decline, the taxes in metropolitan Toronto would rise sharply. [63] Because many grants from both the Ontario and Canadian governments are conditional, it also may happen that metropolitan Toronto will find that the purposes for which it has funds available are not the purposes that are the highest local priorities. [64]

The assessment growth that did occur between 1967 and 1973 was not evenly spread across the municipalities. The total growth in Metro was 22.9 percent. Assessment increased over 40 percent in North York, about 35 percent in Scarborough, and 23 percent in Etobicoke, but it increased only about 13 percent, 12 percent, and 10 percent in East York, the city of Toronto, and York, respectively. The boroughs of Scarborough, Etobicoke, and North York are increasing in their proportion of metropolitan assessment, while the city of Toronto, East York, and York have decreased. This reflects the

fact that some of the boroughs have room to expand—notably North
York and Scarborough—while others are more fully developed and
grow in assessment chiefly through redevelopment. [65]

Trends in Metro and municipal spending are in the direction
of "soft," people-oriented services, such as protection, social
services, and health. These services are labor intensive and will
rapidly increase in cost as labor costs rise. If this does indeed
occur, it may become more difficult to justify use of the property
tax as the major means of funding. [66]

CONCLUSION

Metro's record since its inception has been an impressive one.
Several of its major accomplishments, such as the establishment of
a firm, cohesive base of political support, the trend toward
equalization in educational opportunities, and the organization of
governmental finance, have been noted in preceding sections of this
chapter. Significant progress also has been achieved in several other
areas, some of which had become almost crisis situations by the
early 1950s. Two such areas were those of sewage and water supply.
The rivers in the Toronto region were fast turning into open sewers,
and what few treatment plants existed at the time were laboring at
full capacity. The total water capacity was some 235 million gallons
per day, while actual need was over 300 million gallons. The
resolution of these problems required a large capital outlay for the
construction of reservoirs, water purification and sewage treatment
plants, and distribution lines. These projects were financed in part
by the sale of water to the municipalities. By 1961, the results were
little short of spectacular. The water capacity was increased by
45 percent to 345 million gallons per day; water line distribution was
increased from 85 miles to 201 miles; and sewage treatment capacity
was expanded by 70 percent. The end result has been the creation
of an ample supply of adequately water- and sewage-serviced land
in all parts of the metropolitan area for residential, industrial,
and commercial development. [67]

Other major accomplishments of Metro include the construction
of an integrated, area-wide network of highways; the establishment
of a coordinated public transportation system of subways, streetcars,
and buses; the implementation of a modern and efficient metropolitan
traffic control system; the provision of a unified system of police
administration; and the establishment of a nearly 5,000-acre parks
system.

While a great deal more could be written about the operations,
accomplishments, and continuing problems of the Toronto Metro,
it seems appropriate in concluding our analysis to discuss certain

broader issues that revolve around this Canadian metropolitan experiment. The chief advantages of the Toronto two-tiered system appear to be a flexibility in determining which level of government can best provide a particular service; the ability to take advantage of economies of scale in such areas as borrowing and avoiding duplication of efforts; and the sharing of both resources and burdens among the municipalities that comprise a natural grouping of a central city and surrounding communities.

A logical question to raise, however, is where the lines should be drawn in defining the metropolitan government in order to maximize both the benefits of federation and the benefits of local control. Of the several changes that have taken place since Metro was established in 1954, most have been in the direction of centralization rather than away from it. For example, police protection, welfare services, air pollution control, and property tax assessment have been given over to the metropolitan level, and the number of area municipalities has been reduced to six from the original 13. Here, the central city has been the clear winner in a political sense, especially if one considers the actual elimination of many of the suburban communities in 1967. In the other direction, the size of the Metropolitan Planning Area has been decreased to encompass only metropolitan Toronto itself. The geographic scope of Metro and the functional division of powers between the tiers are issues that are still being debated today, and these debates undoubtedly will continue as long as the federation exists. A less volatile issue, but one also debated, relates to the role that special-purpose boards and commissions should play in governing Metro and its constituent municipalities.

When considering the potential for transferring the structures and procedures of Metro to other metropolitan areas, several factors which are unique to the Toronto experiment, in particular, and to Canada, in general, should be kept in mind. The reorganization in 1953 was facilitated by the social and economic relationships that the city of Toronto maintained with the surrounding communities. The Toronto region was viewed as an economically, socially interacting unit, with the city of Toronto as the clearly recognized hub. This greatly aided the reorganization movement since the population of the entire region already was associated with central Toronto and, accordingly, there was no need for a radical redirection of the people's loyalties.

With respect to the more general Canadian political milieu, the provinces in Canada are given, under the terms of the British North America Act, responsibility for local government. The provinces frequently utilize commissions and boards (such as royal commissions and the OMB in Ontario) to conduct studies and to determine policy objectives concerning local governments, including

their possible reorganizations. The reports of such agencies are
usually strictly adhered to by the provincial governments, a practice
that cannot always be expected with the same degree of consistency in
the United States. The Ontario legislature considered the reorganization
of metropolitan Toronto to be such a success that it established a
series of regional governmental reviews for the purpose of developing
long-range strategies to guide the development of other municipal areas
in the province. [68]

Still another matter to be considered is how successful the
Toronto Metro will be in the long run. Perhaps the federation form
of government is most appropriate only at one stage in an urban
area's life-cycle. Should the six existing municipalities all become
in time fully developed and take on themselves the characteristics of
central urban communities, it may become necessary to add to Metro
other less developed areas in order to provide growth in tax assessment and to maintain economic balance.

Finally, the problem of the complexity and confusion resulting
from a multiplicity of governments is worth mentioning again. If
the metropolitan form of government is to succeed in the long run,
it may be advisable to streamline the electoral system. Citizens who
are confronted with many voting choices and find it difficult to determine
which level of government to hold responsible for a given action may
ultimately become frustrated and alienated from their government.

In summary, the Toronto model of metropolitan government
has much to recommend it, but further experience and experimentation
are needed to determine which elements are most transportable and
which need amending for long-term success.

NOTES

1. Royal Commission on Metropolitan Toronto, Demographic
Trends in Metropolitan Toronto, prepared by N. Cherukupalle Inc.
(Toronto: Royal Commission, 1975), pp. 7, 36-37.

2. Ibid., pp. 6-25.

3. The World Almanac and Book of Facts (New York and
Cleveland: Newspaper Enterprise Association, 1977), p. 655.

4. Business Week, August 19, 1968, pp. 64-68.

5. Horace Brittain, Local Government in Canada (Toronto:
Ryerson Press, 1951), p. 52.

6. Ibid., p. 55.

7. Harold Kaplan, Urban Political Systems: A Functional
Analysis (New York: Columbia University Press, 1967), pp. 45-46.

8. Ibid., p. 45.

9. Ibid.

134   EXPERIMENTS IN METROPOLITAN GOVERNMENT

10. Albert Rose, Governing Metropolitan Toronto: A Social and Political Analysis (Berkeley and Los Angeles: University of California Press, 1972), pp. 11, 14-20.

11. Winston W. Couch, "Metropolitan Government in Toronto," Public Administration Review 14 (spring 1954): 85.

12. Committee for Economic Development, Reshaping Local Government in Metropolitan Areas (New York: CED, 1970), p. 71.

13. Kaplan, op. cit., pp. 45-46.

14. Richard P. Baine and A. Lynn McMurray, Toronto: An Urban Study (Toronto: Clarke, Irwin, 1972), pp. 99-100.

15. Ibid., p. 100.

16. Frank Smallwood, Metro Toronto: A Decade Later (Toronto: Bureau of Municipal Research, 1963), p. 13.

17. Kaplan, op. cit., p. 49.

18. Ontario Municipal Board, Decision and Recommendations of the Board (Toronto: OMB, January 20, 1953).

19. Kaplan, op. cit., pp. 50-55.

20. Smallwood, op. cit., pp. 5-6.

21. Kaplan, op. cit., p. 69.

22. Ibid., "System's Performance," chapters 3 and 4.

23. Ibid., pp. 53-55.

24. Smallwood, op. cit., pp. 12-17.

25. Royal Commission on Metropolitan Toronto, The Organization of Local Government in Metropolitan Toronto, prepared by Ronald C. Smith, Hugh Auld, Jeremy Posner, and Richard Loreto (Toronto, 1975), p. 20. See also Rose, op. cit., pp. 36-42.

26. Rose, op. cit., pp. 30-33.

27. Ibid., pp. 100-102.

28. Ibid., pp. 110-13. In spite of the continuing problems in education, the increase in school enrollment capacity in 1961 was dramatic—46 percent at the elementary-school level and 92 percent at the secondary level. In all, 166,055 pupil spaces were created with construction of 175 new schools and 293 school additions. See Smallwood, op. cit., p. 11.

29. Smallwood, op. cit., pp. 5-6.

30. Ibid., p. 39.

31. Rose, op. cit., p. 114.

32. Ibid., pp. 115-18.

33. Royal Commission on Metropolitan Toronto, The Electoral System for Metropolitan Toronto, prepared by T. J. Plunket, M. J. Powell, and P. Mulligan (Toronto, 1975), p. 16.

34. Ibid., p. 20.

35. Royal Commission, Organization, op. cit., pp. 53-55.

36. Rose, op. cit., pp. 178-79 and 182-83.

37. Royal Commission, Electoral System, op. cit. , pp. 23-26; and Royal Commission, Organization, op. cit. , p. 57.

38. Royal Commission, Electoral System, op. cit. , p. 25.

39. Royal Commission, Organization, op. cit. , pp. 62-64.

40. Ibid. , pp. 66-69.

41. Royal Commission on Metropolitan Toronto, Public Safety Services in Metropolitan Toronto, prepared by Joe Martin, Dr. E. S. Duetsch, Anne McAllister, and Patricia Shelley of P. S. Ross and Partners (Toronto, 1975), pp.. 2-13.

42. Ibid. , pp. 31-41.

43. Royal Commission on Metropolitan Toronto, The Planning Process in Metropolitan Toronto, prepared by John Bousfield Associates and Comay Planning Consultants Ltd. (Toronto, 1975), pp. ix, 11-19.

44. Ibid. , pp. 185-90.

45. Royal Commission on Metropolitan Toronto, Physical Services, Environmental Protection, and Energy Supply in Metropolitan Toronto, prepared by James F. McLaren Ltd. (Toronto, 1975), pp. 8-21.

46. Royal Commission on Metropolitan Toronto, The Planning Process in Metropolitan Toronto, prepared by John Bousfield Associates and Company Planning Consultants Ltd. (Toronto, 1975), pp. 42-51.

47. Ibid. , pp. 53-59.

48. Royal Commission on Metropolitan Toronto, Social Policy in Metropolitan Toronto (Toronto, 1975), pp. 8-11.

49. Ibid. , pp. 13-16.

50. Ibid. , p. 17.

51. Royal Commission on Metropolitan Toronto, Transportation Organization in Metropolitan Toronto, prepared by Juri Pill and Richard Soberman (Toronto, 1975), pp. 18-73.

52. Ibid. , p. 73.

53. Ibid. , p. 18.

54. Ibid. , pp. 23-31.

55. Royal Commission on Metropolitan Toronto, The Provision and Conservation of Housing in Metropolitan Toronto, prepared by Klein and Sears (Toronto, 1975), pp. 3-21.

56. Royal Commission on Metropolitan Toronto, A Financial Profile of Metropolitan Toronto and Its Constituent Municipalities, 1967-1973, prepared by Allen E. Jarrett and Merrill R. Johnston of Jarrett, Goold, and Elliot, Chartered Accountants (Toronto, 1975), p. 41.

57. Ibid. , p. 16.

58. Ibid. , pp. 17-23.

59. Ibid. , p. 42.

60. Ibid. , p. 14. The burden of tax-exempt property, such as government buildings, churches, and charitable institutions, is very unevenly distributed among the area municipalities. For example, the city of Toronto included 56. 5 percent of exempt property but only 38. 9 percent of total assessment in Metro in 1973.

61. Ibid. , p. 65.

62. Ibid. , p. I. The royal commission, the third in Metro's history, was established in September 1974 to review and report on the situation in metropolitan Toronto, and it presented its several-volume report to the provincial government the following year, in 1975.

63. Ibid. , pp. 10-11.

64. Ibid. , p. 65.

65. Ibid. , pp. 8-10.

66. Ibid. , p. 88.

67. Smallwood, op. cit. , p. 11, and Rose, op. cit. , pp. 127-129.

68. Frank Smallwood, "Reshaping Local Government Abroad: Anglo-Canadian Experiments," Public Administration Review, September-October 1970.

PART

III

THE COOPERATIVE
ALTERNATIVE

6

INTERLOCAL
AGREEMENTS AND
THE COOPERATIVE
ALTERNATIVE

DEVELOPMENT OF THE CONCEPT

Interlocal agreements are one of the methods most widely used to deal with metropolitan problems. We first will discuss the general concept of interlocal agreements and then examine in greater detail the practical experience of Los Angeles County and the Lakewood plan.

Interlocal agreements are classified here as two basic types: informal agreements and formal service agreements. Both of these types of interlocal agreements are intended to improve the delivery of municipal services. The actual municipal services themselves are limited only by state law and municipal charters. Municipalities have entered into cooperative contractual ventures for such diverse urban functions as legal advice, personnel services, accounting and other financial services, data processing, planning and zoning, public works, civil defense, law enforcement, fire protection, park and recreation services, library services, and health services.[1] Service agreements have proved to be a rather adaptive procedural response to urban problem solving, since they do not structurally reorganize the governmental system in the area.[2] Interlocal agreements represent a status quo philosophy of dealing with metropolitan problems under the cooperative approach.

Informal agreements can involve almost any service and are based on a nonbinding verbal understanding between two governmental units. Most informal agreements, however, involve either the joint maintenance of highways and bridges or mutual aid pacts. Mutual aid pacts are standby agreements only and do not involve the delivery of a service on a regular basis.[3] An example of a mutual aid pact would

be an agreement between two municipal departments to provide
back-up assistance to each other during emergencies.

Informal agreements are not binding on any municipality and
can be canceled at any time, nor do they usually require any statutory
authorization by the local legislative bodies. Perhaps their greatest
advantage is that of providing certain assurances of supplementary
emergency assistance as in the case of mutual aid pacts. In addition,
the informal exchange of information among jurisdictions can serve
to coordinate the delivery of area-wide services. Thus, in making
their plans in various areas, municipalities may include information
about what actions other communities are pursuing.

The greatest disadvantage of informal agreements is that nothing
is formally written down. This can present problems if one community
questions the performance or responsibilities of another participating
community. Seldom is there any list of total community informal
agreements for public inspection, since most of these agreements
are made through departmental heads.

Formal agreements or service contracts are substantially
different from informal agreements because they are legal documents
with much more detailed provisions that are signed by two or more
communities. State enabling legislation or a joint exercise of powers
act is necessary to permit the initiation of these cooperative interlocal agreements. [4] Some state statutes provide blanket authorization
to local units to provide, jointly or cooperatively, services, without
enumerating each type of service. A number of states, however,
still maintain specific statutory provisions that authorize each type
of agreement. Minnesota, for example, has over 100 separate
authorizing provisions, [5] and in Connecticut, aggreements are
permitted for a duration of 40 years. [6]

Service agreements between municipalities and private concerns
also are very popular methods of providing services. One survey
revealed that over 60 percent of the municipalities with a population
over 2,500 were parties to such agreements. In this same survey,
60 percent of the municipalities had agreements with county governments, while another 40 percent reported intermunicipal contracts.
Service agreements were most common in the West, where they were
found in 78 percent of the surveyed municipalities, and they were
least common in the East and South, where they were found in 53
percent of the surveyed municipalities. [7] Formal agreements are
markedly more popular among council-manager as contrasted with
mayor-council forms of government. The vast majority of these
agreements relate to only one service and two governments—the
provider and the recipient of the service. [8]

Service agreements or contracts can have numerous permutations.
One governmental unit may provide a service to one or more

municipalities. Detroit, for example, provides 16 different services
to 80 governmental units. A municipality might also contract with a
private company to receive such services as refuse collection,
public relations, or the microfilming of documents. [9] Two municipalities might share the cost of a service such as the funding of a
tax assessor, planner, or engineer. In certain instances, a
municipality may even provide a partial service to another. For
example, one town might contract out its tax billing to another unit
of government but would itself assume the responsibility for collecting its own taxes. [10]

In certain cases, a municipality may be ordered by the state
government to provide services to a neighboring community. For
example, Milford, Connecticut, was required to provide waste water
treatment for an adjoining town that had no sewer facilities. [11] Finally,
the municipalities may contract with the state or county to receive
certain services such as police training, crime laboratory services,
police protection, water pollution abatement, election services, and
tax assessing. [12] The second half of this chapter will discuss the
specific use of contracts in Los Angeles County.

There are a number of reasons for the popularity of interlocal
service agreements. Municipalities are often able to obtain a service
or product that they could not provide themselves. If they take
advantage of the economies of scale, the cost may be lower and the
quality of the services may be higher. Services that are needed in
an area with two or more municipalities can be coordinated and
efficiently administered through interlocal cooperation. Services
also can be effectively provided to areas where irregular boundaries
have created service delivery problems; increased efficiency can
be attained by establishing optimum-size operating units on a functional
basis; and natural service areas such as drainage basins, which
sometimes are divided by political boundaries, can be utilized. [13]
Finally, the efficiency and effectiveness of the service delivery is
enhanced with interlocal agreements because a better use can be made
of administrators and specialists through a sharing of personnel costs
on a contract basis.

Perhaps one of the strongest arguments in their favor is that
service agreements enjoy a high degree of political feasibility. They
usually encounter little resistance because they do not restrict the
freedom of action of the recipient government, they do not require
voter approval, and they usually can be terminated on relatively short
notice. [14] The advocates of this cooperative approach stress that
service agreements may help solve select urban problems without
the need for a major structural change such as consolidation or the
formation of a special district.

There have been numerous criticisms raised about the use of service agreements in dealing with urban problems. Critics have pointed out that service agreements are usually confined to the areas of public works and other technical areas as distinguished from social service areas. The bulk of the agreements are found in refuse collection and disposal, police radio communications, libraries, and equipment use. [15] These highly visible functions have little relation to the life-style of community citizens. It has been shown that in many instances where communities enter into service agreements, they do so with communities of similar socioeconomic status, thereby avoiding any possible problems that might be involved with lower-status municipalities. [16] In addition, public works and equipment projects tend to have certain political ramifications. These types of service agreements present more tangible evidence to the public of governmental successes than do the more amorphous and controversial social service programs.

A final area of concern to recipients in a service agreement is the degree of local control over the service. Unless contracts are carefully drafted, a municipality might be forced to live under an undesirable arrangement for an extended period of time. Moreover, unless the contract includes specific provisions for amendment, it may become inflexible and undesirable after a few years. [17]

LOS ANGELES COUNTY
AND THE LAKEWOOD PLAN

The nation's most populated county, Los Angeles, with its 7 million residents, provides an excellent example of the cooperative approach to metropolitan government. In the case of Los Angeles, the approach features an active and powerful county government that has developed over a number of years as the producer of many key services for the municipalities and unincorporated areas.

Los Angeles County is the urban center of an 11-county region in southern California that is widely known for the extent of its area, numbers of people, and burgeoning growth, as well as its topographic, climatic, and economic diversity. For many years, the area was isolated by its location, while its economic capacities remained predominantly agricultural until World War II. At the turn of the century, the population of the city of Los Angeles was only slightly over 100,000, compared to that of New York, which was 3.5 million. Moreover, the entire population of southern California at that time was only 325,000. However, by 1940 the region's population had grown to 3.7 million, and since then it has increased to almost 12 million. Although part of this tremendous increase in population resulted from a natural increase, much of it came through migration.

It has been estimated that about 5 million persons have migrated to southern California since 1940. Americans came to the area for jobs in aircraft plants and shipyards during World War II and continued to be attracted to defense-oriented jobs during the Korean and Vietnam wars and the missile-space age. [18]

The population of Los Angeles County-Long Beach SMSA represents the core of this growth phenomenon, which continued into the 1960s but then in the 1970s began to decrease for Los Angeles County while continuing to increase for the greater Los Angeles region. (See Table 6.1 for the specific population figures.)

The first constitution of the state of California, which was adopted in 1849, directed the state legislature to establish or provide for the organization of a system of county and town governments as well as for cities and villages. These local governments were to be as nearly uniform as practicable, but the legislature had to pass hundreds of special acts for the administration of local governments. [19] Los Angeles County was organized in 1850 as one of the original 27 counties of California.

A new constitution, which was adopted in 1879, established a system of cities by class, which was based on population. Liberal incorporation laws led to a rush of incorporations by new cities without the capacity to provide many of the necessary municipal services. Under California law, a community could incorporate if it had a population of at least 500 persons. In addition, many areas incorporated out of the fear of being annexed by nearby cities, which were always seeking additional territory that would increase their tax base.

TABLE 6.1

Population of Los Angeles-Long Beach
Standard Metropolitan Statistical Area

Year	Population
1974	6,926,000
1970	7,042,000
1960	6,039,000

Source: U.S. Department of Commerce, Bureau of the Census, Statistical Abstracts of the U.S., 1976 (Washington, D.C.: Government Printing Office, 1976), p. 20.

Development of a County
Service Delivery Capacity

From the outset, Los Angeles County has been in an ideal
position to address itself to urban problem solving since California
laws gave the county control over services vital to any city. These
included relief for the poor, public hospital care, assessment of
property for tax purposes, support of the trial courts including jails,
prosecution, probation administration, courtroom facilities and
staffs, registration of voters, and the administration of elections. [20]

By 1912 Los Angeles County had drafted and adopted a home
rule charter. This unique document was the first county charter in
the United States to be written by means of utilizing the home rule
technique, which previously had applied only to municipalities. The
charter was rather brief, written in simple language, and dealt with
matters very broadly. Thus, it avoided the maze of specific details
that characterized many municipal home rule charters of that era. [21]
The charter reduced the number of county elected officials to a
five-man board of supervisors, the district attorney, the assessor,
and the sheriff. The two most important changes were the centralization of general government powers in the board of supervisors
and the introduction of a civil service system.

In 1914 an amendment to the state constitution gave the county
the authority to perform municipal functions for cities through the
device of contractual agreements, and this gave the county a firm
legal basis for certain activities that it already was involved in. [22]
Los Angeles County had first started using service contracts in 1907
when a contract for tax assessment and collection was made with
the city of Loardsbury. This was to become a popular service that
the county has provided ever since to most newly incorporated
municipalities. In 1909 the county established the County Free
Library District, which provided basic library services to both the
unincorporated areas and to municipalities without libraries. This
additional service was supported by an ear-marked tax levy within
the area served.

Another example of the tradition of an active county government
in Los Angeles occurred in 1925 when legislation was passed that allowed
for the formation of county sanitation districts. These new districts
could include municipalities, or combinations of cities and unincorporated areas. By the 1930s, the county had given the cities an option of
transferring the performance of health and library services and tax
assessment and collection to the county. Los Angeles County continued
to expand its level of services prior to World War II by entering into
contracts for the issuance of building permits, animal regulations,
personnel, planning, and traffic engineering services. [23]

The county also has a history of providing the unincorporated areas with many of the same services that were given to the municipalities. In addition to the services offered to the cities, Los Angeles County supplied the unincorporated areas with water, sewage, roads, street lighting, and fire protection. These high-quality services actually helped to thwart the trend of incorporation of the suburban areas. Robert Warren summarizes the effect of these county services on the number of incorporations as follows:[24]

> The policies of Los Angeles County had two basic
> effects in influencing this modification in the tradi-
> tional pattern of utilizing municipal status to obtain
> urban levels of service. The range and level of
> services available from the county and districts
> meant that cities were no longer monopolistic producers
> of urban services, as they had been prior to 1900 and
> even after 1920. The choice available to unincorporated
> residents was no longer incorporation or annexation to
> meet urban needs, but was expanded to include the
> County as an efficient and large scale regional producer
> of basic services and special districts which all allowed
> various combinations of services and service levels to
> be realized.

In effect, the county government was discouraging incorporation and the accompanying governmental fragmentation because it had no desire to lose its clientele group that benefited from county services.

City-county relations have not always been amicable. There have been charges that the county has in effect been subsidizing the unincorporated areas with dollars raised through the general fund, which was paid by the cities. In 1950 a study by the City-County Committee found that a large part of the city dweller's county tax dollar was used to supply police, recreation, and a number of miscellaneous services to the 69 unincorporated areas of the county. For the year 1948/49, the study found that $906 million was spent from the county general property tax funds for special services to unincorporated areas.[25] After this study, other studies were conducted to produce more equitable methods whereby the unincorporated areas might pay for their own level of services. The controversy eventually subsided because of a new wave of incorporations in the 1950s. These new cities hoped to reap benefits derived from contracted urban services. (This very complex system of contract services, to be called the Lakewood plan, will be discussed in the next section.) At the same time, the county had reduced the number of its services available to the unincorporated areas. Nonetheless, many communities have remained unincorporated because of the relatively high level of services they can obtain from Los Angeles County. An indicator of the popularity of the county's services to the unincorporated areas is that the unincorporated population of Los Angeles County has remained at about 1 million for the last two decades, despite a large number of incorporations since 1954. [26]

Thus, there is a rather lengthy record of a highly active county government in Los Angeles that dates back to the turn of the century. Los Angeles has developed its own cooperative model for delivering urban services to its numerous cities and unincorporated areas.

Lakewood Plan

Lakewood began its existence as an unincorporated planned housing development within Los Angeles County in 1950. Prior to this time, the territory was mainly farmland. Over 17,000 single-family, medium-priced houses were included in the Lakewood development along with streets, sidewalks, sewers, schools, parks, landscaping, and a large modern shopping center. The development was built on land that the city of Long Beach had planned to annex to help provide services and increase its tax base. In 1953 Long Beach began a series of annexation proceedings and successfully annexed part of Lakewood, with a population of 24,000, leaving another section of Lakewood, with a population of 20,000, still unincorporated. [27]

Residents in the remaining area of the development began a drive to incorporate in order to save the rest of Lakewood from annexation. A Lakewood Committee for Incorporation was formed and filed an incorporation petition with the county in December 1953. An election was set for March 1954 that would in effect allow the Lakewood residents a choice between annexation by Long Beach or incorporation. The leadership of the city of Long Beach actually campaigned against incorporation because the proposed annexation of the remaining Lakewood development would bring a lucrative area with a good tax base within the boundaries of the city.

Within Lakewood the pro-incorporation faction argued that the city they proposed could be organized and run without the high costs usually associated with municipal government. As an incorporated municipality, they would have local control! The advocates of incorporation also reminded the citizens of Lakewood that a new state law had been passed that allowed a newly incorporated city in California to contract with the county for all essential services. In addition, the advocates projected that Lakewood as a city would receive around $500,000 a year from state collected taxes that were shared with cities and counties. [28]

TABLE 6. 2

Services Available to
City of Lakewood

County-administered Districts
        Consolidated Fire District
        County Library District
        Lakewood Sewer Maintenance District
        County Lighting District (2)
        County Lighting Maintenance District (3)
Self-governing Special Districts
        County Sanitation District No. 3
        Lakewood Park, Recreation and Parkway District
        Southeast Mosquito Abatement District
County Contracts of General Service Agreements
        Animal Regulation
        Assessment and Collection of Taxes
        Health Services
        Emergency Ambulance Service
        Engineering Staff Services
        Industrial Waste Regulation
        Jail Facilities
        Law Enforcement
        Prosecution of City Ordinance Violations
        Planning and Zoning Staff Services
        Street Maintenance and Construction
        Street Sweeping
        Treasury and Auditor Services
        Tree Trimming

Source: City of Lakewood, The Lakewood Plan (Lakewood, Cal., 1960), p. 3.

On March 9, 1954 the Lakewood voters went to the polls and approved the incorporation petition by a vote of 7,254 to 4,868. Lakewood was officially incorporated on April 16, 1954 and immediately had a wide variety of services available to its citizens through the vehicle of the county. These services included the county-administered special districts, the self-governing special districts, and the county contracts or general service agreements. (For a detailed description of these three variations, see Table 6. 2.)

By December 1954, the city of Lakewood was functioning with only ten employees. Its tax rate was very reasonable, even considering the lower cost of public goods and services in the 1950s (29 cents per $100 for 1954-55, 30 cents for 1955-56, and 24 cents for 1956-57). The Lakewood plan was so successful that the trend to incorporate returned to the fast-growing Los Angeles metropolitan area. However, most of the 31 newer cities established a set of voluntary agreements for centralizing the production of services at the county level. The ultimate control over the service levels remained with the cities because the city only purchases specific services that it feels it needs and can afford. [29]

The county had to create additional administrative positions to monitor the efficiency and equity of the plan as more cities became its customers. In 1957 a County-City Coordinator Office was established to handle county policies relating to the Lakewood plan and to coordinate the staff and program.

Under the Lakewood plan, a city receives a package of municipal services from the county government. In some cases, newly created municipalities have received almost all of their services from the county. Although the Lakewood plan follows the general trend in Los Angeles of developing urban services through the auspices of county government, there are several key differences from the earlier city-county service agreements. As Bollens and Schmandt explain, [30]

> It [the Lakewood Plan] entails the purchase of a package of services instead of individual services on a piecemeal basis. It includes for the first time law enforcement and fire protection to cities; previously the sheriff's department did not enter into contracts with municipalities, and newly incorporated areas withdrew from county-administered fire districts. Use of the plan has been confined entirely to communities incorporated since Lakewood became a city in 1954—that is, municipalities not already having their own long-established departments.

Cities operating under the Lakewood plan do not all purchase the same package of services from the county. Lakewood was, of course, the first city to adopt the contract services plan, and even today it relies on it for the delivery of 41 services.

The number of services provided by Los Angeles County has increased as the demand from the newly incorporated cities for these services has increased. In 1963 there were 16 county departments and 5 county-administered special districts producing 55 different services used by cities in Los Angeles County. Service arrangements can take any of three basic forms: (1) a city can simply continue within a county administered special district after incorporation; (2) contracts can be made for specific services; or (3) a city can adopt a general services agreement, which authorizes a city to call upon the county for all services not covered by specific contractual arrangements. By 1973, Los Angeles County had over 1,600 cooperative agreements with its 77 municipalities. Fifty-eight different services are available to cities through contracts and county-administered special districts.

The contracts themselves are limited to five years, but they may be renewed. Some services are self-financing, in which case the users' fees collected from individual cities cover the total cost of the service. Most services have set prices that reflect production costs, while other select services are paid for by a uniform property tax without any relation to the benefits received by the property owner or community. [31]

On the surface, the Lakewood plan appears to have been a splendid success. Richard Cion reports that "its clientele regard it with a euphoric mixture of contentment and admiration."[32] The plan has been praised for being rational, efficient, effective, and politically realistic. It does not create another level of government but instead utilizes the resources of the existing units of government. The county has the ability to produce the desired levels of services that the municipalities want. The municipalities must choose the type of service and the level of the service. As one county official suggested, the plan "is a partnership of cities and the County to provide joint services at the least cost while both agencies retain the power of self-determination and home rule."[33] This viewpoint is usually expressed by most local officials of the 29 municipalities that currently depend on contracts with Los Angeles County for all of their services.

Even when we take into account the many benefits of the Lakewood plan, there are numerous problems that have occurred over the past two decades of its use. Since the county government is the actual producer of the services, the county tends to dominate any bargaining process with the cities over the quality of services and their costs. As Richard Cion argues,[34]

> A city cannot always withdraw from the contract
> system if it wants to. Its actions are not internally
> controlled; rather they are subject to outside
> political influence, particularly from actors in
> the county government whose interests lie in the

continuation of the status quo. The city's great power
in the negotiation process is largely a myth.

The desire of the cities for autonomy has actually resulted in a
restriction of their freedom in most policy areas except for
determining land-use patterns, which remains at the discretion of
the cities.

Moreover, the Lakewood plan has indirectly led to a proliferation
of municipal incorporations in Los Angeles County. The passage of
the plan in 1954 gave tax incentives to suburban residents to incorporate rather than to be annexed or even remain unincorporated. As
Harrigan reports, "Whereas only two cities incorporated in the
county between 1930 and 1950, thirty-two cities have incorporated
since the inception of the Lakewood Plan."35

There also seems to be a clear lack of regional planning
fostered indirectly by the Lakewood plan, since it has rekindled a
paternalistic county government. Since the plan is a way of continuing
and even increasing the county's role, it is a natural tendency of the
county administration to increase their power while at the same time
attempting to ensure that a more general metropolitan government
is avoided. Cion describes the situation well: "They live contentedly
within the framework of the Lakewood Plan, their power already
secure, their reason for seeking metro gone."36

Finally, the plan does not attempt to solve the most pressing
concerns of planning, water supply, sewage, and education. These
policy areas are beyond its intended scope. The Lakewood plan
certainly has eliminated the need for more local departments and
has alleviated the duplication of services that waste metropolitan
resources. However, it tends to avoid the really difficult problems
because as a system of interlocal agreements, it is limited by the
degree of consensus patterns among its subscribers.37

NOTES

1. League of California Cities, Inter-municipal Cooperation
Through Contractual Agreements (Berkeley: League of California
Cities, July 1963), pp. 5-8.

2. Richard J. Guastello and Joseph F. Zimmerman, Intergovernmental Service Agreements in New York State (Albany: New
York Conference of Mayors and Municipal Officials, 1973), p. 1.

3. Joseph F. Zimmerman, "Meeting Service Needs Through
Intergovernmental Agreements," in The Municipal Yearbook
(Washington, D.C.: International City Management Association,
1973), p. 79.

4. Richard C. Hartman, "The State's Role in Regionalism," in The Regionalist Papers, ed. Kent Mathewson (Detroit: Metropolitan Fund, 1975), p. 245.

5. Leigh E. Grosenick, A Manual for Interlocal Cooperation in Minnesota (St. Paul: Office of Local and Urban Affairs, 1969), p. 113.

6. Neil O. Littlefield, "The Legal Framework for Inter-municipal and Regional Action in Connecticut," Urban Research Reports (Storrs, Conn.) (October 1966): 17.

7. Zimmerman, op. cit., p. 79.

8. Vincent L. Marando, "Inter-local Cooperation in a Metropolitan Area: Detroit," Urban Affairs Quarterly 4 (December 1968); 193.

9. Zimmerman, op. cit., p. 85.

10. Guastello and Zimmerman, op. cit., p. 6.

11. Zimmerman, op. cit., p. 79.

12. Ibid., pp. 82-85.

13. League of California Cities, op. cit., p. 2, and Littlefield, op. cit., p. 18.

14. Guastello and Zimmerman, op. cit., p. 3.

15. Henry J. Schmandt, "Intergovernmental Volunteerism Pro and Con," in The Regionalist Papers, ed. Kent Mathewson (Detroit: Metropolitan Fund, 1975).

16. Ibid., p. 156.

17. League of California Cities, op. cit., p. 3.

18. Howard J. Nelson and William A. V. Clark, The Los Angeles Metropolitan Experience (Cambridge, Mass.: Ballinger, 1976), pp. 1-6.

19. Helen L. Jones and Robert F. Wilcox, Metropolitan Los Angeles: Its Government (Los Angeles: Haynes Foundation, 1949), esp. chap. 2, pp. 7-28.

20. Winston W. Crouch and Beatrice Dinerman, Southern California Metropolis (Berkeley: University of California Press, 1963), p. 182.

21. Ibid., p. 183.

22. Robert Warren, Government in Metropolitan Regions (Davis: University of California at Davis, 1966), p. 93.

23. Ibid., pp. 93-104.

24. Ibid., p. 112.

25. Report of the City-County Committee, Los Angeles Division, League of California Cities, December 13, 1950, p. 2.

26. John C. Bollens and Henry J. Schmandt, The Metropolis: Its People, Politics, and Economic Life (New York: Harper & Row, 1975), p. 300.

27. Warren, op. cit., pp. 143-46.

28. Ibid. , p. 159.

29. Ibid. , pp. 202, 155-57.

30. Bollens and Schmandt, op. cit. , p. 302.

31. Warren, pp. 203-09.

32. Richard Cion, "Accommodation Par Excellence: The Lakewood Plan," in Metropolitan Politics, ed. Michael N. Danielson (Boston: Little, Brown, 1971), p. 226.

33. Arthur G. Will, "Lakewood Revisited: Six Years of Contract Services" (Paper presented to the First Annual Municipal Seminar of California Contract Cities, Palm Springs, California, April 29, 1960), p. 1.

34. Cion, op. cit. , p. 228.

35. John J. Harrigan, Political Change in the Metropolis (Boston: Little, Brown, 1976), p. 208.

36. Cion, op. cit. , p. 231.

37. Ibid.

PART

IV

**THE METROPOLITAN
COUNCIL ALTERNATIVE**

7

COUNCIL OF
GOVERNMENTS
APPROACH

TWO DECADES OF EXPERIENCE

The council of governments (COGs) approach is an example of the metropolitan council alternative and represents one of the mildest forms of the metropolitan experiments. In the strictest legal sense, COGs are not really metropolitan governments, but rather represent associations of local governments acting in concert on select issues. The COGs idea is based on voluntary cooperation between local elected officials in metropolitan areas to help solve area-wide problems. The existence of voluntary regional associations of local officials dates back to 1954, when the Supervisors' Inter-County Committee was established in the Detroit area. During this first decade, only nine COGs were formed in the United States, and, according to Royce Hanson, "all of them suffered from uncertainties, inexperience in metropolitan cooperation, and lack of adequate resources."[1]

Since 1965, however, a tremendous period of growth has occurred as the COG model was accepted by most metropolitan areas of the nation. Although the most publicly stated reason for COGs was to ensure better planning and coordination of policies and programs in Cities and Metropolitan Act (Model Cities) stated that after June Federal housing legislation was changed so that COGs would be eligible under section 701 to receive grants, which would pay up to two-thirds of the cost of numerous activities, including studies, data collection, regional plans and programs, and general administration and staffing expenses. During the same year, the Demonstration Cities and Metropolitan Act (Model Cities) stated that after June 30, 1967 all federal grant and aid applications for many types of projects, which were mainly of the public works variety, had to be submitted to an area-wide agency that performs metropolitan or regional planning for the area in which the assistance is to be utilized. [2] It is difficult to minimize the impact that these two federal acts had on the growth of COGs in the mid-1960s, but it would seem safe to conclude that it probably was substantial.

COGs do not have the authority to levy taxes, pass ordinances, or require legislation or action from local governments. [3] These structural and legal limitations have often been posed as one explanation for the popularity of COGs. Local officials find joining these organizations to be politically acceptable because in them membership is voluntary, they lack coercive powers, and they do not pose a serious threat to the integrity of the existing local governments. This alternative appears to be one of the least drastic approaches available because COGs do not disrupt the traditional local decision-making pattern and therefore do not threaten those in power.

COGs are also useful to municipalities in that they serve as information centers in identifying and publicizing the variety and extent of available federal dollars. They help ensure the flow of federal funds to COG members, and they also are able to provide planning assistance and management expertise to municipalities unable to finance such functions within the constraints of their own budgets. [4] Indeed, COGs have often been better received by the smaller suburban municipalities, which can utilize their supplementary services more, than by the core city government, which often already possesses many of the capabilities of a COG.

The membership of COGs generally is composed of the elected officials of the general-purpose governments in the metropolitan area. Cities, towns, and counties comprise the bulk of COGs' membership. In some instances, special districts, interest groups, or citizen groups may be represented in the general assembly or on special committees. As Zimmerman explains, [5]

> The Central Lane Planning Council in Oregon includes
> a park and recreation district, and three school
> districts. The North Central Texas COG and the
> Sabine Neches, [Texas] COG include independent
> hospital, sewer, school, and water districts as
> members. The Greater Topeka Intergovernmental
> Council includes Washburn University as a member.

If COGs are composed of a large number of local governments, their governing bodies are likely to be divided into two levels. The larger unit, often called a general assembly, is the formal policy-making body of the COG. But these large assemblies that usually

meet only once a year are generally too unwieldy to be effective.
During the annual meeting, the general assembly usually adopts the
budget, elects an executive committee, and approves general policies
and the administrative direction of the COG.

Typically, the executive committee will meet on a monthly
basis and in effect carry out most of the major business of the COG,
recommending many of the major policy decisions that are routinely
ratified by the general assembly at its annual meeting. As Royce
Hanson notes:[6]

> The work of the executive committee constitutes the
> most important activity of the councils. These
> committees supervise the staff, maintain liason with
> other regional groups, prepare policy recommendations
> for the general assembly, make budgetary decisions
> and otherwise act on behalf of the entire council. The
> executive committees also assign projects to standing
> committees or ad hoc committees and review the work
> of these committees.

In addition to the general assembly and the executive committee,
other standing committees are often formed to oversee specific
subject areas of continuing concern such as planning and finance.
The more specialized policy areas also usually are handled by
standing committees, which study such problems as air and water
pollution, building codes, law enforcement, metropolitan planning,
open space, parks, recreation, and transportation. Specific
recommendations are channeled back through the executive committee
and eventually to the general assembly before any specific action can
be taken. Most COGs have their own executive director and staff who
are responsible for doing the actual work that has been approved by
the executive committee and general assembly.

The issue of the proper constituent unit form of representation
is a potential constitutional question that has arisen and challenged
the membership structure of most COGs. In the past, COGs have
resembled the General Assembly of the United Nations, since each
governmental unit has an equal say on any given issue. The results
are often bland, consensus-oriented policies. As one critic lamented,
"This structure effectively grants a veto to the very suburban
governments that do not want to lose control over the life style
issues,"[7] such as tax disparities that favor the suburbs, low-income
housing in the suburbs, and the busing of school children to achieve
racial balance. Thus, demands for applying the one-man, one-vote
principle have in effect questioned the legitimacy of COGs, and as a

result, many COGs have responded by establishing a more proportional system of representation.

COGs have been established from a variety of legal bases—specific enabling acts passed by state legislatures, existing general joint exercise of power statutes, as in California, or intergovernmental agreements. If there is nothing in state law to facilitate the creation of a COG, it has proved to be possible to create a COG through the device of a nonprofit organization. A nonprofit organization, while giving considerable legal power to the COG, has built-in limitations on legislative activities imposed by the Internal Revenue Service.

There is no standard form or model in a COG. Its ultimate composition, organization, membership, and responsibilities will depend on such variables as the geographic area of the country in which it is formed, the situation that existed at the time of its creation, the history of interlocal cooperation and regional planning in the area, and the legal means by which it was created.

The proponents of COGs have made numerous claims about the functions of these organizations. The major activities of COGs involve regional planning and the formulation of regional policies. By virtue of their COG organization, members are able to identify needs in their area that go beyond the scope of their local boundaries. COGs provide a forum for elected local leaders to discuss the pressing regional issues, and after debate, possibly to concur in joint, coordinated regional efforts. Finally, the COG can conceivably be used to implement the details of the cooperative action by utilizing such devices as interlocal agreements, joint performance of services, or the adoption of parallel ordinances. [8]

However, the most publicized function of COGs is their ability to provide a forum for local government leaders to talk over their problems. Through their COG, local leaders can become acquainted with each other and become accustomed to working together in an amicable and mutually beneficial relationship. In many cases, the relationship among local officials before the creation of a COG had been a hostile one, with one government vying against another for federal and state grants, or arguing about how much each should pay to support such area services as airports or hospitals.

Once local officials are able to converse and accept the institutionalized setting of a COG, they can begin the task of identifying mutual regional problems. Proponents of COGs also have argued that these regional affiliations can serve to forestall the loss of local power. Because COGs are voluntary organizations, a unanimous or nearly unanimous vote is generally sought before it considers an issue or problem in the region. Thus, COGs tend to avoid those major regional problems that could cause controversy—in effect avoiding all serious problems that might entice a disgruntled member to exercise a veto. [9]

COGs seem to gravitate toward problems offering simple, agreeable solutions, leaving the more difficult issues for future discussion. As Henry Schmandt has written, "Services which have social implications of significant import on how people live and whom they come into contact with in their neighborhood—zoning, education, housing and law enforcement, in particular—are those which localities guard most jealously."[10] COGs have become too timid to be effective, shying away from anything that might appear to be overtly regionalistic or controversial or that might be interpreted as a grab for power. [11]

Another problem inherent in the structure of COGs is the potential divisiveness of the forces of local interest versus the forces of regional interests. These forces work against every COG member, who is called on to serve two constituencies, the voters in his local government and the concerns of the region or county at large. The member has no direct political link with his COG, since he becomes a COG member by virtue of being elected as a COG representative by his fellow elected officials. In the event of a conflict of interest between the interests of his local government and the interests of the region, most observers have discovered that the member is usually compelled to vote for the interest of his local community. Yet another related problem is that every COG member has additional demands placed upon his time, interests, and responsibilities by virtue of his affiliation with the COG organization. Since local officials must frequently run for reelection to be recertified for COG membership, there is often a loss of continuity in the organization when the defeated local candidates are also ineligible for the COG as a consequence of their electoral defeat.

One of the greatest limitations of regional cooperation for any COG is its basic lack of authority. Once the planning and policy-making stages of the administrative process have been accepted, it logically follows that the proposed program should be implemented. However, without the political power or legal authority of a true government, a COG is usually at a loss to enforce its regionwide plans. Without these important political resources to invoke sanctions, the COG must try to talk the program through to inform, enlighten, and convince, not only other elected officials, but the general public as well. Here, COGs resemble interest groups in performing the functions of education and salesmanship of policies.

It is important to remember that just because the representative to COG has endorsed a particular plan of action, this does not guarantee that either his community or his fellow elected officials will support his decision. For their own political survival, COG representatives must be very careful that they do not lose contact with local sentiment concerning regional issues.

One of the greatest incentives for the growth and development of COGs has been the role of the federal government in channeling money to local governments. COGs are dependent on federal grants for much of their funding as well as for the emphasis of their specific activities. As federal interests change over the years, so must COGs be able rapidly to adjust their staffs and priorities in an effort to maximize their chances in the competition for federal money.

The Intergovernmental Cooperation Act of 1968 contained a section that asserted the need to coordinate federally assisted programs and projects with area-wide comprehensive planning considerations as well as with state and local plans and programs. The Office of Management and Budget (OMB) was assigned the responsibility of implementing this government-wide review procedure, and in 1969, it issued the now famous Circular A-95, which outlined the review process in accordance with the following description:

> The circular sought to stimulate a network of state,
> regional, and metropolitan planning and development
> clearinghouses to receive and disseminate information
> about proposed projects, to coordinate between
> applicants for federal assistance, to act as a liaison
> between federal development projects, and to conduct
> an evaluation of the state, regional or metropolitan
> significance of federal or federally assisted
> projects. [12]

In theory, the A-95 procedures were designed to serve as a screen for comprehensive planning, but in practice the project-by-project review and comment process tends to preclude any initiatory role in comprehensive planning for the reviewers. Despite the development of the A-95 review process and its potential for giving teeth to COGs, most local applications have been approved routinely by COGs and without much criticism. Bollens and Schmandt have attributed this to two basic reasons: the ability of the COG and grant seeker to strike a bargain over areas of disagreement through informal talks before the application is officially submitted and the general lack of meaningful comprehensive regional plans among COGs. [13]

Another limitation to rigorously applying A-95 is that COGs are usually trying to build consensus through the volunteer approach, and, accordingly, cutting off certain communities from select grants could have detrimental political effects for the relevant COG. Moreover, since the review process allows COG members to review each other's grant requests, it would make little political sense to criticize harshly or deny a fellow member's grant application, especially if one's own application is pending.

With all their inherent limitations, what can the over 300 COGs in the United States hope to accomplish? Because COGs are voluntary organizations, they have proven to be politically palatable—much more feasible than other types of regional organizations and formal metropolitan governments. Usually they are easily created through state enabling legislation, a private organization, or some other similar formative device. Even such political barriers as state boundary lines have not proven to be insurmountable obstacles to the formation of a COG.

The structure of a COG also makes it a flexible device which can adjust to any changes in a metropolitan environment without going through numerous political hurdles such as legislative action, referenda, renegotiation of contracts, or interstate compacts. This flexibility is illustrated by the fact that several COGs have changed their names, structures, and membership bases as they have become more fully developed.[14] In addition, COGs have been able to foster a level of regional awareness among previously locally oriented officials. After advocates of local power have served for a while on a COG, they have often been imbued with an ardent spirit of regionalism.[15]

As has been mentioned, one of the major concerns of COGs is with regional planning, especially due to the impetus of the A-95 review process. As Schmandt commented: "COGs have played their most valuable role in formulating plans for land use, transportation, sewer and water facilities and the conservation of natural resources."[16] Despite the criticism of COGs' use of the A-95 review process, other advantages have been derived from its use. The A-95 process has worked to create a modest coordinating function in the local decision-making process that occurs before a government submits its grant application for official review. Indeed, Melvin B. Mogulof views the use of the A-95 procedures as the single most potentially powerful and widespread device available to affect the distribution of resources in a region according to a regional point of view.[17]

COGs also give technical assistance to members who might not otherwise be able to afford the services of a professional planner. This arrangement allows planners to work for a number of communities on a part-time basis. Previously, the costs of the planners' expertise would have been prohibitive for many of the smaller suburban communities. Thus, the community has access to a professional planner while the COG has a chance to establish a closer working relationship with the individual community and its planning board as well as to influence indirectly the community's plans toward regional objectives.

Certain COGs have also been able to provide their membership with economies of scale and other efficiencies inherent in the pooling of resources. COGs have helped to convince local governments to participate in such cooperative ventures as joint purchasing programs, data collection and information sharing for select services, and joint studies of specific problems.

Very few COGs have attempted to assume operational responsibilities for regional services as facilities. Usually COGs seem to be more comfortable in their roles of planning and policy making and avoid getting into the actual implementation of specific programs.

GREATER PORTLAND
COUNCIL OF GOVERNMENTS

The Portland metropolitan area is located in the Casco Bay area of Cumberland County, Maine. This is the largest and most densely populated county in the state, with a 1970 population of 192,528, which represented a 5.8 percent increase over the 1960 population. The county covers 886.1 square miles and is located approximately 100 miles north of Boston. [18] In 1970 the two largest cities of the area were Portland, with a population of 65,116, and South Portland, with a population of 23,267. Typical of many American cities, recent growth in the Portland area has been concentrated in the suburban municipalities that surround the core cities of Portland and South Portland. The Portland area is the largest New England metropolitan area north of Boston, with an estimated population of 227,300 in 1974. [19] The Portland SMSA also contains the major industries, transportation facilities, businesses, banks, maritime facilities, commercial fisheries, hotels, recreational areas, and education, cultural, and religious institutions in Cumberland County. The 20 other municipalities within the county vary in size and character, ranging from coastal, fishing, and farming towns and inland farming and residential towns to resort and lumbering towns in the Sebago Lake region in the northeastern sector of the county.

There is a mixture of local governmental forms in Cumberland County, including the selectman form with a town meeting, selectman-manager with a town meeting, council-manager, and mayor-council with a city administrator. By national standards, the county government is very weak, and its functions are mainly connected with the court system, the sheriff's office, and the county jail. The state government is very important in providing social services.

In Maine, the development of regional planning was primarily a reaction to the 1954 Federal Housing Act. In 1955, the Maine legislature passed enabling legislation that permitted cities and towns to form regional planning commissions. Most of the federal planning funds were directed toward the problems of urban areas, and in 1956 the Greater Portland Regional Planning Commission (GPRPC) became the first of its kind to organize in the state. The GPRPC was designed to develop comprehensive plans for the Portland region, but it had no real enforcement powers.

The GPRPC was somewhat successful in its endeavors. It produced a Policy Plan for Regional Development, which included an inventory of the area's various resources such as highways, airports, open space and recreational areas, solid waste disposal facilities, community-type facilities, and commercial and industrial land-use zones. However, a general sense of frustration developed due to certain inefficiencies of the GPRPC and its failure to establish any real relationship between planning and implementation. This need to close the gap between planning and implementation was a major rationale for involving locally elected officials in a more structured regional decision-making process. As the situation turned out, GPRPC itself was to have an important role in the formation of a COG in Portland.

Formation of the Greater Portland Council of Governments

The idea of a council of governments for the Greater Portland area was first publicly suggested by Maine's U. S. Senator Edmund S. Muskie in a conference with Falmouth town officials concerning a cleanup of the Presumpscot Estuary in June 1967.[20] Muskie suggested that a COG would help in achieving the cleanup as well as assisting with other area-wide problems. The possibility of establishing a COG was also raised at the 22d New England Managers Institute, which was held in August 1967 at the University of Maine at Orono. Richard C. Hartman, director of the National Regional Council, addressed the meeting and spoke enthusiastically about the COG concept. He stressed that the formation of a COG would satisfy the federal requirements of local involvement at the regional level and also would buy time for local governments that wanted to prevent further federal encroachment into the affairs of the small local units.[21]

A survey of local officials taken by the Portland Press Herald in September 1967 showed a highly favorable interest in the idea of creating a COG for the Portland area.[22] The local officials surveyed in the poll generally predicted that something of a regional nature was bound to come sooner or later, and they concluded that a COG would be a good start. The only opposition at this stage came from several small suburban towns that felt that the outlying communities would not benefit from area-wide planning.

The impetus for the formation of the GPCOG has been credited
to three key people: Portland bank president and Falmouth Council
Member Halsey Smith, Portland attorney Barnett Shur, and then
Falmouth Town Manager Osmond Bonsey. In February 1968 a dinner
meeting hosted by Smith's bank was held at the Portland campus of
the University of Maine and was attended by several officials from
12 area communities. Also participating in the session were the
University of Maine's Bureau of Public Administration, the Maine
Municipal Association, and the director of the National Association
of Regional Councils. The object of the session was to introduce the
concept of COG to local community officials. The municipal officials
were impressed by the concepts presented at the meeting, and they
agreed to have a second meeting in April at the Portland campus. [23]
The second meeting of the group was addressed by Muskie, who
urged that the communities seriously consider forming a COG to force
the federal government to take a more active role in mandating local
governments to cooperate in problems of a regional nature, if the
communities did not do so voluntarily. [24] Muskie was a well-liked and
respected politician, and those attending the meeting recognized his
expertise as chairman of the Senate's Subcommittee on Intergovernmental Relations. At this same meeting, there was established a
committee comprised of representatives of each community in the
area and the GPRPC to propose and approve bylaws for the proposed
organization. After these bylaws were approved, each community was
to adopt a "declaration of intent," if it wished to become a member
of the COG. The bylaws were accepted on October 17, 1968, and the
GPCOG was officially established under the sponsorship of GPRPC
on November 13, 1968. [25] A total of ten communities finally decided
to join GPCOG, which at the time of its inception was only the second
COG in New England. [26]

Ironically, the regional planning commission, which had been
the source of many complaints from local officials, became actively
involved in helping to form the new council by lending office space
and contributing money for the initial planning. At first the new
council was called the Greater Portland Regional Planning Commission
and Council of Governments. However, by January 1, 1970, when
the enabling legislation became effective, the planning commission's
legal status and assets were turned over to the council, which was
renamed the Greater Portland Council of Governments. The planning
commission was transformed into a committee for the council, but
that too was soon dissolved. This dissolution of the regional planning
commission caused considerable anguish and contention between the
supporters of the commission and those of the proposed COG, with
the former losing out in the end. [27]

The formation of the GPCOG was by no means devoid of politics. However, it was a rather restricted form of interest-group conflict and cooperation that only rarely is seen in the public arena. Interested and knowledgeable local officials simply succeeded in convincing each other that the GPCOG was an improvement over the GPRPC, that it would provide them with a useful vehicle for discussion and cooperation, and that it represented a possible insurance policy against further federal pressures for regional government.

Organizational Structure of GPCOG

The full GPCOG jurisdiction extends to the 22 municipalities that comprise the Cumberland Planning and Development District, which includes most of the Portland SMSA and Cumberland County. The current dues-paying members are the county and 18 eligible communities. Other ex-officio members include the People's Regional Opportunity Program, the Cumberland County Soil and Water Conservation District, and the Portland Water District.

GPCOG's purposes were defined as fostering cooperative efforts in considering problems, formulating appropriate policies, and developing plans that involved more than one community. To achieve these purposes, GPCOG operates as a forum to identify, discuss, and study regional challenges and opportunities, provides the organizational machinery to make possible effective communication and coordination among the area's governments and governmental agencies, provides a mechanism for the preparation, maintenance, and distribution of regional plans, maintains liaison with members and their governmental units, and speaks out with a single, united voice in the areas where the membership agrees to such a role. [28]

GPCOG is composed of two major bodies—a general assembly and an executive committee. As in most COGs, the general assembly is the legal policy-making body for the COG, but the de facto policy-making body is the executive committee. Each member government has at least two representatives on the assembly and an additional representative for each 10,000 persons or fraction thereof as determined by the last U. S. census. State legislation stipulates that "at least half of the representatives of each member shall be municipal officers." [29] The general assembly meets annually in April to adopt formally the budget and membership fee schedule and to establish guidelines for the executive committee. [30]

The president of the assembly, who is elected by the membership, automatically becomes chairperson of the executive committee. The executive committee is composed of one elected official from each of the member towns, the chairperson of the GPCOG planning

committee, and a Cumberland County commissioner. There also are
provisions to include nonvoting ex-officio members such as representatives of the county conservation district, the water district, and
the low-income segment of the county. [31] The executive committee,
which meets at least monthly, has the power to propose annual budget
and fee schedules; to appoint special committees; to appoint, fix the
salaries of, and remove staff; to consider and recommend action on
regional policies, studies, and plans; to render technical assistance
on the request of a member government; and to afford such technical
assistance on a fee basis to any nonmember government of Cumberland
County. The GPCOG also has several standing committees dealing
with such matters as land-use planning, environmental improvement,
intergovernmental relations, criminal justice, housing, and water
quality planning.

      The current executive director of GPCOG, Osmond Bonsey, is
the third director to work for the council, the first having taken
another job in 1970 and the second apparently having been fired,
according to newspaper accounts in 1973. Bonsey began work in early
1974, after serving several years as the town manager of Falmouth.
In addition to the executive director, there are currently 24 other
GPCOG employees, including planners, administrators, secretaries,
and grant coordinators. The size of the staff, of course, varies
according to the GPCOG's utilization of specific federal grants.
Currently, GPCOG has a director/coordinator for transportation, a
criminal justice coordinator, an assistant director of finance and
program development, a director of planning, and a director of
area-wide water quality planning. These administrators act as
program managers of their specific policy areas.

Building a Record

      The record of GPCOG has developed rather slowly since the
official inception of the organization in 1968. By November 1969, the
membership finally reached an agreement about how their dues would
be assessed. The agreement was based on a formula that considered
evaluation, tax effort, and population. Equipped with a financial base
and formalized by enabling legislation, GPCOG was finally ready in
1970 to become an active council.

      The charter members had high expectations for the infant
organization, and most elected local officials had their own ideas as
to what the priorities of GPCOG should be. Some preferred to
emphasize joint purchasing, police communications systems, and
canine control, while others wanted to stress service activities in
the public works area. At times, GPCOG's new executive committee
seemed euphoric about the multitude of activities that awaited the

council's approval. Once the dues formula was accepted, committee members spoke glowingly of becoming involved in such numerous and varied activities as housing, law enforcement, solid waste disposal, data processing, zoning, mass transit, canine control, air pollution, and site selection. [32] At this point, many observers in effect expected GPCOG to perform as a formal metropolitan government, which, of course, was legally and politically impossible.

What seemed like an auspicious beginning did not develop as the membership had hoped. Almost as soon as members left the table of their organizational meeting, in-fighting began. As John Menario, the former city manager of Portland, recalls, there was bickering about financing, about who would be president, and about where the office would be located: "COG needed an accomplishment to demonstrate its value. But the first several years, instead of solving problems, it created problems."[33]

Some members were upset about the abuse and eventual elimination of the GPRPC, others were concerned about the rapid growth of GPCOG's staff, which seemed to be publishing massive studies while ignoring the needs of its membership, and still others felt the executive committee was virtually dysfunctional because so few members were attending its sessions. [34] The criticism about the large number of studies is consistent with the earlier criticism of the GPRPC. In the period between 1970 and 1972, GPCOG produced over 20 studies, reports, model ordinances, and model regulations. In spite of the plethora of written materials, many local officials in the Portland area either seem unfamiliar with this research or view it as useless and not related to achieving desired results. GPCOG reports on regional data-processing centers, central records-keeping facilities, environmental improvement, sign controls, transportation, recreation, public works, mobile homes, canine control, and air pollution, to mention only a few, were published and then largely forgotten.

One might assume that the previously mentioned A-95 review process could provide GPCOG with the teeth needed to conduct a successful regional planning process. However, it has been estimated that GPCOG receives about one state or federal grant request per day for review. Rarely has GPCOG really critically reviewed any grant or loan application. It simply does not have the time, money, or staff to take a hard look at each application. In 1975, for example, the Department of Housing and Urban Development (HUD) gave GPCOG $3,000 for the review process. The director and staff accept the grant proposals and claim that "we ruffle them quick like" before sending them along. [35] The current executive director believes that HUD must tacitly agree with the process because the agency has never demanded a more intensive review process from the council than that

FIGURE 7.1

Greater Portland Council of Governments,
Revenues and Expenditures

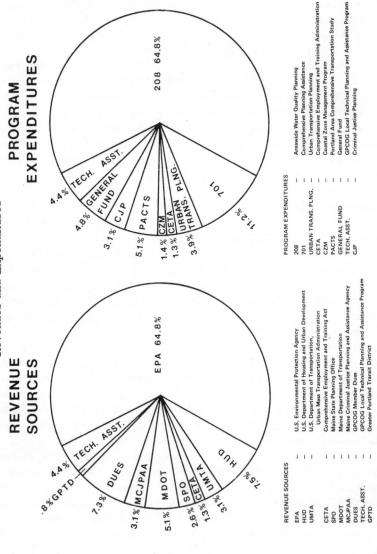

REVENUE SOURCES

PROGRAM EXPENDITURES

REVENUE SOURCES

EPA	–	U.S. Environmental Protection Agency
HUD	–	U.S. Department of Housing and Urban Development
UMTA	–	U.S. Department of Transportation, Urban Mass Transportation Administration
CETA	–	Comprehensive Employment and Training Act
SPO	–	Maine State Planning Office
MDOT	–	Maine Department of Transportation
MCJPAA	–	Maine Criminal Justice Planning and Assistance Agency
DUES	–	GPCOG Member Dues
TECH. ASST.	–	GPCOG Local Technical Planning and Assistance Program
GPTD	–	Greater Portland Transit District

PROGRAM EXPENDITURES

208	–	Areawide Water Quality Planning
701	–	Comprehensive Planning Assistance
URBAN TRANS. PLNG.	–	Urban Transportation Planning
CETA	–	Comprehensive Employment and Training Administration
CZM	–	Coastal Zone Management Program
PACTS	–	Portland Area Comprehensive Transportation Study
GENERAL FUND	–	General Fund
TECH. ASST.	–	GPCOG Local Technical Planning and Assistance Program
CJP	–	Criminal Justice Planning

Source: Greater Portland Council of Government.

168

which is conducted. Thus, GPCOG seems basically satisfied with its review, or nonreview, process, which is based on a philosophy that clearly contradicts the intentions of the A-95 review process.

While the GPCOG budget for fiscal year 1976 was $792,015, membership dues were only $58,031, or 7 percent of the total budget. Over $33,000 of the local dues were used as matching funds for two major programs—HUD 701 and Coastal Zone Management Planning. Federal money for GPCOG was estimated to be $606,817, or about 70 percent, and state funding was $86,031, or 11 percent. Local funds other than dues consist of $6,200 from the Greater Portland Transit District and $34,936 from technical planning assistance fees. [36] (See Figure 7.1 for a more specific breakdown of revenues and expenditures.)

The major program expenditure was for the Water Quality Planning Program funded by the U.S. Environmental Protection Agency for a two-year period at $770,000. The Comprehensive Planning Assistance Program (701) received increased support from HUD, primarily to support two new major requirements in the program—land-use planning and housing planning.

A very tangible benefit for most COG members is the savings that have been derived from joint purchases. For example, for a number of years, members have pooled their money to buy rock salt. During the first year of the pool, members saved up to $3 per ton in a total purchase of 17,000 tons. It has been estimated that savings from the salt purchase have equaled the local dues paid to the COG. While attempts have been made to broaden the joint purchasing concept, success has been rather limited. Members have made joint purchases of small items such as fire fighting equipment and a pavement stripe-marking machine, and two communities bought their police cruisers together. However, more systematic efforts at joint purchasing, such as the standardization of police patrol cars, have failed. Moreover, the city of Portland has its own purchasing department and does not participate in the joint purchasing arrangement.

As with COGs elsewhere, most of the activities of GPCOG involve providing technical assistance to the smaller suburban communities. Many of these communities never had the services of a planner before GPCOG developed a uniform approach to planning services, which provides for some consistency while still allowing for local variations. A standardized methodology for collecting land-use information, soils analysis data, zoning data, and other types of information has been developed. Special assistance from GPCOG has helped communities comply with state and federal guidelines for shoreland zoning, solid waste disposal, and flood insurance regulations. [37]

Since 1973 technical assistance planning has also been provided to the Greater Portland Transportation District (GPTD). Although

the district is responsible for carrying out program activities,
GPCOG has prepared grant applications, conducted special studies.
and provided a degree of regional transportation coordination. [38]

Thus, the pattern remains fairly constant regardless of the
specific policy area in which GPCOG is involved. The emphasis is
on regional planning and attempts at formulating regional policies
for the various functional areas—housing and development, criminal
justice, health, and human services. GPCOG seems to cherish its
role of providing research assistance, advice, and recommendations
while attempting to coordinate regional planning in the metropolitan
area.

In the case of GPCOG, it seems rather unlikely that the Maine
legislature will expand its authority in the near future. The demand
for a more potent COG that would have greater authority and could
be transformed into a legal metropolitan government simply does not
exist. Indeed, as has been noted earlier, part of the basis for the
local support for the creation of GPCOG was the desire to resist
further federal encroachment and to increase the capabilities of
the local governments. A dominant theme of COG advocates (both in
Maine and nationwide) was "regionalism is local power." Local
officials seem to regard COG as an experiment in cooperation, but
certainly not as a future replacement of their own political and
administrative responsibilities.

It is ironic to note that in the GPCOG enabling legislation, there
is a provision that stipulates: "The council may . . . exercise such
other powers as are exercised or capable of exercise separately or
jointly by the member governments."[39] It is unlikely that local
governments will exercise their rights as stated above because of the
many local differences that still prevail. The bylaws of GPCOG
seem to limit the COG's role more than does the enabling act itself.
The bylaws state that the goal of GPCOG is "to strengthen local self-
government while combining total resources for meeting regional
challenges beyond our individual capacities."[40] Implicit in this
statement is the belief that regional action should be taken only after
local efforts have failed. This would seem to preclude any real,
comprehensive effort to attempt to resolve a problem before it
reaches the crisis stage and to confine the COG to the role of "plugging
up the holes" in the present methods of handling metropolitan
problems.

NOTES

1. Royce Hanson, Metropolitan Councils of Governments
(Washington, D. C.: Advisory Commission on Intergovernmental
Relations, 1966), p. IV.

2. John C. Bollens and Henry J. Schmandt, The Metropolis: Its People, Politics, and Economic Life (New York: Harper & Row, 1975), p. 304.

3. B. Douglas Harmon, "Councils of Governments and Metropolitan Decision Making," in 1969 Municipal Yearbook (Washington, D. C.: International City Management Association, 1969), p. 10.

4. Melvin Mogulof, Governing Metropolitan Areas (Washington, D. C.: Urban Institute, 1971), pp. 31-33.

5. Joseph F. Zimmerman, Subnational Politics (New York: Holt, Rinehart and Winston, 1970), p. 434.

6. Hanson, op. cit., p. 18.

7. John J. Harrigan, Political Change in the Metropolis (Boston: Little, Brown, 1976), p. 12.

8. William Coleman, "What Is the Role of Regional Councils?," Speech to workshop on local intergovernmental cooperation, New Orleans, July 1966.

9. Hanson, op. cit., p. 7.

10. Henry J. Schmandt, "Intergovernmental Volunteerism: Pro and Con," in The Regionalist Papers, ed. Kent Mathewson (Detroit: Metropolitan Fund, 1975), p. 156.

11. Ibid., p. 152.

12. Mogulof, op. cit., p. 6.

13. Bollens and Schmandt, op. cit., p. 306.

14. Hanson, op. cit., p. 16.

15. Schmandt, op. cit., p. 156.

16. Ibid., p. 154.

17. Melvin B. Mogulof, "Metropolitan Councils of Governments and the Federal Government," Urban Affairs Quarterly 7 (June 1972): 492.

18. State of Maine, Department of Economic Development, 1971 Pocket Data Book (Augusta: DED, 1971).

19. Statistical Abstract of the United States, 1976, U. S. Department of Commerce, Bureau of Census (Washington, D. C.: Government Printing Office, 1976), p. 909.

20. Portland Evening Express, June 27, 1967.

21. Ibid., August 27, 1967.

22. Ibid., September 19, 1967.

23. "Officials Support Formation of Regional Councils," Portland Press Herald, March 1, 1968, p. 12.

24. Portland Press Herald, April 17, 1968.

25. Greater Portland Council of Governments, Bylaws, March 23, 1972 (Portland: GPCOG, 1972).

26. "Regional Council Faces Vital Test in 1970," Maine Sunday Telegram, December 14, 1969, p. 18A.

27. "Community Leaders Seen Key to COG's Future," Portland Press Herald, December 21, 1970, p. 14.

28. Greater Portland Council of Governments, Bylaws, March 23, 1972 (Portland: GPCOG, 1972), p. 1.

29. Title 30, M. R. S. A. , section 1982.

30. Greater Portland Council of Governments, Bylaws, June 1, 1974, pp. 1–12.

31. Ibid.

32. "Communities to Get Word on Regional Council Levy," Portland Press Herald, November 18, 1969, p. 15.

33. Interview with John Menario, city manager of Portland, November, 1975.

34. "Regional Council Faces Test in 1970," Maine Sunday Telegram, December 14, 1969.

35. Interview of Osmond Bonsey, executive director of GPCOG, in South Portland, October 1975.

36. Greater Portland Council of Governments, Annual Report, 1976, p. 39.

37. Greater Portland Council of Governments, Annual Report, 1975, pp. 17–18.

38. Ibid. , p. 29.

39. Title 30, M. R. S. A. , Section 1983, (2).

40. Greater Portland Council of Governments, Bylaws, June 1, 1974.

CHAPTER

8

MINNEAPOLIS-ST. PAUL:
THE TWIN CITIES
REGION APPROACH

BACKGROUND

The Twin Cities region of Minneapolis–St. Paul is the largest
and most politically fragmented area to be organized in America during
this century along the lines of a metropolitan government concept.[1]
This analysis will focus on the creation and development of the metropolitan council, which serves an area encompassing 3,000 square
miles and about 1,865,000 people. It is comprised of seven counties:
Hennepin, Ramsey, Anoka, Dakota, Washington, Scott, and Carver;
two major cities, Minneapolis and St. Paul; and approximately 290
other units of government. Among the latter group are 25 cities,
105 villages, 68 townships, 77 school districts, and 20 special service
districts.

Problems of a metropolitan nature had arisen for the
usual reasons: an expanding population, relocations of populations,
scattered and uncontrolled growth, and the accompanying need for
services such as sewers, waste disposal, housing, and transportation.
Unlike many metropolitan areas, however, this area had no great
disparity between the central cities and the suburbs. By the time
it was recognized that some problems would have to be dealt
with from a metropolitan perspective, there was almost an even
balance between the central cities and the suburban areas, both in
population and in property valuation. The practical effect of this
balance was that neither could clearly dominate the other.[2] The
Twin Cities area was also extremely important to the state economy
as a whole since it contained approximately half of the state's total
population and more than half of its wealth. What disparities there
were in the region tended to be between the individual suburbs.

173

There was also a history of rivalry between Minneapolis and
St. Paul that was of long duration. Although separated by only 11
miles, Minneapolis had become oriented toward the West and served
as a post for trade and settlement of the western lands. On the other
hand, St. Paul was eastern oriented, being tied to the heavily settled
Midwest and East coast. The Twin Cities area is blessed with
considerable diversity in its economic base. There is a solid group
of well-known, stable industries that are quite well distributed among
the cities and the suburbs. In addition there is a major university,
the University of Minnesota, and a large medical center affiliated
with the university.

Overall, the population of the Twin Cities region is remarkably
homogeneous. Minority groups represent only a little over 2 percent
of the total population. Of this 2 percent, about 1. 4 percent are black,
0. 5 percent are Indian, and the remainer are primarily Spanish
American. This is approximately the same proportion as exists in the
state as a whole, and accordingly, there tends to be little cultural
cleavage or clash between the metropolitan area and the rest of the
state. As compared with other cities in the United States, there is
relatively little unemployment, and incomes are comparatively high.

The political culture of the Twin Cities area is best described
as one of high citizen participation and "good government." Although
Minnesota is a competitive two-party state, both state and local
elections are usually nonpartisan. There is "high respect for government and politics as a field of human endeavor and widespread public
support and participation."[3] There have been few problems with the
governmental structure itself or with its operations and activities.
This is reflected in the fact that regional problems were not seen as
the result of incompetent government or a bad system, but rather
were simply viewed as being beyond the capability of any one governmental unit to handle. The opinion of the general public that existing
agencies were doing their assigned tasks with considerable competence
was to have a significant impact on the future structure of the
metropolitan reform. [4]

The governmental system in Minnesota tends to be dominated
by the legislative bodies. The state government is dominated in many
respects by a strong state legislature, which legally maintains rather
tight control over local governmental units. [5] The legislature
generally has played a passive role, however, when it comes to initiating local policy issues. Prior to World War II, the combined
population of the core cities constituted about 90 percent of the population of the total region, but since the 1950s there has been tremendous growth in the surrounding areas. The suburbs have grown by
nearly 72 percent as compared with approximately 53 percent for the
central cities. In attempting to cope with this expansion, there was a

proliferation of governmental units. As some have argued: "The
metropolitan problem is the inability of government to make
necessary decisions about area-wide development as a consequence
of the high degree of political fragmentation in our metropolitan
areas. "6

There were three main reasons why the existing local governments were unable to handle metropolitan problems in the Twin Cities
region. First, there were the extended problems that tended to have
a spillover effect on other jurisdictions. For example, water
pollution would need to be handled on a cooperative basis. Secondly,
solutions could be very costly and beyond the means of a single
governmental unit. A third reason was that no single unit possessed
the authority to make the decisions necessary for the entire
metropolitan area. 7 Traditionally, the counties in Minnesota have been
weak governments. Compared with those in other states, they possess
few powers and often do not utilize those they do possess. They are
characterized as "essentially administrative agencies of the state. "8
It is interesting to note that after the establishment of the metropolitan
council, this role began to change, particularly in Hennepin County.

THE POLITICS OF ACCEPTANCE

The questions of why and how governmental change occurs in
a particular metropolitan area are not only interesting and important
questions for the purpose of analyzing the specific case under
consideration but also are vital to any attempt to determine what, if
any, elements of the alteration might be replicated in other
metropolitan areas where reform is needed and desired. While no
two situations are ever exactly alike, there are often areas of
similarity where certain generalizations can be applied. In the case
of the Twin Cities area, the reasons for the structural change were
rooted both in past history and in several current issues, which
served as the catalytic forces. The history of the area had emphasized
good government, and reform was a positive attitude, not a response
to negative feelings about government. As early as 1933, signs of
movement toward regional planning occurred with the creation of the
Minneapolis-St. Paul Sanitary District, and ten years later, in 1943,
a Metropolitan Airports Commission was formed. Another decade
passed, and in 1953, Clarence C. Ludwig, executive director of
the League of Minnesota Municipalities, began to lobby for the creation
of a metropolitan planning commission. Although a bill to this effect
was defeated in both the 1953 and the 1955 legislatures, it passed in
1957. The Metropolitan Planning Commission (MPC) was charged with
making "plans for the physical, social, and economic development
of the metropolitan area with the general purpose of guiding and

accomplishing coordinated and harmonious development of the area. "9
The work of the MPC was to culminate in a "metropolitan guide."
This plan was issued just after the formation of the metropolitan
council but was not endorsed by it. One should note that the MPC
had only advisory powers, and this greatly impeded its ability to
implement its plans. It could only promote cooperation through its
limited powers of persuasion, and, accordingly, its success depended
on good communications and public relations. Understandably, this
system simply could not function in an atmosphere of conflict.

There were certain obstacles to reorganization. Minnesota had
a home rule law that necessitated a referendum on any law that
affected local government. The traditions of good government and
citizen participation required political accountability for all governing
bodies or any other groups engaged in making policy decisions. This
requirement could be satisfied by making all decision-making bodies
elected agencies, but this in turn would mean, essentially, the
creation of additional units of government. As in most areas, there
was in the Twin Cities region a suspicion of big government, centering
mostly around the issues of personalized services and access to
decision makers. These issues were very important to a population
that valued high citizen participation.

There were also certain legal and constitutional problems that
had to be resolved. The most critical issue that focused attention on
reorganization was that of sewers. In 1959, the State Department of
Health found that 47.5 percent of water wells in suburban communities showed serious contamination of ground water. Over 250,000
people "were drawing water from the same soil formations that
sewage was being discharged into."10 The wells were being
contaminated by nitrates recirculating from backyard septic tanks.
As a result of this finding, the Federal Housing Authority directed
that no more home loans be issued until a central water system was
developed. The first solutions proposed centered mainly on the
sewer and water problems. The MPC recommended that a state
agency should collaborate with local government on service and
prepare a plan for the area's future needs. Another special report,
the Robbie report, recommended that a single multipurpose agency
should assume responsibility for problems of the entire area. As far
as sewers were concerned, the MPC, the Minneapolis-St. Paul
Sewer District (MSSD), and most of the suburban communities agreed
on the need for a metropolitan-wide system. 11

A bill for a metropolitan sanitary district was defeated in the
state legislature in both 1961 and 1963. Opposition to the idea arose
for the usual reasons. There was concern over the establishment of
another level of government and over the possible loss of local
autonomy. Most important, however, was the fear of Minneapolis

and St. Paul that they would end up paying for the problems of the
suburbs. After all, they already had a sewer system, and why should
they pay more to help build one for the suburbs? This hostility toward
the sewer district proposal continued for three years with little being
accomplished. In 1961, Governor Elmer Andersen initiated a
conference to debate metropolitan problems, but nothing substantive
materialized from the discussions. In 1964, two events occurred
that significantly contributed to a renewal of the debate. The town
of New Hope wished to tie in with the MSSD on a contract basis, but
MSSD refused. New Hope then made plans to build its own plant,
which, if implemented, would have caused the effluent to go into
streams that ran through Minneapolis's parks. New Hope eventually
got its contract but at a very high price. An appeal to the state
legislature barred municipalities from profiting from the selling of
services. This ruling, of course, increased the already tense
relationships, but it also highlighted the need for a workable solution.
A second major factor that contributed to the movement toward
structural reorganization was the direction provided by the Hennepin
County League of Municipalities. Led by President Milton Honsey,
the league argued for a more permanent solution on a metropolitan level
rather than merely on the county level. The Honsey-Bergstrom
report provided both a catalyst for thinking in metropolitan terms
and a specific document around which to rally support.

There were also four elements whose convergence at approximately the same time proved critical for metropolitan reorganization.
The first was legislative reapportionment. Extreme malapportionment
existed in Minnesota, with the Twin Cities area itself being greatly
underrepresented. Court-ordered reapportionment improved this
situation somewhat, but this was done in 1965 and was based on the
1960 census, which did not take into account the increase in the
population of the area. Another significant event was a special
census of the Twin Cities areas and suburbs that was taken in 1965
and that created pressure for an even more extensive reapportionment
in 1967. A third element that seemed to facilitate reorganization was
the passage of the federal Demonstration Cities and Metropolitan
Development Act of 1966. The MPC did not possess the powers for
the planning and review functions required by this federal law, and
this fact probably helped to motivate the state legislature into taking
some appropriate actions in order that federal assistance would be
available. A fourth factor contributing to the reorganization was the
elimination of home rule. Minnesota had long had a home rule law,
but just before the bill for a metropolitan council went to the legislature, the law was rescinded. Accordingly, a local referendum was no
longer required for reorganization. [12]

Overall, there was little organized opposition to the idea of
a metropolitan council. One reason for this was that most people
agreed that something needed to be done. Another advantage for the
proponents of the idea was that there was no pressure for a comprehensive consolidation type of metropolitan government. Instead,
there developed out of the discussions over the sewer system something of a consensus with which to work as the boundaries of the
debate were drawn. This consensus resulted from an "informal
coalition of various groups and individuals which was conspicuous in
its lack of centralized leadership and strategy. " It served to transform
general feelings "into a precise statement of desires representing
virtually all elements of the metropolitan community. "[13] It is
important to remember that since the state legislature was dominated
by rural and out- of-state interests (reapportionment had not yet
fully taken place), a degree of unity was needed to spur it into action.
It was felt that a consensus would "give a sense of urgency to
metropolitan demands and create momentum to force the legislature
to act; it could modify demands, but it could not deny them. "[14]

The metropolitan reorganization movement was certainly not
one of grass-roots origins, but it was characterized by high participation among those who had an awareness of metropolitan problems.
The Citizens League was extremely influential in developing a
favorable climate of opinion toward metropolitan-wide institutions.
The Citizens League is a nonpartisan, good-government group with
a long history of positive and respected action. Its leadership
represented a cross-section of the metropolitan communities.

Another extremely important factor in developing the consensus
was the role of the MPC. First, the MPC strove to educate the
populace of the Twin Cities area, and its endeavors in this regard
were primarily responsible for the changed attitude toward metropolitan-wide planning. Moreover, the MPC focused on the process
of development and the manner by which decision making would
occur within a metropolitan framework. The MPC also produced a
series of proposals on metropolitan governmental organization.
There is no question that the activities of the MPC had a major
impact on the development of a favorable climate of opinion, but the
fact that it lacked legal powers emphasized the need for the creation
of a body that would be capable of developing and implementing
appropriate plans.[15]

Other major participants in the drive for metropolitan reorganization were the Metropolitan Section of the League of Minnesota
Municipalities, which was the semiofficial voice of local government
officials, and the County Leagues of Municipalities and Local Officials.
Both major political parties strongly endorsed metropolitan government, and the matter even became an issue in the 1966 gubernatorial

election. In addition, the League of Women Voters contributed an
educational program for the general public. Very significantly,
both city, and most suburban, newspapers supported the metropolitan
government concept, and they provided thorough coverage of the
various discussions. The business community also actively supported
the idea of reorganization, and the various Chambers of Commerce
put together an Urban Study and Action Committee. The business
community, of course, was concerned with growth and development
in terms of its own interests. Their rationale was that metropolitan-
wide planning and enforcement would help minimize risks and increase
services.

The opposition was never very significant in its impact. It
was extremely late in forming and remained weak and almost totally
ineffective. As was mentioned earlier, a general consensus developed
at an early stage and its momentum tended to force the opposition to
be reactive and negative. Indeed, the opposition itself agreed that
some type of solution was necessary; they simply disagreed with the
form being proposed. County officials were inclined to be opposed
because of their fear of losing some of their power, which was
already quite minor. Led by the suburb of Bloomington, a few of the
wealthy and rapidly developing outer-ring suburbs objected because
they feared that they would be forced to support the development of
other areas. The Suburban Sun newspapers were also vocal in their
opposition, mainly for the same reason.

There was one other interesting event that contributed to the
changes that were eventually to occur. Briefly, in 1964, a utility
revealed its plan to build an electric power facility with an 800-foot
smoke stack. An intense debate ensued over the location of the smoke
stack, and, out of this debate, conclusions emerged that proved to
be extremely important to the governmental structure that ultimately
was decided upon. The first was that municipal tax base considerations could defeat any effort to plan land uses in an orderly manner
since there was considerable economic competition between the
municipalities for tax purposes. Secondly, the MPC, or any other
body composed of representatives from local governmental units,
could not effectively handle an issue where serious conflict resulted.[16]

THE NEW SYSTEM

The consensus that developed during the period from 1965 to
1967 was for an area-wide governmental body to handle such issues
as sewer works, open space, transit, airports, and a zoo. One of
the major reasons for the decision to concentrate on these areas was
the fact that the "functions which they had identified had never been
handled (and were not then sought) by municipalities individually."[17]

This is not to say that these services were not being performed, but
rather, that they were under the jurisdiction of special-purpose
districts. In other words, functions would not be taken away from
municipalities but would be coordinated by a central agency.

By 1967, the consensus group was ready to present its position
to the legislature. Initially, there were four separate bills, but
because of their differences and similarities, it is possible to consider them as two major alternatives. The Ogdhal-Frenzel bill
represented essentially the consensus position described above. The
bill called for an elected council that would have planning and operating
control of regional functions. Senator Gordon Rosenmeier, who was a
dominant figure in the legislature at the time, felt that the legislature
should be more involved, and, accordingly, he was instrumental in
developing the alternate plan for metropolitan reorganization.
Rosenmeier's so-called state solution mandated creation of a small
council that would be appointed at large by the governor and would
be responsible for planning and coordinating the operation of the
existing regional state agencies or any future agencies that might be
created. Both this bill, which was labeled the Newcome-Ashbach
bill, and the previously cited Ogdahl-Frenzel bill would cover only
those districts created by the state legislature in separate acts. The
council would not be able, for example, to set up a transit district.
The main differences between the bills were over elections and
whether or not the council would be an operating or coordinating
body.

Due largely to his political influence, Rosenmeier's concept
was the one that prevailed. Support was bipartisan in nature. The
house passed the Newcome-Ashbach bill 103 to 20, and the senate
approved it 46 to 18. A last-minute amendment to make the council
elective failed by an extremely narrow margin—66 to 62 in the house
and 33 to 33 in the senate.[18] The bill was signed by the governor and
went into effect.

Shortly thereafter, the attorney general ruled that the metropolitan council was "neither an agency of state government nor an
agency of local government, but a new unique agency lying somewhere
between possessing some of the powers and characteristics of
each."[19] It can be classified as a metropolitan government because
it is comprised solely of area representatives, and it is concerned
only with area-wide interests, decisions, services, and needs. Moreover, the council is empowered to levy an area ad valorem tax to
finance its operations. It can also be viewed as a state agency, since
the governor appoints the representatives who comprise the council.
The legislature also assigns the council its powers, controls its
finances, determines its structure, and requires it to submit reports.
In the Minnesota tradition, the council is a fairly strong legislative

FIGURE 8.1

Metropolitan Council of the Twin Cities Area

1 SPRING PARK
2 ORONO
3 MINNETONKA BEACH
4 TONKA BAY
5 EXCELSIOR
6 GREENWOOD
7 WOODLAND
8 MEDICINE LAKE
9 VICTORIA
10 ROBBINSDALE
11 SPRING LAKE PARK
12 U. S. GOVT
13 HILLTOP
14 COLUMBIA HEIGHTS
15 ST. ANTHONY
16 LAUDERDALE
17 FALCON HEIGHTS
18 MENDOTA
19 LILYDALE
20 GREY CLOUD
21 LANDFALL
22 DELLWOOD
23 PINE SPRINGS
24 MAHTOMEDI
25 GEM LAKE
26 BIRCHWOOD
27 WHITE BEAR
28 BAYPORT
29 WILLERNIE
30 OAK PARK HEIGHTS
31 LAKELAND SHORES
32 ST. MARY'S POINT

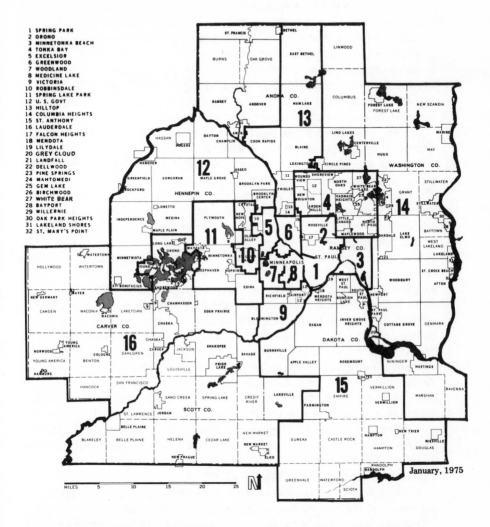

January, 1975

The Council members and their districts are as follows: Chairman - John Boland, North St. Paul

1 - John J. Costello,
      St. Paul
2 - Todd J. Lefko,
      St. Paul
3 - Charles L. Rafferty,
      St. Paul
4 - Stanley B. Kegler,
      Maplewood

5 - E. Peter Gillette, Jr.,
      Minneapolis
6 - Joan Campbell,
      Minneapolis
7 - Gladys S. Brooks,
      Minneapolis
8 - Alton J. Gasper,
      Minneapolis

9 - Robert L. Hoffman,
      Bloomington
10 - Alice Kreber,
       Crystal
11 - Robert Short,
       Edina
12 - Charles R. Weaver,
       Anoka

13 - Marcia Bennett,
       Columbia Heights
14 - Opal M. Petersen,
       Stillwater
15 - Paul A. Thuet, Jr.,
       West St. Paul
16 - Kingsley H. Murphy, Jr.,
       Orono

Source: Metropolitan Council of the Twin Cities Area,
January 1975.

181

body that could easily become elective at a future time, although thus far all attempts to make it so have failed.

Another point that should be mentioned is that the council does not really constitute a two-tier system as many experts advised. It is more nearly a three-tier system since the county governments are beginning to provide more services. The transfer of services to the county level has occurred primarily in Hennepin County and has involved such functions as the court system and the welfare system. Other local governments such as municipalities, of course, continue to deliver their traditional services.

The council itself is composed of 16 members, all of whom are appointed by the governor for overlapping six-year terms on the basis of a combination of two senatorial districts of equal population size. Each member represents approximately 100,000 persons. The chairman is selected at large and serves at the governor's will. The districts and their boundaries are depicted in Figure 8.1. The council's powers are mostly of a coordinating nature. Specifically, it is directed to perform three functions. First, it must review all metropolitan plans and projects of special districts, including independent commissions, boards, and agencies. It may indefinitely suspend, in total or in part, any project that it finds (within 60 days of its submission) to be inconsistent with its development guidelines. Second, it reviews and comments on long-term municipal comprehensive plans and any other matter that may have a substantial effect on metropolitan area development. The council alone determines whether a plan has "a metropolitan effect," which can be a rather thorny question. Local plans are not subject to veto, and if one local unit objects to the plans of another unit, the council may hold hearings and mediate any differences. Third, the council performs an advisory evaluation, through the A-95 review process, of applications for federal grants emanating from local governments, boards, or agencies. In addition, open space land acquisition funds require unqualified approval or disapproval. [20]

The primary purpose of the metropolitan council is to plan policies and not to become an operating agency. This distinction is extremely important because of the willingness to move toward regional planning but not toward program operations. Although the council is not an implementing body, it is in actuality responsible for numerous operations. To help carry out this responsibility, there are numerous policy boards and advisory committees. By September 1975, the council had been divided into four committees of seven members each: (1) the Human Resources Committee, (2) the Physical Development Committee, (3) the Personnel and Work Program Committee, and (4) the Environmental and Transportation Committee. There are also three metropolitan commissions that are legally

FIGURE 8.2 Organization of Twin Cities Approach

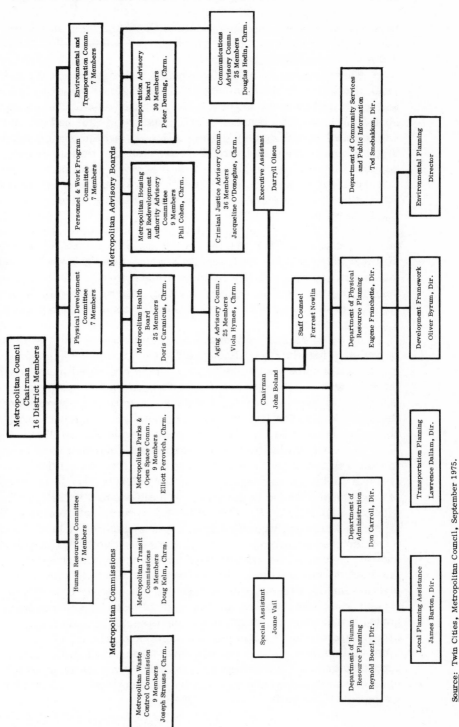

Source: Twin Cities, Metropolitan Council, September 1975.

183

separate but nonetheless subordinate to the council and six metropolitan advisory boards, which aid in policy planning. (See Figure
8. 2 for the detailed organization.)

There was some initial controversy between the council and
local officials over the membership of the regional operating board
as a consequence of the latter's belief that they should also be represented on the various boards. The legislature in 1969 had set up the
sewer board to include only private citizens, and the council followed
this model with the park board because it felt that private citizens would
be more metropolitan in their outlook than would local officials and
also would have more time to devote to board activities. The advisory
committees, on the other hand, consisted of both private citizens
and local officials.

The activities of the council are implemented through a series
of regional agencies that are legally separate from the council but
still subordinate to it. Each separate agency owns its own facilities
and is charged with actually carrying out its program. Although the
relationship varies from agency to agency, the prototype is the sewer
board, whose members are appointed by the council and represent
specific geographic areas.

As noted earlier, any new metropolitan agency must be created
by the state legislature. Although all such agencies must conform to
the council's plans and policies, they can be organized in any one of
three basic ways: as a program of state government on a seven-
county basis, as a new agency for the seven-county area, or as a
region-wide effort of local units. The council also appoints one
nonvoting member to each board of an area-wide special district.

The council also was made responsible for maintaining programs
of research and study in the following areas: (1) air pollution, (2)
regional parks and open space, (3) water pollution, (4) development
of long-range planning in the area, (5) solid waste disposal, (6) area-
wide tax disparities, (7) metropolitan tax assessment practices,
(8) storm water drainage facilities, (9) consolidation of local government services according to need, (10) advance public land acquisition,
and (11) governmental organization, including recommendations on
the mechanisms most suitable to accomplish all of the above. [21] The
policies for the region are to be included in a Metropolitan Development
Guide. The guide "shall consist of a compilation of policy statements,
goals, standards, programs, and maps prescribing guides for an
orderly and economic development, public and private, of the
Metropolitan area. The comprehensive development guide shall
recognize and encompass physical, social, or economic needs of
the Metropolitan area and those future developments which will have
an impact on the entire area . . . . "[22]

FIGURE 8.3

Intergovernmental Relationships
of Metropolitan Council

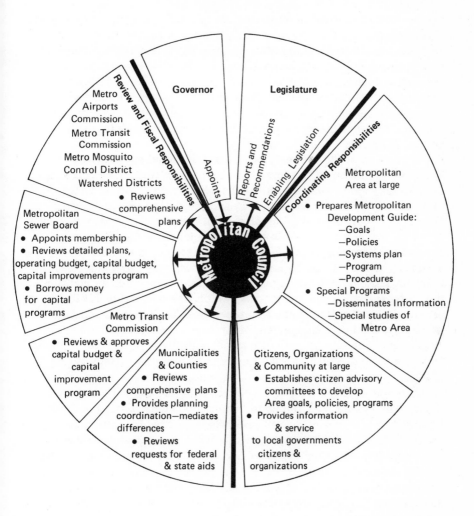

Source: Advisory Commission on Intergovernmental Relations, Regional Governance: Promise and Performance—Substate Regionalism and the Federal System, vol. II—Case Studies (Washington: D. C.: Government Printing Office, 1973), pp. 113-38.

The council operates on a budget based about equally on a
region-wide property tax levy of 0.7 mills, and federal grants. In
1973, the budget was $3 million. The council does not have a capital
fund nor does it allocate funds for grants. The regional programs
are usually financed through user charges and ad valorem property
taxes. One must keep in mind that the operating agencies are separate
legal bodies, and the council merely oversees their budgets. For
example, in the case of the Metropolitan Sewer Board, the council
both approves its budget and sells its bonds. The costs are then
apportioned among the various municipalities responsible for raising
the money. The Metropolitan Transit Commission, as another
example, combines user charges for bus rides with a property tax
levy in a "transit taxing district," which covers areas that are
served by buses. (See Figure 8.3.)

The use of the property tax for the regional agencies was made
available by means of an overall tax reform in 1971. The financing
of counties, municipalities, and school districts also was changed
significantly by increased state aid and the device of state revenue
sharing. In the interest of keeping down the share of local property
taxes for financing, the state legislature passed a 4 percent sales
tax and a 22 percent increase in the state income tax. The
legislature also passed legislation prohibiting any local unit itself
from initiating or increasing taxes on sales or income. In addition,
the Metropolitan Development Act, which was adopted in 1971,
provided for a limited sharing in the growth of the nonresidential
property tax base of the seven-county area. As a matter of fact,
40 percent of the net growth of nonresidential valuation was excluded
from entering directly into the local tax base of the jurisdiction
where the buildings were located. Instead, this amount was pooled
at the seven-county level, to be shared in by all the various jurisdictions. The system was implemented on a population basis but was
weighted in such a way that an area where per capita valuations were
above the regional average would receive a smaller share. [23]

The impact of the metropolitan council on the existing governmental system is rather difficult to assess. Perhaps the impact can
be viewed best in terms of what would have existed if the council had
not been established. Put quite simply, prior to the council's creation,
there was no body performing the functions that the council now
performs. Each governmental unit attempted to handle its own
problems individually. There can be no question that the individual
units were competent; the problem was that they were seriously
hampered by their limited jurisdictions. It is extremely important
to realize that this problem, and the professional consensus that
developed as a means of resolving it, produced essentially a
coordinating agency in the form of the metropolitan council. There was

no real change in the structure of the local governmental units. All
of their functions and powers were left intact, just as long as the
scope of the problem to be dealt with remained within their boundaries.
However, when a problem arose that extended beyond local boundaries,
the Metropolitan council could become involved. This is not to suggest
that the council has no real power, because it can, of course, enforce
its coordinating function. However, the basic task of the council is
to represent regional interests in certain designated areas over that
of the more narrow local interests. This was one of the major
reasons why the council membership was not composed of local unit
officials or other representatives who might reflect only parochial
viewpoints.

Therefore, most local units were left completely unchanged in
so far as their structures were concerned. Admittedly, a few of the
older regional commissions and, of course, the new ones, were made
subordinate to the metropolitan council. The council also may have an
advisory member on other region-wide boards, but it has no direct say
in their affairs. The impact of local government has been experienced
primarily through such means as the A-95 review procedures (which
give the council a veto on federal funds to be used for planning in
the region), the Metropolitan Development Guide, and the review of
municipal comprehensive plans. But the real impact of this metropolitan alternative seems to be that in practice it has encouraged
more intergovernmental cooperation instead of forcing conflict
through the use of the more drastic legal and structural options, such
as consolidation. These council activities may have tended to reduce
somewhat the autonomy of local units, but, at the same time, they
have motivated them to consider the effects of their actions on each
other. Moreover, the council seems to have stimulated

> . . . governmental action, especially by the major
> urban counties in social service activities such as
> community health and criminal justice planning.
> . . .   it has also saved some expense by curtailing
> the over-zealous construction programs of the single
> purpose districts. 24

Thus, the metropolitan council has served as the focal point for the
discussion of area-wide issues. More specifically, it has promoted
the development of thinking in terms of regional approaches to
solving area-wide problems. [25] It is a new and unique level of
government between state and local governmental units. Initial
evaluations of the council have stressed the fact that it performs
functions not previously performed by the local entities. These
functions of policy formulation and planning can have far-reaching

effects, even if limited to a relatively few regional services. By way
of example, at present, the council does not possess authority in the
area of direct land-use planning. However, siting of airports, highways, and mass transit systems can have a considerable impact on
the ability of local governments to do their own planning. Generally,
the council's job is to prepare regional guidelines within which
localities can do their planning and development. [26]

EVALUATION AND ANALYSIS

Much of the record pertaining to the metropolitan council
following its inception revolves around the three legislative sessions
that have occurred since 1967. Since the state of Minnesota has the
power to determine the structure, functions, and continued existence
of any new agencies, the metropolitan council must spend a good deal
of time in developing proposals to present to the legislature.

The 1967 enabling legislation required that the initial work
program consist of seven priorities to be studied and presented to
the 1969 legislative session. These priorities were (1) a metropolitan
zoo, (2) a metropolitan open space system, (3) a sewage plan to
solve the area's water pollution problem, (4) a solid waste disposal
plan, (5) a mass transit plan, (6) a method of resolving highway
planning disputes, and (7) the Metropolitan Development Guide. [27]
An initial problem was where to locate the council, and this provided
an interesting first look at whether the competing interests would be
regional or local. There was a fair amount of conflict, and this
involved rivalry not only between the two cities of Minneapolis and
St. Paul but among the suburbs as well. Once St. Paul was finally
approved as the site, the conflict evaporated, and this was interpreted as a hopeful sign for the future.

The first real test of the viability of the council revolved
around the sewer issue. The council labored from the fall of 1967 to
early 1969 to prepare plans and translate the plans into the form of
a bill to be introduced in the 1969 session of the legislature. While
the sewer plan was drawn up directly by the council, other issues were
delegated to advisory committees for plans and recommendations.
Most observers considered the 1969 session to be a triumph for the
council. [28] Four main requirements were established by statute: (1)
the creation of a Metropolitan Sewer Board, (2) the adoption of a
public program in solid waste disposal, (3) the setting up of a board
to plan for a zoo, although it would be a state zoo and not a metropolitan one, and (4) the enactment of a major parks and open space
program. The parks and open space program was later invalidated by
the state supreme court, but the board was retained in an advisory
capacity. The financing of the parks system had been provided by

appropriating a share of the state cigaret tax to parks. This money
now would go directly to the council.

The implementation of the sewer and solid waste programs
was carried out directly so that by January 1971, all sewer facilities
were owned by the sewer board, guidelines were issued for comprehensive sewer plans, and the first bond was issued in April 1971.
A controversy soon arose between the board and the council over the
fringe communities. The board was moving interceptor sewers out
to the fringe communities, but the council was more concerned about
opening up large areas of land to development once the sewers had
been installed. The council required the board to prepare a five-year
advance plan for future construction, and this program would have
to be approved by the council. Solid waste management seemed to
be fairly effective. Planning was local with council approval, while
the counties implemented and operated the land-fill sites. Additional
actions taken by the council in 1968 and 1969 involved setting up an
advisory health planning agency for the region as required in federal
law and appointing a housing advisory committee. However, there
were still several key issues that were unresolved after the 1969
session. The Metropolitan Airport Commission twice submitted a
proposed site to the council, and twice it was rejected. Finally, the
commission applied for funding to prepare an airport plan. Transportation planning itself became a complex mix of authorities and
numerous requirements. A contract was established whereby the
highway commissioner delegated to the council his responsibility
under a 1962 federal law that required the development of a continuous,
comprehensive, and coordinated transportation program. [29]

The council was not as well prepared for the 1971 legislative
session as it had been for the one in 1969. Complicating the council's
ability to articulate its viewpoint was a change in the make-up of the
legislature resulting from the fact that some of the council's strongest
supporters did not stand for reelection. However, Wendell Anderson,
the new governor, did support the council. Among the council's
failures were the park and open-space plan and the housing authority.
A movement to elect the council members also failed, as did the
attempt to make the airport commission subordinate to the council.

Successes were rather marginal: the Metropolitan Transit
Commission was required to follow the transportation section of the
council's guide; county plans were made subject to the same review
as municipal plans; and watershed districts were made subject to
the council's planning controls. After the disappointing 1971 session,
the council moved ahead as far as it was able on its own. A new Park
Advisory Board was established, and it recommended a program of
state-financed, regionally planned, county-operated parks. In dealing
with housing, the council adopted a policy of distributing federally

subsidized housing more widely around the region. In 1972, it vetoed
for the first time an application for open space funding from a community that had not made an effort on low-income and moderate-
income housing. [30]

The 1974 legislative session proved to be another good one for
the council. A Metropolitan Parks and Open Space Commission was
set up as an agency of the council. The Commission received
authority to issue $40 million in bonds for park acquisition and
development. It was able to implement its plan through its ability to
use these funds as grants to counties and municipalities. In addition,
the council was officially designated as a Metropolitan Housing and
Redevelopment Authority, and within the year, it received federal
funding for 500 low-income units. Another important issue was a
proposal for a metropolitan land planning bill. The council felt this
was necessary to carry out the Development Framework Plan for
guiding future growth. This plan proposed to slow down development
in the rural parts of the metropolitan area and to encourage growth in
the developed areas where public facilities already existed. Each
local unit was to formulate a plan for its own development. However,
the council could review those local plans and require modifications
for consistency with the regional plans. [31] Unfortunately for the
council, the bill failed to pass in the 1974 session.

In addition to its responsibilities in the area of regional
problem solving, the council also performs many review functions,
especially with regard to local plans and applications from local
units for federal funds. This review power tends to reduce local
autonomy, and accordingly, it is not surprising that the local units
jealously try to guard their right to develop as they wish. The council
has been inclined to remain aloof from local officials, and the latter,
in turn, have tended to view the council with some mistrust and
suspicion. This attitude results from several factors. First, there
is a fear by local officials that regionalism will mean the loss of local
autonomy. Second, there is a lack of understanding of the extent to
which the metropolitan council is controlled by the legislature. Since
there is little public awareness of the council and its activities, little
citizen input is given to elected officials. Finally, the council had a
large portion of its staff involved in human service planning, and
this was not viewed by many cities as the intention of the enabling
legislation. [32] The council also has remained somewhat remote from
the people and has not attempted to cultivate grass-roots support.
As Dennis Farney lamented, "You know it's hard to appreciate the
beautiful symmetry of a metropolitan sewer system . . . . The
Council has yet to be seen by the man in the street as a problem-
solving agency that's doing good for him. "[33]

The current chairman of the council, John Boland, should help with these problems. A former legislator, Boland has stressed the point that the top priority of the council should be the physical development of the region. In addition, public relations need to be improved and methods need to be developed to facilitate access and input to the council from the general citizenry. As one former council member remarked, "The Metropolitan approach should develop more of a 'service' image to replace the prevailing 'control' image."[34] Thus, communication and relations with elected officials remain extremely critical. Boland seems well aware that the legislature listens to local officials, as evidenced by his statement that "if things ever get head to head with the local communities we're going to lose."[35]

Other problems of the council center around the delay involved in the review procedures and the confusion in the relationships between the council and the agencies. There is a definite need to standardize these relationships to clarify the respective responsibilities. At the present time, each agency tends to have its own unique position, and there is no real guideline for the relationships of future agencies. The delay of the review process is a serious impediment to the council in coordinating area development. As it currently operates, the process usually occurs only after final local or final agency plans have been made and action has started. As Baldinger reports,[36]

> Too often it [the Council] has been forced to act
> unfavorably or to give qualified approval to plans
> that had progressed so far that unfavorable action
> would have created undue cost, legal or develop-
> ment problems. Too often commitments on projects
> have been made before the Council is brought in to
> coordinate or review . . . . Review without an
> opportunity to determine priorities often is wasteful.
> The Council must have the power to provide needed
> policy solutions.

To evaluate the metropolitan council, one must first consider what it was expected to accomplish—namely, to make regional decisions and to coordinate governmental relations. Its effectiveness should be determined by its ability to assert a region-wide policy interest in the programs of operating agencies.[37] As was indicated earlier, the council was able to do this for sewers, transportation, airports, housing, parks, and open space. It succeeded, by means of reviewing the relevant plans, to keep all

units within the region in accord with the suggestions outlined in the
Metropolitan Development Guide. Its sanction over these plans is
weak, however, and may need to be strengthened in the future. The
council does have the power to suspend plans for 60 days while it
attempts to mediate differences, but there is no recourse if such
differences are not resolved. As also has been noted, the policies
of the metropolitan council have tended to increase the tension of
intergovernmental relations. [38] This is due at least in part to the
uncertainty of the local units with respect to their position versus
that of the council. One should remember that the council is a political body, and, undoubtedly, decisions are made with this fact in
mind. Though the members of the council are chosen to represent
certain areas, they are not directly elected and thus do not have to
answer to the people.

Other criteria for evaluation pertain to the metropolitan
reorganization. Few expected that there would be a reduction in
service costs or taxes, since many of the regional activities would
be undertaken for the first time. Costs had previously been assessed
in terms of pollution or undesirable development, but these "social
costs" are rather difficult to measure. There was some saving
through economies of scale and coordination of projects. For example,
instead of two separate hospital improvement projects, a joint
project has saved an estimated $4 million in construction costs and
about $1 million per year in operating costs. [39]

The role of state government has been considered essential for
metropolitan reorganization efforts, and this certainly was true in
the Twin Cities area. Not only was the metropolitan council
established by the state legislature, but it continues to remain
dependent on the legislature for organizational structure and funding.
The difference between the council approach and approaches adopted by
other states is that the state bureaucracy does not get involved in
the actual administration at the regional level.

The issue of centralization and decentralization is of particular
importance since it involves the entire spectrum of citizen participation. Certainly the council does centralize policy decision making
for the region in certain areas, and this fact can influence the entire
future direction and growth of the region. Most of the discussion on
the council and its activities has been in the direction of centralization.
However, decentralization has also been an issue of concern.
Approximately two years after the metropolitan council was established,
the Citizens' League proposed a system of community councils for
the city of Minneapolis. The idea proved to be popular and the
Citizens' League proceeded to develop a system for the Model City
area. In St. Paul, which does not have district representation, the
community councils proposal became an issue in the mayoralty

campaign in 1972, and subsequently the proposal has been studied
for possible implementation. One suburban community in its long-
term plan called for the community to be organized around a number
of villages of about 6,000 persons each. [40]

The Metropolitan Reorganization Act of 1974 has produced the
only adjustments to the council thus far. Under the terms of this
act, the membership was increased from 14 to 16 and the districts
were redefined (see Figure 8.1). The act also provided that
metropolitan commissions be composed of eight members appointed
by the council, with the chairman appointed by the governor. The
law required that the council adopt regulations establishing standards
and guidelines for determining how a proposed project should be
evaluated for its "metropolitan significance." The council also was
directed to establish a procedure for a regular review process.

REPLICABILITY

The metropolitan council is regarded as a fairly successful
institution. It is quite different from any other attempt at metropolitan reform, and, hopefully, it might serve as a model for other
communities searching for a way to cope with their metropolitan
problems. Needless to say, not all of the features can be borrowed.
Regions differ in the procedures they have for implementing and
operating programs, and the distribution of specific functions among
various levels of government also differs. The exact structure of the
council could not be duplicated in all metropolitan areas, but it could
serve as a guide. The council's structure would seem to be best
suited to a large multicounty area. It is a compromise between a
voluntary planning body, such as a council of government, and a
city-county consolidation, both of which have a number of limitations
pointed out elsewhere in this text. The council exhibits several
unique features. One is the distinction between programs that have
their own operating facilities, such as sewers, and those that need
to be operated as part of a larger system, such as parks. The
council also provides a model for a regional planning and policy
body that is separate from the usual associations of local governmental units.

It would be difficult to replicate the Twin Cities traditions of
good government, its characteristics of a homogeneous population,
a high degree of citizen participation, and a high level of education,
its solid economic base, and its relatively low unemployment rate.
However, there are at least four lessons to be learned by communities wishing to achieve a reorganization on a regional level. One is
to work for a repeal or revision of home rule laws, since in most
cases home rule provisions require a referendum, a device that

often inhibits change. A second factor in any consideration of replicability is the role of state government. Only the state legislature can create a body with the necessary jurisdiction, powers, and finances. Thus, a lesson can be learned from the Twin Cities' recognition of the necessity of working with an eye toward legislative approval. As has been seen, the Twin Cities' reformers were keenly aware of the need to develop a consensus to present a united front to the legislature. Thirdly, the actual initiative for reorganization can come from the communities themselves rather than from the state or federal government. Local initiative, however, requires a fairly cohesive and motivated community. Finally, another essential lesson is that both informed citizens and local officials must be convinced that regional problems do indeed exist and, in addition, that a metropolitan level remedy is available for the resolution of the problems.

The metropolitan council of the Twin Cities area in Minnesota offers a viable "solution" to restructuring government to handle metropolitan problems. Its actual form may not be applicable to many areas, but it does offer a useful example of what can be done.

NOTES

1. Stanley Baldinger, Planning and Governing the Metropolis: The Twin Cities Experience (New York: Praeger, 1971), p. 3.
2. Advisory Commission on Intergovernmental Relations, Regional Governance: Promise and Performance (Washington, D. C., 1973), p. 114.
3. Baldinger, op. cit., p. 29.
4. Advisory Commission on Intergovernmental Relations, op. cit., p. 118.
5. Ibid., p. 114.
6. Baldinger, op. cit., p. 8.
7. Ibid., p. 8.
8. Ibid., p. 39.
9. Ibid., p. 63.
10. Ibid., p. 77.
11. Ibid., p. 79.
12. Ibid., pp. 134-38.
13. Ibid., p. 90.
14. Ibid., p. 91.
15. Ibid., p. 114.
16. Advisory Commission on Intergovernmental Relations, op. cit., p. 115.
17. Ibid., p. 115.

18. Baldinger, op. cit., pp. 154-58; and Advisory Commission on Intergovernmental Relations, op. cit., p. 116.

19. Advisory Commission on Intergovernmental Relations, op. cit., p. 118. The following discussion of structure and operations is based on this section unless otherwise noted.

20. Baldinger, op. cit., p. 160.

21. Ibid., p. 161.

22. Metropolitan Council, "Development Framework" chapter of the Metropolitan Development Guide (St. Paul, March 27, 1975), p. iii.

23. The section on financing the metropolitan council and agencies was based on Advisory Commission on Intergovernmental Relations, op. cit., pp. 127-30.

24. Terry Novak, "Twin Cities Regionalism: A Local Perspective," Public Management 56 (January 1974): 20.

25. Camille André, "Twin Cities Regionalism: A Metropolitan Perspective," Public Management 56 (January 1974): 18.

26. Advisory Commission on Intergovernmental Relations, op. cit., p. 131.

27. Baldinger, op. cit., p. 171.

28. Advisory Commission on Intergovernmental Relations, op. cit., p. 120.

29. Ibid., p. 121.

30. Ibid., p. 124.

31. The Metropolitan Council, a synopsis of the council's work put out by the council—(St. Paul: Metropolitan Council, n.d.).

32. Novak, op. cit., p. 22.

33. Dennis Farney, "The Twin Cities Experiment," Wall Street Journal, March 21, 1974, p. 12.

34. André, op. cit., p. 20.

35. Farney, op. cit., p. 12.

36. Baldinger, op. cit., p. 177.

37. Advisory Commission on Intergovernmental Relations, op. cit., p. 130.

38. Ibid., p. 131.

39. Ibid.

40. Ibid., p. 134.

CHAPTER

9

CONCLUSIONS

For some persons, a text written about metropolitan governmental experiments might seem somewhat passé. Although considerable interest was generated in this area in the 1950s, few cities actually established metropolitan governments. Moreover, since most of the metropolitan experiments that have been reviewed in this study tended in the direction of greater centralization, they might seem to run counter to the decentralization, community control, and citizen participation literature of the late 1960s and 1970s. [1] Indeed, the renowned political scientist Robert Dahl has suggested that for ideal, widespread civic participation, the optimum size for a contemporary American city is probably between 50,000 and 200,000 persons. Dahl questions whether the citizen can truly identify with or participate in local governments that are larger than 200,000. [2] Yet many cities, after experiencing such reforms as consolidation, the comprehensive county plan, or federation, have grown beyond these limits. Certainly the experiments of Nashville, Indianapolis, Jacksonville, Miami, and Toronto would fit this description.

The continued interest in governmental reform and the accompanying changes in the balance of community power serve to encourage more scholarly attention to this subject. Academicians and administrators alike have certainly sustained their interest in discovering ways of more effectively dealing with urban problems. In order to progress beyond the campaign rhetoric both in favor of reform and against it, more attention must be given to the collection of information based on the actual records of metropolitan government. Here we find something of a vacuum in the available literature. With the exception of the royal commission's evaluation in Toronto, there appears to be a real lack of comprehensive policy evaluation studies for most of the major metropolitan experiments that we attempted to analyze. The actual performance of most metropolitan governmental experiments has been obscured by chamber-of-commerce-type rhetoric and boosterism. This especially appears to be the case with Jacksonville and Indianapolis, where glowing statistics of great savings and more and better progress are usually reported. Miami officials, on the other hand, admit that they have not created a panacea to their many problems and express the hope that conflict will be minimized.

We have examined in this study several reorganizations that were exceptions to the general rule of resisting the formation of a metropolitan government. In the more drastic forms of metropolitan government, where basic structural change occurred, there appeared to be a general pattern that was adhered to. Several authors have posited theories of the politics of acceptance in the cases of consolidation to account for the relatively few successful implementations of this approach as compared with the numerous attempts.[3] Rosenbaum and Krammerer developed a typology with three stages: a crisis climate, power deflation, and the accelerator. Marando emphasizes community problems that lead to reform consideration, the establishment of a reorganization study, the charter commission and its proposals, the reorganization campaign with its proponents and opponents, and the voter response, characterized by a low turnout. Bollens and Schmandt discuss the impetus for reorganization in terms of such initiators as civic and business groups, the press, local officialdom, political parties, and racial groups.

While there have been noticeable similarities in the politics of consolidation, most authors also have pointed to the presence of unique circumstances or conditions. These unique factors, of course, cannot be transported from one area to another, and yet they often appear to be the most salient factors influencing the voters' response to reorganization efforts. Examples of such unique circumstances are the exposure of corruption and the disaccreditration of the schools prior to the referendum in Jacksonville. In Nashville, the use of the green sticker tax on all automobiles, the aggressive behavior of the mayor toward the suburbs, and the persistant disagreement between the two major city newspapers on the consolidation issues tended to give the 1962 referendum a more unique set of circumstances than those that pertained to the 1958 referendum.[4] In Indianapolis the unusual circumstances of Republican control at all levels of government and the ability of Mayor Lugar to promote the reform proposal without a referendum proved to be extremely important factors. It has been argued that such unique factors are usually positive in their effect on the support for reorganization. Moreover, some have suggested that it is these unique factors that seem to be the necessary ingredients to any successful reform. However, unique conditions by themselves may not be enough to achieve reorganization. [5]

With the two-level alternative as evidenced by the Miami and Toronto variations, there is a basic problem of determining the areas of functional responsibility. Which level of government should perform which specific function? Functions may be performed solely by the upper or area-wide tier, the lower or local tier, or by both tiers on a shared basis. In Miami, the shared and separate functions were not very clear until after the reorganization, when it was quite apparent that the elastic clause of the charter favored the county. This caused a severe crisis of identity among the smaller municipalities and a tremendous amount of hostility between the two tiers. Consequently, a great deal of energy was drained from the new government, which was hard pressed to address the more pressing regional problems. In Toronto we found an entirely different situation, since the shared and separate functions were more clearly defined prior to the reorganization, which did not involve a referendum. Accordingly, when Metro Toronto was formed, it was able immediately to begin to attact the critical problems that were identified, however narrowly, by the first chairman.

As we have seen, in Canada the provinces play a much more direct and active role in the public policy-making process of municipalities than it usually the case with the states in the United States. Through its hearings and recommendations to the provincial government, the Ontario Municipal Board strongly influenced the creation and structure of Metro Toronto. The provincial government played an important role in the planning as well as the implementation phase of Metro. This can be contrasted to the usual situation in the United States where the urban area itself determines the type of government it desires and then approaches the state for support and enabling legislation. In Canada then, and particularly in the case of Toronto, the two-tier alternative of metropolitan government appears much easier to attain. For the United States, it apparently is considered a more drastic reform than even the one-level approach of city-county consolidation. The fear of core-city dominance is another basic reason why federation is not more widely accepted. If a mechanism could be perfected that would at least partially divide the large central city as a political unit within the federation, some of the objections to metropolitan federation might be overcome. [6]

The milder approaches to dealing with metropolitan problems such as the cooperative alternative through interlocal agreements and the metropolitan council alternative, either the council of governments model or the Twin Cities model, seem to possess a number of common ingredients. The politics-of-acceptance contest is usually low key with respect to both of these alternatives. Local officials, convinced that they are dealing with numerous regional problems that go beyond their won governments' capacities, have suceeded in convincing each other that different alternatives can and should be pursued. From their perspective, it is very critical, however, that whatever alternative is chosen preserves the status quo. This is especially true with regard to councils of governments. In Los Angeles the Lakewood plan did not deter governmental fragmentation and municipal incorporations, but it did reduce the need for additional departments in the newly created cities. Most importantly, the Lakewood plan appeared to offer local officials choices in services and in the amounts of these services. The county would thus continue its long-standing tradition of being the major producer of services, thereby making unnecessary any new metropolitan structure.

Noticeably absent in these milder forms of metropolitan experiments is the existence of much citizen participation and involvement in the establishment or daily operations of the new systems. The general public has not been called upon to evaluate the experiment through the election process in the GPCOG, the Minneapolis-St. Paul council, or Los Angeles County.

It is indeed ironic that, in most of the metropolitan experiments, a problem-solving capacity has been created that is superior to the one that existed prior to the change. However, many of the communities have failed to utilize fully this potential in solving the major social problems of the metropolitan area. This phenomenon tends to be found in both the mild and the more drastic experiments and can be explained by a number of factors. Issue or service selection in both Toronto and Portland tended to favor the easy problems where consensus already had developed. In most cases, these problems involved physical services rather than social services. Successful metropolitan reforms of all varieties have enjoyed the support of the community elites, while support from the poor has usually been lacking. In order to correct this situation, a newly created political system should make a special effort to address itself to the problems of all segments of the community. This is especially true in those metropolitan experiments that do not require a referendum.

As Marando has concluded:[7]

In all but a few metropolitan areas, the following political process conditions exist: first, city-county governmental reorganization is not basically a grass-roots movement. It springs from the desires of only an interested few persons—namely, the civic groups, academics, and community business leaders.

> Hence, reorganization campaign efforts have great
> difficulty in reaching large numbers of people when
> the issue is not one of widespread public concern.

The above generalizations could easily apply to a number of the
metropolitan experiments that have been examined here, allowing
for the unique circumstances that have been outlined in each separate
account.

There have been in the past and will continue to be in the future
major political obstacles to all metropolitan reorganizations, but
especially for the more drastic forms of city-county consolidation,
federation, and the two-tier urban county approach. These obstacles
are formidable where voter approval is required, and they tend to be
almost insurmountable in the largest metropolitan areas. An active
state role in the reorganization of local government for urban areas
and the absence of a referendum appear to be two ingredients that
will facilitate, but certainly not guarantee, metropolitan reform.
When the state government assumes an involved role with metropolitan
governmental structure, the state's influence on that structure will
likely expand. [8] In this regard, the Twin Cities' approach probably
offers the most promising benefits for the metropolitan reform of the
1970s. It has all the necessary elements for metropolitan government
such as authority, multifunctional capacity, a geographic scope
approximating the urban area, and power to levy taxes. But, most
importantly, the Twin Cities metro council is a creature of the state,
and the state has even more potential power for metropolitan policy
making, though it rarely uses its full capacities. [9]

The metropolitan governments have usually generated a degree
of conflict with the first-tier local governments, but nevertheless,
when all factors are taken into consideration, they have built
impressive records of achievement. As Melvin Mogulof reports
on his evaluations of Jacksonville, Miami, the Twin Cities, and
Toronto:[10]

> They have generally done well the things they set out
> to do—they almost always seem to have done them
> with more skill than was displayed in the metro-
> politan area prior to the restructuring. This is not
> to suggest that these achievements could not have
> been accomplished under the previous governing
> structure of the area. But they were not. The fact
> is, in each of the operating metro areas, the new
> structure has brought a sense of governmental
> competence and buoyancy, which is a rare com-
> modity on the American governing scene.

We have examined eight metropolitan experiments that have all claimed to improve the urban environment. The future will determine which of these approaches has made the most contributions to urban problem solving at the metropolitan level.

NOTES

1. For example see Milton Kotler, Neighborhood Government: The Local Foundations of Political Life (Indianapolis: Bobbs-Merrill, 1969); and Mario Fantini and Marilyn Gittell, Decentralization: Achieving Reform (New York: Praeger, 1973).

2. Robert R. Dahl, "The City in the Future of Democracy," American Political Science Review 61 (1967). Also see Joan Carver, "Responsiveness and Consolidation," Urban Affairs Quarterly 9 (December 1973): 211-14.

3. For example see Walter A. Rosenbaum and Gladys M. Krammer, Against Long Odds: The Theory and Practice of Successful Governmental Consolidation (Beverly Hills and London: Sage, 1974); Vincent L. Marando, "The Politics of Metropolitan Reform," Administration and Society 6 (August 1974); and John C. Bollens and Henry J. Schmandt, The Metropolis: Its People, Politics, and Economic Life (New York: Harper and Row, 1975), chap. 14, "The Politics of Reform".

4. Bollens and Schmandt, op. cit., pp. 510-12; and Marando, op. cit., pp. 244-45.

5. Marando, op. cit., p. 245 and T. M. Scott, "Metropolitan Government Proposals," Western Political Quarterly, June 1968, pp. 498-507.

6. Conrad J. Weiler, Jr., "Metropolitan Federation Reconsidered," Urban Affairs Quarterly 6 (June 1971).

7. Marando, op. cit., p. 256.

8. Ibid., pp. 255-60.

9. Melvin Mogulof, "A Modest Proposal for the Governance of America's Metropolitan Areas," American Institute of Planners Journal, July 1975, pp. 250-55.

10. Melvin B. Mogulof, Five Metropolitan Governments (Washington, D.C.: Urban Institute, 1972), pp. 136-37.

SELECTED BIBLIOGRAPHY

Abler, Ronald, John S. Adams, and John R. Borchert. The Twin Cities of St. Paul and Minneapolis. Cambridge, Mass.: Ballinger, 1976.

Adam, Graeme Mercer. Toronto, Old and New. Toronto: Coles Publishing, 1972.

Advisory Commission on Intergovernmental Relations. Regional Governance: Promise and Performance—Substate Regionalism and the Federal System, vol. 2: Case Studies. Washington, D. C.: Government Printing Office, 1973, pp. 6-35, 113-38.

André, Camille. "Twin Cities Regionalism: A Metropolitan Perspective." Public Management 56 (January 1974): 17-29.

"Another Crisis for Metro." Business Week, February 18, 1961, p. 102.

Baine, Richard P., and A. Lynn McMurray. Toronto: An Urban Study. Toronto: Clarke, Irwin, 1972.

Baldinger, Stanley. Planning and Governing the Metropolis: The Twin Cities Experience. New York: Praeger, 1971.

Bollens, John C. Special District Governments in the United States. Berkeley and Los Angeles: University of California Press, 1957.

———, and Henry J. Schmandt. The Metropolis: Its People, Politics, and Economic Life. New York: Harper and Row, 1975.

Booth, David A. Metropolitics: The Nashville Consolidation. East Lansing: Institute for Community Development and Services, Michigan State University, 1963.

Brittain, Horace. Local Government in Canada. Toronto: Ryerson Press, 1951.

Carver, Joan. "Responsiveness and Consolidation: A Case Study,"
    Urban Affairs Quarterly 9 (December 1973): 211-45.

Cion, Richard. "Accomodation Par Excellence: The Lakewood Plan."
    In Metropolitan Politics, edited by Michael N. Danielson,
    pp. 224-31. Boston: Little, Brown, 1971.

"City-County Consolidations, Separations, and Federations."
    American County 35 (November 1970): 12-17.

City of Jacksonville, Florida. Financial Summary, 1974-1975.

——. Financial Summary, 1973-1974.

——. Bold View—Special Report: Two Years of Consolidated Govern-
    ment, March, 1971.

Coleman, William. "What Is the Role of Regional Councils?" Speech
    to workshop on local intergovernmental cooperation, New Orleans,
    July 1966.

Committee for Economic Development. Modernizing Local Govern-
    ment to Secure Balanced Federalism. New York: CED, 1966.

——. Reshaping Local Government in Metropolitan Areas. New
    York: CED, 1970.

Coomer, James C., and Charlie B. Tyer. Nashville Metropolitan
    Government: The First Decade. Knoxville: Bureau of Public
    Administration, University of Tennessee, 1974.

Crouch, Winston W. "Metropolitan Government In Toronto." Public
    Administration Review 14 (Spring 1954): 85-90.

——, and Beatrice Dinerman. Southern California Metropolis.
    Berkeley: University of California Press, 1963.

Dade County Metropolitan Study Commission. Final Report and
    Recommendations. June, 1971.

Dahl, Robert. "The City in the Future of Democracy." American
    Political Science Review 61 (December 1967): 953-70.

Dortch, Carl R. "Consolidated City-County Government Indianapolis-Marion County, Indiana Style." Indiana Chamber of Commerce, unpublished manuscript, October 1974.

Easton, David. A Framework for Political Analysis. Englewood Cliffs, N.J.: Prentice-Hall, 1965.

Elazar, Daniel J. A Case Study of Failure in Attempted Metropolitan Integration. Chicago: National Opinion Research Center and Social Science Division, University of Chicago, 1961.

Erie, Steven P.; John J. Kirlin; and Frances P. Rabinovitz. "Can Something Be Done? Propositions on the Performance of Metropolitan Institutions." In Reform of Metropolitan Governments, pp. 7-41. Baltimore and London: Johns Hopkins University Press, Resources for the Future, 1972.

Fantini, Mario and Marilyn Gittel. Decentralization: Achieving Reform. New York: Praeger, 1973.

Farney, Dennis. "The Twin Cities Experiment." Wall Street Journal, March 21, 1974, p. 12.

Fischer, John. Vital Signs, U.S.A. New York: Harper & Row, 1975, pp. 57-74 ("The Minnesota Experiment"), 86-97 ("The Rescue of Jacksonville").

———. "Jacksonville: So Different You Can Hardly Believe It." Harpers, July 1971, pp. 20-24.

Forstall, Richard L. "Changes in Land Area for Larger Cities, 1960-1970." In Municipal Yearbook, 1972, pp. 84-87. Washington, D.C.: International City Management Association, 1972.

Glendening, Parris. "The Metropolitan Dade County Government: An Examination of Reform." Ph.D. diss., Florida State University, 1967.

Grant, Daniel R. "Political Access Under Metropolitan Government: A Comparative Study of Perceptions by Knowledgeables." In Comparative Urban Research: The Administration and Politics of Cities, edited by Robert T. Daland, pp. 249-71. Beverly Hills: Sage, 1969.

————. "A Comparison of Predictions and Experience with Nashville 'Metro'," Urban Affairs Quarterly 1 (September 1965): 35-54.

————. "Opinions Surveyed on Nashville Metro." National Civic Review 54 (July 1965): 375-78.

————. "Metropolitics and Professional Political Leadership: The Case of Nashville." Annals of the American Academy of Political and Social Science 353 (May 1964): 72-83.

Graves, W. Brooke. American Intergovernmental Relations: Their Origins, Historical Developments and Current Status. New York: Scribner's, 1964.

Grosenick, Leigh E. A Manual for Interlocal Cooperation in Minnesota. St. Paul: Office of Local and Urban Affairs, 1969.

Guastello, Richard J., and Joseph F. Zimmerman. Intergovernmental Service Agreements in New York State. Albany: New York Conference of Mayors and Municipal Officials, 1973.

Hanson, Bertil. A Report on Politics in Nashville. Cambridge, Mass.: Joint Center for Urban Studies of MIT and Harvard, 1960.

Hanson, Royce. Metropolitan Councils of Governments. Washington, D.C.: Advisory Commission on Intergovernmental Relations, 1966.

Harmon, B. Douglas. "Councils of Governments and Metropolitan Decision Making." In The Municipal Yearbook 1969, pp. 10-16. Washington, D.C.: International City Management Association, 1969.

Harrigan, John J. Political Change in the Metropolis. Boston: Little, Brown, 1976.

Hartman, Richard C. "The State's Role in Regionalism." In The Regionalist Papers, ed. Kent Mathewson, pp. 236-53. Detroit: Metropolitan Fund, 1975.

Hawkins, Brett W. Nashville Metro: The Politics of City-County Consolidation. Nashville: Vanderbilt University Press, 1966.

Hester, Lex. "The Jacksonville Story." National Civic Review 59
    (February 1970): 76-80, 95.

Hetland, James L. "The Metropolitan Council." Minnesota
    Municipalities 53 (February 1968): 41-42, 53-54.

Hill, R. Steven, and William P. Maxam. "Unigov: The First Year."
    National Civic Review 64 (June 1971): 310-15.

Jones, Helen L. , and Robert F. Wilcox. Metropolitan Los Angeles:
    Its Government. Los Angeles: Haynes Foundation, 1949.

Kaplan, Harold. Urban Political Systems: A Functional Analysis.
    New York: Columbia University Press, 1967.

Kean, E. Gordon, Jr. "East Baton Rouge Parish." In Guide to
    County Organization and Management, pp. 31-35. Washington,
    D. C. : National Association of Counties, 1968.

Key, V. O. , Jr. Southern Politics. New York: Alfred A. Knopf, 1955.

Kolderie, Ted. "Reconciling Metropolis and Neighborhood: The Twin
    Cities." National Civic Review 62 (April 1973): 184-88.

————. "Strength in Unity." National Civic Review 58 (April 1969):
    154-58.

Kotler, Milton. Neighborhood Government: The Local Foundations
    of Political Life. Indianapolis: Bobbs-Merrill, 1969.

Lawrence, David M. , and H. Rutherford Turnbull, III. "Unigov,
    City-County Consolidation in Indianapolis." Popular Government,
    November 1972, pp. 18-76.

League of Women Voters of Indianapolis. Unigov: What It Is—What
    It Isn't. Indianapolis: Chamber of Commerce, 1972.

League of Women Voters of Nashville. Your Metropolitan Government:
    A Handbook About Nashville and Davidson County, Tennessee.
    Nashville, 1973.

Levy, Frank S. , Arnold J. Mettsher, and Aaron Wildavsky. Urban
    Outcomes: Schools, Streets, and Libraries. Berkeley: Univer-
    sity of California Press, 1974.

Lineberry, Robert L. , and Edmund P. Fowler. "Reformism and
    Public Policies in American Cities." American Political
    Science Review 61 (September 1967): 701-16.

————, and Ira Sharkansky. Urban Politics and Public Policy.
    New York: Harper and Row, 1974.

Local Government Study Commission of Duval County. Blueprint for
    Improvement. Jacksonville, 1966.

Longbrake, David B. , and Woodrow W. Nichols, Jr. Sunshine and
    Shadows in Metropolitan Miami. Cambridge, Mass. : Ballinger,
    1976.

Lotz, Aileen R. "Strong Mayor Plan Defeated in Dade." National
    Civic Review 61 (June 1972): 303-04.

Marando, Vincent L. "Inter-local Cooperation in a Metropolitan
    Area: Detroit." Urban Affairs Quarterly 4 (December 1968):
    185-200.

————. "The Politics of Metropolitan Reform." Administration and
    Society 6 (August 1974): 229-62.

Marion County Republican Central Committee. The Record Speaks
    for Itself. Indianapolis: Marion County Republican Central
    Committee, n. d.

Martin, Richard A. Consolidation: Jacksonville-Duval County.
    Jacksonville: Crawford Press, 1968.

Metro Government, Model for Action. Office of County Manager,
    November 1975.

Metropolitan Council. "Development Framework." In Metropolitan
    Development Guide. St. Paul, Minn. , March 27, 1975.

Miller, James Nathan. "A City Pulls Itself Together." Reader's
    Digest, July 1967, pp. 132-36.

Minnesota. The Metropolitan Council Act as Revised and Amended
    Through May 1, 1974 statutes. Chapter 473B.

Mogulof, Melvin B. Governing Metropolitan Areas. Washington,
    D. C. : Urban Institute, 1971.

——. "Metropolitan Councils of Governments and the Federal Government." Urban Affairs Quarterly 7 (June 1972): 489-507.

——. "A Modest Proposal for Government of America's Metropolitan Areas." Journal of the American Institute of Planners 41 (July 1975): 250-57.

"Nashville, A Story of Progress." Forbes, May 15, 1968, pp. 51-57.

Nelson, Howard J., and William A. V. Clark. The Los Angeles Metropolitan Experience. Cambridge, Mass.: Ballinger, 1976.

Novak, Terry. "Twin Cities Regionalism: A Local Perspective." Public Management 56 (January 1974): 20-22.

Ontario Municipal Board. Decision and Recommendations of the Board. Toronto: OMB, January 20, 1953.

Ostrom, Vincent. Water and Politics: A Study of Water Policies and Administration in the Development of Los Angeles. Los Angeles: Haynes Foundation, 1953.

"Panel Discussion of Regionalist Paper #10." In The Regionalist Papers, ed. Kent Mathewson, pp. 229-35. Detroit: Metropolitan Fund, 1975.

"Questions Most Frequently Asked About Unigov." Unpublished paper prepared by the Indianapolis Mayor's office.

Rogers, Bruce D., and C. McCurdy Lipsey. "Metropolitan Reform: Citizen Evaluation of Performances in Nashville—Davidson County, Tennessee." Publius 4 (Fall 1974): 19-34.

Rose, Albert. Governing Metropolitan Toronto: A Social and Political Analysis. Berkeley and Los Angeles: University of California Press, 1972.

Rosenbaum, Walter A., and Thomas A. Henderson. "Explaining the Attitude of Community Influentials Toward Government Consolidation: A Reappraisal of Four Hypotheses." Urban Affairs Quarterly 9 (December 1973): 251-72.

Rosenbaum, Walter A., and Gladys M. Krammer. Against Long Odds: The Theory and Practice of Successful Governmental Consolidation. Beverly Hills and London: Sage, 1974.

Royal Commission on Metropolitan Toronto. <u>Demographic Trends in Metropolitan Toronto</u>. Prepared by Cherukupalle Inc. Toronto: Royal Commission, 1975.

———. <u>The Electoral System for Metropolitan Toronto</u>. Prepared by T. J. Plunkett, M. J. Powell, and P. Mulligan. Toronto: Royal Commission, 1975.

———. <u>A Financial Profile of Metropolitan Toronto and Its Constituent Municipalities, 1967-1975</u>. Prepared by Allen E. Jarrett and Merrill R. Johnston, of Jarrett, Goold, and Elliot, Chartered Accountants. Toronto: Royal Commission, 1975.

———. <u>The Organization of Local Government in Metropolitan Toronto</u>. Prepared by Ronald C. Smith, Hugh Auld, Jeremy Posner, and Richard Loreto. Toronto: Royal Commission, 1975.

———. <u>Physical Services, Environmental Protection, and Energy Supply in Metropolitan Toronto</u>. Prepared by James F. MacLaren Ltd. Toronto: Royal Commission, 1975.

———. <u>The Planning Process in Metropolitan Toronto</u>. Prepared by John Bousfield Associates and Comay Planning Consultants Ltd. Toronto: Royal Commission, 1975.

———. <u>The Provision and Conservation of Housing in Metropolitan Toronto</u>. Prepared by Klein and Sears. Toronto: Royal Commission, 1975.

———. <u>Public Safety Services in Metropolitan Toronto</u>. Prepared by Joe Martin, Dr. E. S. Duetsch, Anne McAllister, and Patricia Shelley. Toronto: Royal Commission, 1975.

———. <u>Transportation Organization in Metropolitan Toronto</u>. Prepared by Juri Pill and Richard Solverman. Toronto: Royal Commission, 1975.

———. <u>Social Policy in Metropolitan Toronto</u>. Prepared by Mary Collins Consultants Ltd., and Community Social Planning Associates. Toronto: Royal Commission, 1975.

Schmandt, Henry J. "Intergovernmental Volunterrism: Pro and Con." In <u>The Regionalist Papers</u>, ed. Kent Mathewson, pp. 149-58. Detroit: Metropolitan Fund, 1975.

Schreiber, William. "Indianapolis-Marion County Consolidation: How Did It Happen?" Unpublished manuscript.

Scott, Thomas M. "Metropolitan Governmental Reorganization Proposals." Western Political Quarterly 21 (June 1968): 252–61.

"Self-Help and the Cities." Nation's Business 59 (June 1971): 22–26.

"Shakeup in Jacksonville." Newsweek, August 13, 1973, p. 61.

Sharkansky, Ira, and Richard I. Hofferbert. "Dimensions of State Politics, Economics, and Public Policy." American Political Science Review 63 (September 1969): 867–79.

Sloan, Lee and Robert French. "Jacksonville-Duval County Consolidation: Black Rule in the Urban South?" Trans-Action 9 (November/December 1971): 29–34.

Smallwood, Frank. Metro Toronto: A Decade Later. Toronto: Bureau of Municipal Research, 1963.

—. "Reshaping Local Government Abroad: Anglo-Canadian Experiments." Public Administration Review 30 (September-October 1970): 521–30.

Sofen, Edward. The Miami Metropolitan Experiment. Bloomington: Indiana University Press, 1963.

—. "Quest for Leadership." National Civic Review 57 (July 1968): 346–51.

State of Minnesota Senate. A Bill for an Act Relating to Land Planning in the Metropolitan Area 69th Leg., S. F. No. 1653, April 19, 1975.

Tanzler, Hans. "Both City, Business Profit From Partnership." Industry Week, January 29, 1973, p. 57.

—. "Business Is Solving a City's Problems." Nation's Business 57 (July 1969): 56–59.

—. "Jacksonvillians Like Consolidated City Government." American City 85 (April 1970): 79–81.

Tennessee Taxpayers' Association. A Financial Analysis and Evaluation of the Proposed Metropolitan Government Charter for
Nashville and Davidson County. Nashville, 1962.

"Three Mayors Review Their Government." Nation's Cities 7
(November 1969): 26-32, 38, 40-41.

Tunley, Roul. "The City That Married Its Suburbs." Reader's Digest,
May 1973, pp. 2-6.

U. S. Department of Agriculture. The Impact of Metropolitan Govern-
ment on the Rural-Urban Fringe: The Nashville-Davidson
County Experience, by Robert E. McArthur. Washington,
D. C. : Government Printing Office, 1971.

Urban Observatory Report. "City Taxes and Services: Citizens
Speak Out." Nation's Cities 9 (August 1971): 9-23.

Warren, Robert O. Government in Metropolitan Regions: A
Reappraisal of Fractionated Political Organization. Davis:
Institute of Governmental Affairs, University of California at
Davis, 1966.

Weiler, Conrad J. "Metropolitan Federation Reconsidered." Urban
Affairs Quarterly 6 (June 1971): 411-20.

Will, Arthur. "Lakewood Revisited: Six Years of Contract Services."
Paper read at the First Annual Municipal Seminar of California
Contract Cities, April 29, 1960, Palm Springs, California.
Mimeographed.

Willbern, York. "Unigov: Local Government Reorganization in
Indianapolis." In The Regionalist Papers, ed. Kent
Mathewson, pp. 207-29. Detroit Metropolitan Fund, 1975.

Young, Ed. "Nashville, Jacksonville, and Indianapolis Examine for
Possible Lessons for Future." Nation's Cities 7 (November
1969): 26-32.

Zimmerman, Joseph F. "Indianapolis Consolidates." American
City 85 (January 1970): 76.

——. Intergovernmental Service Agreements for Smaller Municipalities. Washington, D. C. : International City Management
Association, Urban Data Service, 1973.

————. "Intergovernmental Service Agreements and Transfer of Functions." In Substate Regionalism and the Federal System, ed. Advisory Commission on Intergovernmental Relations, pp. 29-52. Washington, D. C. : Government Printing Office, 1974.

————. "Meeting Service Needs Through Intergovernmental Agreements." In The Municipal Yearbook: 1973, pp. 79-88. Washington, D. C. : International City Management Association, 1973.

————. "The Metropolitan Area Problem." Annals of the American Academy of Political and Social Science 416 (November 1974): 133-47.

————. Subnational Politics. New York: Holt, Rinehart and Winston, 1970.

JAMES F. HORAN is an Associate Professor of Political Science at the University of Maine at Orono. Professor Horan's research interests are in state and local government and comparative politics. His publications include Downeast Politics: The Government of the State of Maine, The Legislative Process in Maine, and Studies in American Politics. Dr. Horan holds a B. A. and Ph. D. from the University of Connecticut, Storrs, Connecticut.

G. THOMAS TAYLOR, JR. is an Assistant Professor of Political Science at the University of Maine at Orono. Professor Taylor's research interests are in urban politics and local public management. His articles and reviews have appeared in Urban Affairs Quarterly, Journal of Politics, and National Civic Review. Dr. Taylor holds a B. A. and M. A. from the University of Virginia and Ph. D. from the University of Colorado.

RELATED TITLES
Published by
Praeger Special Studies

*COMMUNITY AND REGIONAL PLANNING: Issues in
Public Policy, 3rd edition
> Melvin R. Levin

INNOVATIONS FOR FUTURE CITIES
> edited by Gideon Golany

POLICY EVALUATION FOR COMMUNITY DEVELOPMENT:
Decision Tools for Local Government
> Shimon Awerbuch and
> William A. Wallace

THE POLITICAL REALITIES OF URBAN PLANNING
> Don T. Allensworth

SYSTEMATIC URBAN PLANNING
> Darwin G. Stuart

*Also available in paperback as a PSS Student Edition.